W9-CNB-571

COMPARATIVE ESSAYS IN EARLY GREEK AND CHINESE RATIONAL THINKING

Comparative Essays in Early Greek and Chinese Rational Thinking

JEAN-PAUL REDING
University of Zurich, Switzerland

ASHGATE

Published by
Ashgate Publishing Limited
Gower House
Croft Road
Aldershot
Hants GU11 3HR
England

Ashgate Publishing Company
Suite 420
101 Cherry Street
Burlington, VT 05401-4405
USA

Ashgate website: http://www.ashgate.com

British Library Cataloguing in Publication Data
Reding, Jean-Paul, 1950–
    Comparative essays in early Greek and Chinese rational thinking
    1. Philosophy, Ancient 2. Philosophy, Chinese – To 221 B.C.
    3. Philosophy, Chinese – 221 B.C.–960 A.D.
    I. Title
    181.1'1

Library of Congress Cataloging-in-Publication Data
Reding, Jean-Paul, 1950–
    Comparative essays in early Greek and Chinese rational thinking / Jean-Paul Reding.
        p. cm.
    Includes bibliographical references (p.) and index.
    Contents: "Contradiction is impossible" – The origin of logic in China –
Philosophy and geometry in early China – Greek and Chinese categories –
Words for atoms, atoms for words – Light and the mirror in Greece and China –
"To be" in Greece and China.
    ISBN 0-7546-3803-0 (alk. paper)
    1. Philosophy, Chinese–To 221 B.C. 2. Philosophy, Ancient. 3. Philosophy,
Comparative. I. Title.

B126.R435 2004
180–dc21

2003045369

ISBN 0 7546 3803 0

Typeset in Times New Roman by Bookcraft Ltd, Stroud, Gloucestershire
Printed and bound in Great Britain by Athenaeum Press Ltd, Gateshead,
Tyne and Wear

Contents

Acknowledgements

1   '"Contradiction is Impossible"' is a previously unpublished contribution.
2   'The Origin of Logic in China' is an original contribution. Part of its research material goes back to an earlier paper that appeared in *Etudes Asiatiques* **40**/1 (1986), 40–56, under the title 'Analogical Reasoning in Early Chinese Philosophy'.
3   'Philosophy and Geometry in Early China' is a completely rewritten and expanded version of a paper that appeared in *Etudes Asiatiques* **47**/4 (1993), 623–44, under the title 'Les philosophes-géomètres de la Chine ancienne' (in French).
4   'Greek and Chinese Categories' appeared first in *Philosophy East and West* **36**/4 (1986), 349–74. The present version is updated, corrected and enlarged.
5   'Words for Atoms – Atoms for Words: Comparative Considerations on the Origins of Atomism in Ancient Greece and on the Absence of Atomism in Ancient China' is a previously unpublished contribution. It originated as a series of lectures ('*Warum gibt es keinen Atomismus im alten China?*') delivered at the University of Zürich in 1990/91. An earlier version of it was presented at the conference 'Thinking through Comparisons' in Eugene, Oregon (May 1998).
6   'Light and the Mirror in Greece and China: Elements of Comparative Metaphorology' was first presented at the Asian Studies Annual Meeting in Honolulu, Hawaii (April 1996), and also later in the same year at the annual meeting of the 'Société romande de philosophie' at Rolle, Switzerland (June 1996). A shorter and less technical French version has appeared in the *Revue de théologie et de philosophie* **129** (1997), 1–30, under the title 'L'utilisation philosophique de la métaphore en Grèce et en Chine. Vers une métaphorologie comparée' (in French). The present version has not been published before.
7   '"To Be" in Greece and China' is a previously unpublished contribution.

I am grateful to the editors of *Philosophy East and West* (Honolulu, Hawaii), *Etudes Asiatiques* (Zürich, Switzerland) and the *Revue de théologie et de philosophie* (Lausanne, Switzerland) for the permission granted for reprinting material that first appeared in their publications.

Introduction

Comparing ancient Chinese to ancient Greek philosophical thinking is certainly a fascinating enterprise. But it is also a questionable one. What is the philosophical justification for such an undertaking? And why should we compare ancient Chinese to ancient Greek thought, rather than to Indian, Arabic or African ways of thinking? We might ask, further, if we have at our disposal a comparative method adaptable to a project of this scope.

Let me begin by trying to answer the last question first. The comparative method is firmly established in the natural sciences, where we have a number of comparative disciplines, such as comparative zoology and comparative anatomy. Historical linguistics, comparative law, religious studies and comparative mythology also deserve to be mentioned in this context. Comparative philosophy, however, is rather ill famed, and has never acquired the status of a unified and independent philosophical discipline.[1] Even the very notion of comparative philosophy as a discipline distinct from pure philosophy is rejected sometimes.[2]

Comparative philosophy is also seen very often as nothing more than a broader approach to the study of the history of philosophy, by including Indian, Chinese and African philosophies as appendices to standard histories of Western philosophy.[3] The most common way of practising comparative philosophy, however, is to spot marked differences or similarities between specific doctrines or global attitudes of Western and Eastern philosophy. The goal I have set myself is to rehabilitate the comparative method as a more rigorous way of doing philosophy with a cross-cultural perspective.

The comparative method must not be confused with the mere act of comparing. Everything may after all be similar to – or different from – everything else.[4] The comparative method is part of a whole scientific and epistemological procedure. The comparative sciences are located midway between historical and empirical sciences. Based on historical data such as texts, archaeological finds or recorded history, they nevertheless are, like

---

1 Denominations such as 'geophilosophy' (Ohji and Xifaras 1999) or 'ethnophilosophy' have an implicit relativistic ring. Interesting is Deutsch's 'contrastive philosophy' (Deutsch 1970: 320). For a critical discussion of the comparative method and its relation to philosophy, see Wu Xiaoming 1998; Benesch 1997; Reding 1998 (with bibliography). See also the impressive collection of texts in Mazaheri 1992. On the new school of intercultural philosophy and hermeneutics, see Holenstein 1994; Mall 1995; Schneider 1997; Schneider 1998; Wu Kuang-Ming 1998.
2 See Allinson 2001.
3 Brunner 1975: 252.
4 'Whatever you can affirm about Eastern or Western thought, it is always possible to quote a doctrine which says exactly the opposite.' (Regamey 1968: 503) See also Segal 2001: 349–50.

1

empirical sciences, in the position of emitting and testing hypotheses. Comparative sciences, it has to be said, never predict anything. Comparative disciplines cannot rely, as the natural sciences do, on facts freely reproducible under laboratory conditions. They rather 'retrodict', which means that they can put forth theories, hypotheses and explanations dealing with what we may call 'diverging evolutionary chains'.

There are two essential aspects to the comparative method. The first has already been mentioned: it is a method to confirm or invalidate hypotheses. The observed similarities and differences must appear as meaningful elements in a cluster of hypotheses, not as learned curiosities in a description of exotic mentalities. The second aspect is much harder to explain, because it seems, at first sight, to be a *petitio principii*: the structural unity of the comparative domain and of the data has to be presupposed.

To clarify this second issue, take an example from historical linguistics.[5] If we consider the Greek word *oikos* ('home') and the Latin *vicus* ('village') from the point of view of their phonological evolution, the hypothesis of a common Indo-European ancestor **uoikos* imposes itself. The Greek *oikos* and the Latin *vicus* hence are really one and the same word. The rationale for comparing these different forms lies in the fact that Latin and Greek, just as Sanskrit or Old Persian, have branched off from a presumed common ancestor, namely Proto-Indo-European. It is, of course, possible to emit hypotheses in historical linguistics, and put them to test by trying to find words or verbal forms that fit or do not fit a proposed reconstruction. If we have the Latin *vinum* ('wine'), we can predict ('retrodict') that the corresponding Greek form must be *oinos* ('wine'), if our earlier hypothesis of the relationship between *vicus* and *oikos* is to be confirmed. The scientific task then is to describe and explain the process whereby these words have developed in different ways. We do not need to explain their similarity. In a simplified manner, we could say that Greek still *is* Proto-Indo-European. The right question to ask here is not 'why is Greek different from Latin?' but rather 'why is Greek not the same as Latin?'[6] The similarity is the original *datum*; the *explanandum* is the difference.

In an analogous way, we can compare fins to wings. It will be much more difficult, in this case, to specify the common ancestor of these two organs, although we can, with reasonable certainty, point to a common 'locomotive function'. The important factor here is the medium in which the corresponding locomotive organs had been placed. It is indeed the medium, water or air, which is responsible for the diverging ways in which locomotive organs have evolved.

These examples show that the comparative method, as it appears in historical linguistics or in comparative zoology, is generally used to deal with differences, and more precisely, as I have indicated above, with diverging evolutionary

---

5　This discipline is rightly called '*grammaire comparée*' in French.
6　The French grammarian Ferdinand Brunot wrote at the beginning of his *Histoire de la langue française*: 'French really is no more than Latin spoken in Paris [...].'(Brunot [1905] 1966: 15).

chains.[7] These chains may nevertheless, in some way, be seen as identical to each other, because they can be related to a supposed common ancestor. In 'neutral' conditions, Greek and Latin would not even have started to branch off from Proto-Indo-European, just as aquatic life might never have left the ocean.

In comparative philosophy, the basic unity of philosophical thinking must also be our initial postulate. In the case of comparative philosophy, however, we cannot point to a common philosophical ancestor. The great philosophical traditions of India, China and Greece all have an origin that can be historically specified, and it is certain that Greek and Chinese philosophies have sprung up independently from one another.[8] Even if we do not have any compelling reason, at least at the start, to believe that what the first Greek, Chinese, Indian, African or other philosophers did was essentially the same,[9] the basic unity of philosophical thinking must be our initial postulate, just as Proto-Indo-European is the starting hypothesis for historical linguistics, or law-abiding communities for comparative law.[10] The commensurability[11] of the facts that are to be examined has to be presupposed; otherwise, the comparative discipline as such cannot even be established. An expert in comparative linguistics could never start an investigation if first it had to be proved that the signs of the languages examined are words in the same way as are those of the languages already known. This is not to say, of course, that every word or linguistic datum from another language is of interest to the comparativist. Comparative material is drawn together with an eye to possible applications; as a consequence, not every phenomenon from another culture is immediately significant to the comparativist. Only those instances that may further existing knowledge about the concerned domain are investigated by the comparativist. Moreover, the comparativist approaches this domain with hypotheses already in mind, which are confirmed or invalidated through examination of the comparative material.[12] The role of these hypotheses is to isolate the parameters that have caused these evolutionary chains to become different.

---

7 The link of the comparative method to evolution is also stressed in Segal 2001.

8 I cannot discuss here Bernal's hypothesis of a possible Afroasiatic origin of Greek civilization (Bernal 1987; Bernal 1991).

9 It is Heidegger's – and ultimately Hegel's – thesis that philosophy is a purely European phenomenon, incommensurable with the thought of other ethnic groups (Heidegger [1943] 1987: 3). Husserl ([1938] 1977) and Gadamer (1972: 362) also share this assumption.

10 Proto-Indo-European is, of course, not to be considered as the language spoken by some Indo-European ancestors. It is a hypothetical, artificial and formal reconstruction. Its goal is to explain the relations between the different branches of Indo-European, not the reconstruction of the primitive language. On the comparative method in historical linguistics, see Meillet [1924] 1984.

11 For a discussion of this aspect, see Yu Jiyuan 2001: 296.

12 It may also happen that the comparative method is rejected on ideological grounds. Segal (2001) quotes cases where the comparative method is rejected in biblical studies because it levels religions and does not account for the peculiar status of the religion of ancient Israel in its environment.

The question we should ask in comparative philosophy is not 'why is Greek philosophy *different* from Chinese philosophy?' but 'why are they not *the same*?' Without this methodological postulate, we are left with bare differences, which we cannot investigate, or mysterious points of contact, which we cannot explain. In other words, the goal of the comparative method is to get hold of the parameters that cause these evolutionary chains to become different. But these parameters act in equal ways on all the chains that are under consideration.

Let me use a simile to further clarify this situation. Take the example of two rivers coming from two different springs. We know that the flowing of rivers obeys scientific laws, codified by the science of limnology. In one sense, there is only one basic law: flowing water always takes the shortest possible way. Ideally speaking, every river should flow, as many canalized rivers nowadays do, in a straight line. But if we follow up their meanders on a map, the actual course of our two rivers may appear to be totally divergent, and even incommensurable. We have to imagine Chinese as well as Greek philosophy as two meandering rivers, and not Greek philosophy as the ideal straight line, and only the Chinese as being of the meandering type. Nevertheless, the scientific approach to the seemingly random meandering of rivers is rendered possible by the fact that the postulated ideal line of their flow is modified by a number of parameters common to all meandering rivers, such as the nature of the geological substratum on which the rivers flow, or their pluvial or nivo-pluvial rate of flow. This simile may help us to understand how it is possible that two diverging and apparently unrelated phenomena nevertheless may obey exactly the same laws.

One sees at once that this way of practising comparative philosophy also establishes much stronger initial conditions. If the comparative approach is to yield more than a mere *description* of what is felt strange or different in another philosophical culture, and eventually lead us on to the way of an *explanation* of these differences, we will also have to start from much stronger assumptions, namely: in a comparative undertaking the 'home philosophy' and the 'other philosophy' must be on one and the same epistemological level. There can be no room for a norm-defect structure. To be fair, we have to admit that the principles explaining the presence, the absence, or the particular configuration of a facet of the 'other philosophy' must also at the same time explain why this facet is present, absent, or different in our 'home philosophy'.

This bold hypothesis now raises another problem, namely that of the status of these different philosophies. The relations between Eastern and Western philosophies have been characterized in a great variety of ways. All attempts to put these different modes of thinking on a par have ended up, in one way or other, by postulating that they were complementary to one another: Western thought is good at logic and science, Indian thought at religion, Chinese at ethics.[13]

---

13   See, for example, Suzuki 1914: 47; Scharfstein and Daor 1978: 120–21.

This kind of explanatory model is clearly not viable under the conditions just laid down. It is simply unsatisfactory to claim that the first Chinese philosophers had been bad logicians compared to their Greek counterparts, or that the first Greek philosophers had neglected economics. We cannot admit a 'division of labour' in philosophy. There can be no radical and unbridgeable difference in this sense between Greece and China.[14]

On the other hand, my initial thesis is not that we are dealing with identical types of philosophizing. What I would like to show, rather, is that there is a common set of initial conditions that are modified by several 'parameters'. This view implies – paradoxically – that it is at the beginning that different cultures are closest to each other. But this really means no more than that the possibility that either culture could develop one way or the other had been – theoretically at least – the same in the beginning.[15] The conviction of the comparativist is, precisely, that those differences are nowhere contingent, but that they must appear as different, and not the only possible, solutions within one and the same framework. Moreover, these solutions must appear as conditioned only by different and equally applicable 'parameters', and not by irreducible 'mentalities' or 'world-views'.[16]

Even on these assumptions, however, we do not yet have the material that would permit us to carry out a comparative investigation meeting the standards just described. If both cultures have nothing in common in the way they have unfolded their possibilities, we still lack the means – the *tertium comparationis* – that would make them comparable at least in some aspect. The most important presupposition of the method outlined here, therefore, is that it is possible to find threads that are, for some time at least, common to both cultures[17] and that it is possible to pick up these common threads. In other words, it should be possible to go back to the crossroads where Greek and Chinese philosophers stood before making opposite choices.

To pick up those threads it is necessary to turn away from the mainstream of ancient Chinese philosophy and study its rather neglected facets of rational and logical thinking. We shall concentrate, therefore, not on Confucianism, Daoism or Legalism, but on the work of the Later Mohists, Zhuangzi and Gongsun Long. It might be objected that these thinkers are perhaps not sufficiently representative of the Chinese mind, because their fundamental options – rationalism and utilitarianism – were not retained in the great summa of Chinese thought elaborated during the Han dynasty. But their example shows in a significant way that rationalism did offer itself as a *choice* to the Chinese. It is legitimate, therefore, to compare Chinese to Western rationalism, and

---

14 The postulate of the fundamental unity of cultures is prominent, though in a different way, in many other comparative works. See, for example, Needham 1962: xxxv; Todorov 1982; Schwartz 1985; Jullien 1995; Hall and Ames 1995; Mall 1995; Wiredu 1996.

15 On this problem, see also Jullien 1998: 57–67.

16 For a devastating critique of the notion of mentality, see Lloyd 1990.

17 Note that this approach is totally different from that of Jullien (1995), who tries to locate the Chinese ways of approaching reality at the very outskirts of *Western* ways of thinking.

observe both fighting on the same battleground, because we still move in an as yet unshaped – potential – cultural universe. So, even if this strain of thought is not characteristic of Chinese thinking as a whole, it illustrates quite vividly its *potentialities* and provides us with unique and ideal comparative material. We can only regret that the number of comparative investigations that can be conducted under such criteria is very limited, because the meeting points are scarce and because not many of the writings of this tradition of the buried *logos* survive.[18]

The unifying theme of the essays collected in this volume is, precisely, an investigation into the remnants of this form of rationality. My central claim is that this is not a kind of Chinese rationality, but simply rationality in China.[19] There are, as we shall see, a great number of elements that appear to be the same in both cultures, such as, for example, the discovery of the axiomatic method, the art of definition, the principle of contradiction, logical syntax, and categories. The hypothesis developed in these essays is that Greek and Chinese rational thinking are different facets of one and the same phenomenon. It is not the case that one of these chains would be the standard whereas the other one would be deviant, that Greek culture is the norm, whereas Chinese culture would be the 'exception'. The present series of essays on the theme of the buried *logos* in China could well have as its counterpart a corresponding series of essays on a buried *dao* of economical philosophy in ancient Greece.

The methodological hypothesis is, as I have already indicated, that we should have ended up, in China as well as in Greece, with one and the same type of rational philosophy. If we cast the problem in these terms, we have to ask then for the parameters that can account generally for the most basic differences between Greek and Chinese data. It should also be clear that it is impossible for some particular form of philosophical thinking to become a universal standard of reference for comparative studies. The standard of reference in comparative philosophy, if such a standard exists, cannot be an idealized or artificial construction, because there is no ideal way of philosophizing. The standard of reference can only be an inexhaustible pool of possibilities, towards which the parochial nature of our thought blocks our access until we see our own ways of thinking as one of many possible solutions within a much larger framework.

This is why the comparativist looks rather for extreme differences in comparable evolutionary chains, because these cases are most likely to suggest fruitful hypotheses or enlightening explanations.[20] For a comparative

---

18   Jullien (1998: 90–96) applies only hesitatingly the name 'philosophy' to these more rationalist strands of Chinese thinking (Later Mohism) while he tries to reinterpret all the lore traditionally qualified as Chinese philosophy in terms of wisdom (*sagesse*).

19   This 'golden age of rational logical inquiry' (Harbsmeier 1998: xxi) is still a largely neglected chapter in the history of Chinese philosophy.

20   This conception owes much to the French comparativist Masson-Oursel. See my discussion of his views in Reding 1985: 25 and Reding 1998.

undertaking in philosophy, Greece and China are therefore ideal starting-points, because both have developed, in their beginnings at least, in total independence from each other and have also, moreover, totally different linguistic backgrounds.[21]

There is then another question we may ask: what are the results a comparative philosopher may expect? Undoubtedly, the comparative philosopher will try to get a better understanding of philosophy.[22] Just as a linguist cannot expect to explore the subject thoroughly through the study of only one language, the philosopher too hopes to broaden and deepen his knowledge about philosophy by examining the philosophical productions of other cultures. There is no more sense in saying that a language is inferior to another or is a primitive language than to say this of a philosophical theory. Comparative philosophy, therefore, is in principle incompatible with a Hegelian approach to the history of philosophy.[23] A Western philosopher cannot really claim to know philosophy if he is not ready to investigate the totality of philosophical facts.[24] The Hegelian philosopher, who establishes a theory of the global evolution of philosophy that tries to prove that there can be philosophy only in the West, very much resembles a linguist who would leave aside African, American Indian and Sino-Tibetan languages because he believes that Indo-European languages can teach him all there is to know about language.

Rather than stressing the extreme differences between both cultures – as do most other writings on this subject – my aim is more precisely to look for the parameters that have to be restored to see the similarities. I have focused my attention essentially on two parameters: the difference in the starting-points of philosophy and the difference of language.

In ancient Greece, philosophical thinking begins with natural philosophy and with theory of knowledge, whereas in ancient China, economics and social philosophy come first into focus. The Mohists begin their philosophical adventure with a definition of the basic properties of human nature. Their attitude is, nevertheless, typically rational: their problem is to secure a foundation to their doctrine that would, on the intent at least, go back to an absolute and unshakeable – Cartesian – starting-point. What makes these attempts comparable and commensurable, is that both focus on the problem of finding a starting-point, not only for the specific problem of the foundation of ethics, but for philosophy *tout court*. The specific problem that early Chinese philosophy had to solve was to provide a reasoned account of the transition from impulse (yu^a) to virtue (de^b), from impulse to social and legal order (fa^c), or from impulse to ritual behaviour (li^d).

---

21 On this problem, see below.
22 Comparative philosophy, as Kwee Swan Liat had already noticed, is a meta-philosophy. See Kwee 1953: 64.
23 This problem is further discussed in Reding 1985: 14–19.
24 The notion of 'philosophical fact' is borrowed from Masson-Oursel 1941. See also Masson-Oursel 1911; Masson-Oursel 1926.

Philosophy is thus like an unknown continent, which is discovered, almost simultaneously, in China and in Greece. However, each culture has its own landing-place, from where the exploration of the other, yet unknown parts, starts. Although it is the same continent for all, it does make a difference, if rational thinking, logic and argumentation are approached and conceptualized, as they are in ancient China, from the point of view of politics and economics or if they are approached from the side of natural philosophy and theory of knowledge, as they are in ancient Greece.

The second and most important parameter is, of course, language. The originality of my work in this domain lies in the fact that it tries to explain in a non-relativistic way and with the help of many detailed examples how and to what extent language inflects the development of philosophical theories, in China as well as in Greece. My global aim is to show that the bringing together of two different and independent traditions enables the philosopher to reach a unique vantage-point from where he can gain new insights into the basic structures of philosophical thinking.

Comparisons, as I have already indicated, require some kind of philosophical justification. The main interest of the themes treated in the seven essays proposed here lies in the fact that they are all centred around a common project, namely to test the hypothesis of linguistic relativism. If we look for the parameters that can possibly explain the diverging evolution of Greek and Chinese rational philosophy, we have indeed to consider in the first place the linguistic influence. What kind of philosophical differences are imputable to the language used by the first Greek and Chinese philosophers? There is no *a priori* answer to this question. We have rather to set up a crucial experiment, to decide whether linguistic structures and philosophical ways of arguing are in some way correlated to one another or whether they are independent of each other, even if it is not yet clear what correlation, independence, influence or interference should mean in this context.

The reason why Indian philosophy cannot help us here is all too evident. Indian philosophy shares with Greek philosophy a common Indo-European cultural and linguistic background, which makes it impossible for us to distinguish, of the observed similarities, those that are of strictly philosophical origin from those which are merely linguistic. The relation between Greek and Indian philosophy might be compared to two rivers sharing the same upper reach (namely the Indo-European culture), which means that they cannot be studied without at the same time taking into account the parameters governing these common 'upper reaches'. In the same vein, Buddhist China might be compared to the confluence of two rivers.

There is yet another condition that has to be fulfilled if our crucial experiment is to succeed: the language we analyse must belong to a stratum of 'pure' ordinary language, that is, a language that is as yet untouched by philosophical manipulations. Philosophical arguments have a life of their own. Once the first arguments are developed (such as Parmenides' ontological deduction), subsequent philosophers respond to them and create thereby an interrelated texture of technical terms, arguments and theories, likely to change the very structure of ordinary language. Many of the distinctions embodied in our ordinary ways of speaking, for example, are themselves remnants of earlier philosophical distinctions sunk into the collective 'linguistic unconscious', like Aristotle's 'substance' and 'essence', 'actual' and 'potential'. Nietzsche, and after him the French deconstructionists, have made us conscious of the fact that our 'normal' ways of speaking are far from being philosophically innocent, but are undermined by a whole labyrinth of hidden philosophical terminology.[25] Our experiment, therefore, can only be successful if it is possible to have access to a state of language that is prior to the coining of philosophical terminology, which means nearly prior to the origin of philosophy itself.[26] Surprisingly enough, these rather strict experimental conditions can also be met.

It should have become clear by now that the comparison between China and Greece, right at the beginning of philosophy, that is, prior to the retroactive influence of philosophy upon language, is, for the time being, *our only chance* to find out if, and possibly how, language interferes with philosophical thinking.[27] As long as we try to solve the problem of the influence of language on philosophical argumentation within our own culture, we very much resemble Baron Munchhausen who, after he got caught in a swamp, pulled at his own hair to get out of it again. It is impossible, for us, to find out how philosophical thinking would have developed in ancient Greece with a linguistic substratum different from Greek ... unless we postulate that rational philosophical thinking as it has developed in ancient China is just what we are looking for.

Why at all, one might ask, is the problem of language important in a philosophical perspective? The reason why a philosopher should feel concerned with this problem is easy enough to state. If it can be proven that language has a deep and systematic influence on the manner in which thought and experience are organized, the traditional claim of philosophers, at least since Descartes and Spinoza, but probably as early as Plato, to have access to an objective and neutral grasp of reality is untenable. If reality can only be perceived through the

---

25 Derrida 1981. The principle is also recognized by Owen (1979b: 145): 'Modern English can be more precise because it is heir to so much analytic thought on the issues, including Aristotle's.' Owen, of course, thinks that Aristotle has improved our ways of speaking, whereas Derrida clearly implies that he has ruined them.

26 On this aspect, see also Kahn 1995.

27 Graham (1989: 389) writes: 'Chinese thought before the introduction of Buddhism from India is the unique instance of a philosophical tradition which, as far as our information goes, is wholly independent of traditions developed in Indo-European languages (Arabic philosophy descends from Greek, Tibetan from Indian). It therefore provides the ideal test case for Whorf's hypothesis that the thought of a culture is guided and constrained by the structure of its language.' Creel (1970: 2) notes: '[...] the Chinese setting is so isolated and divergent from that of the West as to provide almost a "laboratory" situation.' See also Reding 1985: 37.

10 *Early Greek and Chinese Rational Thinking*

veil of language, the direct and immediate contact with the real nature of things at which the philosopher aims is impossible.[28]

Descartes and Locke had been aware of the potentially pernicious influence of language upon thinking. They could not imagine, however, that this influence might itself be tied up, not to language in general, but to a particular tongue, such as Greek, Latin, English or German, or to a group of historically related languages, such as Indo-European, and thus be opaque to detection and to conscious reflection before the awareness of structurally totally different types of languages.

If the search for pure and absolute knowledge really is the one thread running through Western philosophy, the efforts made to track down and eliminate the distorting influences that prevent the philosopher from reaching the object of his quest are no less important. The attitude of the great rationalists, such as Descartes, Spinoza, Leibniz or Locke, is still quite optimistic. They subscribe to the fundamental postulate of rational philosophy, namely that the philosopher first has to make – and has the means to do so – *tabula rasa* of all his preconceptions and presuppositions, before he can start building a new philosophical system. Descartes even places himself in the most unfavourable conditions for knowing, only to show that absolute knowledge is possible whatever the epistemological condition and position of the knowing subject. The *cogito ergo sum* is the cornerstone of Descartes' system precisely because this principle is the only one that is invulnerable to the worst imaginable distorting influences on knowledge.[29]

This ideal of the foundations of knowledge, inherited from axiomatic geometry, has been shattered rather late in Western philosophy. The starting-point is perhaps Bacon's theory of *idola*, exposed in his *Novum Organum*. The most important for our context are the *idola fori*, under which all the bad influences of language upon thinking are to be ranged.

However, the Western philosophers' attitude to these distorting influences has itself changed radically. Feuerbach, Nietzsche, Freud, Marx, Derrida and many others have pointed out that the philosopher is influenced by factors acting secretly and at a rather subliminal level. Psychological, sociological, ideological and psychoanalytic factors, cognitive styles, the simple fact of being a man or a woman – all have a strong and definite, though less overt, influence on the way in which reality is grasped by the philosopher. This concept of influence is therefore crucial for the understanding of the making of late modern and contemporary philosophy, whose development is due mainly to a reaction against the postulate of the *tabula rasa* of rational philosophy.

---

28 Gadamer 1999.
29 Descartes' argument, however, is open to an objection that becomes immediately evident to someone familiar with the *Zhuangzi*, especially with the 'butterfly-dream': instead of proving that thought is inseparable from the existence of the individual person having this thought, the *cogito* only shows that 'there is thinking going on', the 'I' being totally idle. On this argument (known as the 'Lichtenberg objection'), see Katz 1986: 118–30.

Nietzsche's philosophy is the most radical attempt to show that the philosopher, while constructing his system, is secretly influenced by subjective and psychological factors that are simply below his limits of consciousness, not factors a philosopher could think out or imagine, as Descartes believed. Unaware of these elements, the philosopher nevertheless thinks his system to be 'pure' and freed from any conditioning influences. Nietzsche reveals in a quite merciless way these hidden assumptions, located mostly in what he calls '*Vorurteile*' (prejudice), right at the beginning of his *Beyond Good and Evil*. A few pages later, Nietzsche then renders the nature of the Indo-European languages directly responsible for some of the main structures of Western metaphysics.[30] Had he known Chinese, Nietzsche's critique of philosophy might have been even more devastating.

The gradual unveiling of all these distorting features has also provoked a strong counter-reaction, sometimes formulated as a revival of Cartesianism. Phenomenology and analytical philosophy are perhaps, among the major contemporary philosophical options, the most consistent attempts to demonstrate that below all these conditioning factors there is still a layer of unconditioned and universally valid knowledge. Although I basically agree with the philosophical ideals of phenomenology, namely the intent to free thinking from its conditioning factors and go back to a stratum of pre-theoretic and idealized conditions of knowledge, I do not believe that we can reach this goal without knowing how and when these influences act on our modes of thinking. It is useless, to my mind, to devise a method telling us *a priori* how to avoid the pernicious influences of language upon our ways of philosophizing if we do not even know how language may exert this influence. As long as we stay within one single cultural tradition, we can never know how philosophy would have developed had the linguistic substratum been not an Indo-European language but a Semitic or a Sino-Tibetan, or even an African language.[31]

The empirical research work that has been carried out in this domain rather corroborates the hypothesis of linguistic relativism. We owe the modern formulation of this tenet to Benjamin Lee Whorf, who had studied under Sapir and who had worked in the field of American Indian languages. For Whorf and the linguistic relativists in general, the conceptual structure of a natural language is even considered to be the condition of possibility of experience. Knowledge and experience of the world can only be gathered, according to Whorf, through language, as appears from the following quote:

> We cut up and organize the spread and flow of events as we do, largely because, through our mother tongue, we are parties to an agreement to do so, not because nature itself is segmented in exactly that way for all to see. Languages differ not

---

30   Nietzsche [1885] 1930: 27–28 (§ 20).
31   This critique also applies to Husserl's conception of a purely logical grammar in his
      Logische Untersuchungen (especially *Untersuchung 4*). On this problem, see Lohmann
      (1948) who tries to establish a difference between Indo-European, Semitic and Chinese.

only in how they build their sentences but also in how they break down nature to secure the elements to put in those sentences.[32]

Whorf insists upon the fact that the languages differ from one another not only in their surface structures, but also in that the conceptual structures embedded in them are incommensurable. Language, according to Whorf, is not only a medium for expressing thought or for picturing reality. It has a cognitive significance of its own. The cognitive systems exemplified by different languages however are judged by Whorf to be mutually incompatible.[33] Whorf's relativistic conclusions, gained from his anthropological fieldwork on Hopi, an American Indian language, have to be checked against the thought and the language of many more civilizations. Whorf's major contribution to philosophy – even if his conclusions are exaggerated – is his effort to clarify the problem of the influence of language on philosophical thinking in a pragmatic and cross-cultural way, not in a speculative one.[34] But Whorf did not choose the right comparative material. The truth is that we cannot say what the intellectual outfit of the Hopi really is, for there is no Hopi philosophy or science, except the one Whorf himself has reconstructed for us.

Nevertheless, Whorf's hypothesis has importance beyond anthropology. If Whorf is right, the Western philosophers' ideal of pure and universal knowledge is impossible, because language and thought simply can never be separated.[35] If the philosopher is entrapped in his native language, then every cognitive insight he provides can do nothing else but redescribe the fundamental structures of his linguistic outfit. Benveniste had tried to show that Aristotle's system of the categories at best recapitulates certain basic structures of the Greek language.[36] Linguistic relativism is possibly brought back to life again in a different shaping by Lakoff and Johnson.[37] Their claim that human thinking, perceiving and acting is structured by metaphors, and the fact that metaphors differ from one language to another, strongly implies relativism.

What is needed, then, in order to go beyond this crude type of linguistic relativism? From the philosophical point of view, it would be enough to show that there are cognitive structures that are independent of language, which is, of course, very difficult, because these structures always have to be expressed within language. Nevertheless, there is another way of conducting the experiment, if we reverse the terms of the problem. Instead of starting with *different* cognitive contents, we shall try to demonstrate that one and the same

32 Whorf 1956: 240.
33 See Whorf 1956: 57–64.
34 See Bloom 1981; Bloom 1989 (focusing on native modern Chinese speakers) and Hansen 1983.
35 The inseparability of thought and language seems to be the central claim of linguistic relativity. See Slobin 1996. This conception goes back to Wilhelm von Humboldt.
36 See the essay 'Greek and Chinese Categories' in this volume.
37 Lakoff and Johnson 1980.

cognitive insight can be expressed through the medium of structurally very different languages. This is the plan that I shall try to follow throughout the seven essays collected in this volume. The basic idea that has guided me through all of these studies is this: before answering the question, is there an influence (good, bad or whatever) of language upon thinking, we have to know first how this influence shows up. We cannot take it for granted, as Whorf and many others seem to do, that the relation between language, thought and reality is invariable from one culture to another. To describe the action of language, with Whorf, as 'dissecting' is, as we shall see, a very poor metaphor.

In the Western philosophical tradition there is the firm belief that, whatever the relationship between language and thought might be, the two domains that are linked together, namely thought (and hence philosophy) and language, are both autonomous and separate, even antagonistic elements.[38] Even if Whorf and his followers seem, at first sight, to disagree with this position, their approach still places them within the typical Western paradigm, at its very edge, because thought appears to be totally dominated and crushed by language. If language and thought are antagonistic factors in one culture, this does not mean that this relationship will be the same in another culture as well. The main goal of these essays will be to show that the frontiers between both domains are shifting, which means that one and the same cognitive insight may turn up as a philosophical theory in one culture and as a grammatical rule or a semantic structure in another. In this way, we shall be able to leave behind us the problem of linguistic relativism and even show that this problem is itself relative to Western ways of conceiving the relations between language and thought.[39]

I shall also try to show that the very nature of the linguistic substratum of a culture already defines its attitude to philosophy, because language and philosophy are by their very essence complementary means of grasping reality. Many philosophical theories can indeed be viewed as proposals for a new way of speaking – and thinking – about the world; on the other hand, our ordinary ways of describing things as appearing, seeming or being, or events as actual or potential, show that much philosophical ground had already been cleared by former (Western) generations of native speakers and philosophers.[40] Philosophy is not entrapped in language. Philosophy is at the outermost cognitive edge of language.

There is thus a dynamic interchange of functions between 'ordinary language' and philosophical theories, depending on how generous the linguistic substratum is to philosophical impetus. If ordinary language is felt as

---

38   Wardy (2000) finds the right formula to criticize these attempts and show their limitation: thought is either 'positively guided' or 'negatively constrained'.

39   See also Derrida 1981.

40   This problem emerges most clearly out of Austin 1964. The point had already been made by Boas (1911: 66): '[…] our European languages as found at the present time have been moulded to a great extent by the abstract thought of philosophers.'

illogical, as it certainly is by the first Greek philosophers, there is a strong need to clear up its dark regions by philosophical theories and terminology. The comparison with the solutions devised by the first Chinese philosophers when faced with the same problems shows, on the contrary, that this attitude is only the typical reaction of our own, Indo-European culture.

The first essay, '"Contradiction is Impossible"', focuses on a curious paradox that is shared by logicians of both cultures. Contradiction, it is argued, is impossible, since each object has one and only one proper and true name by which it can successfully be called. If both interlocutors use the same name, there is no contradiction; if they use different names, they speak about different objects, and there is no contradiction either. In spite of these common initial assumptions about the nature of contradiction, the notion of contradiction itself is approached from the direction of political discourse and human interaction in ancient China, and from the angle of epistemology in Greece, thus causing the notion to develop in different ways in both cultures. The parameter of language, on the other hand, does not seem to have acted in this case, because the philosophical notion of contradiction that had been mastered in ancient China, at least by the more rationally minded thinkers, does not substantially differ from the early Greek concept.

The second essay, 'The Origin of Logic in China', uses the comparative approach to search for an explanation of the absence of formal logical theory in ancient China. My aim here is to show that analogical reasoning, as it had been practised in ancient China, bears unsuspected germs of logical thinking that had been left unexplored in Greece. Moreover, this essay also shows that Chinese logical thinking had started with the discovery of logical syntax, and not with formal logic as in ancient Greece.

Whereas the two preceding essays deal with logical concepts and methods, the third essay, 'Philosophy and Geometry in Early China', sets out to compare the impact that the discovery of the axiomatic method has had upon philosophy and geometry in Greece and in China. The essays show that there is wide agreement as far as the nature of the axiomatic method is concerned. The observed differences are explained by a rather complex interaction of linguistic as well as social parameters.

The fourth essay, 'Greek and Chinese Categories', offers a comparative approach to the origin and to the formation of categories in Greek and Chinese thought and addresses specifically the problem of linguistic relativism.

'Words for Atoms – Atoms for Words' tries to find an explanation for the absence of atomism in ancient China and its presence in ancient Greece.

'Light and the Mirror in Greece and China' proposes a comparative study on the use and the role of metaphors in philosophical discourse. This essay shows that metaphors, in ancient Chinese philosophical discourse, are used in a notably strict and rational way, in total contrast to Greek and Western uses.

The last piece, '"To Be" in Greece and China', is an essay in comparative ontology. Its goal is to show the ambivalent role that the Greek language has played in the development of ontology. This essay builds upon a sharp criticism of Graham's and Kahn's approaches. The Greek language is often depicted, along with German, as one of the – if not *the* – most metaphysical of all languages. This essay tries to show, on the contrary, that the Greek language was considered, by the first Greek thinkers, as a supremely illogical language, and that ontology had originated as a philosophical reaction and as a corrective to faulty ways of speaking rather than as a ready-made gift of a 'philosophical language'.

The main difficulty in my approach lies, perhaps, in the choice of the comparative material. The restriction to themes related to rational thinking, argumentation, logic, linguistic philosophy and metaphor has been dictated to me by methodological imperatives, because these domains offer the most suitable and the most fruitful terrain for comparisons, even if this may give a somewhat distorted picture of ancient Chinese philosophy.[41]

---

41 This picture has now been rectified by the work of Harbsmeier (1998) who shows that the Chinese language is well equipped to deal with all the important notions of rational philosophy. Unconvincing is Bronkhorst (2001) who tries to exclude China to show that rationalism is restricted to Greece and India.

Chapter 1

'Contradiction is Impossible'

Early Greek and Chinese philosophers seem to agree on an axiom that now looks very curious to us, namely that 'contradiction is impossible', and with it also debating, refuting and lying.[1] In the *Euthydemus*, an early Platonic dialogue, two sophists, Dionysodorus and Euthydemus, attempt to persuade their pupil Ctesippus of the validity of this paradox.

> Dionysodorus then said: 'Do you pretend, Ctesippus, that there is such a thing as contradiction?'
>
> 'Perfectly so,' Ctesippus said, 'and I am entirely convinced of it. And you, Dionysodorus, do you think that there is no contradiction?'
>
> 'At least,' he said, 'you cannot prove that you have ever heard anybody contradicting anybody else.'
>
> 'Is that really so?' he answered, 'for just now I am proving to you that Ctesippus contradicts Dionysodorus.'
>
> 'Would you like to hear the explanation of it?'
>
> 'Yes,' he answered.
>
> 'Well then. Is there for each thing a proper way of calling it?' (*eisin hekastôi tôn ontôn logoi*)[2]
>
> 'Yes,' he said.
>
> 'The way the thing is or the way it is not?'
>
> 'The way the thing is.'
>
> 'You remember, Ctesippus,' he said, 'that we have demonstrated before[3] that nobody speaks of things the way they are not. What does not exist, nobody can call it, as we have seen.'
>
> 'What should this mean for the present case? Is it not less true that you and I contradict each other?'
>
> 'Do we contradict each other if both of us call the object by its name? Would we then not say exactly the same?'
>
> 'Yes,' he said.
>
> 'If, on the contrary, neither of us calls the object by its name, could we then contradict each other? In this case, then, would either of us say anything about this object?'

---

1   In ancient Greece, this paradox is ascribed to the sophist Euthydemus, but also to Protagoras, Antisthenes and Prodicus. See Plato, *Euthydemus* 286C; Diogenes Laertius IX, 53 (Protagoras); Aristotle, *Metaphysics* 1024b33f. (Antisthenes); Binder and Liesenborghs 1966 (Prodicus). For an overview, cf. Denyer 1991: 24f.; for Antisthenes, see Brancacci 1990.

2   This argument presupposes that there is for each thing one and only one 'proper' way of calling or naming it. We might term it the law of the one-to-one correspondence between names and things.

3   *Euthydemus* 284C.

'No,' he said.

'Do we contradict each other if I name one object and you name some other object? Is it not, then, that I say something about the object at issue and you do not say anything about it at all? How could the one who does not say anything contradict the one who does say something about the object?'

(Plato, *Euthydemus* 285D–286B)

If two interlocutors speak the truth about one and the same subject matter, then they must also say the same about it. If they do not, then either the object they speak about is not the same, and in this case there is no debate, since everybody speaks about something different, or else, one of them does not speak at all, because his discourse simply does not reach the object. Finally, if neither of them speaks about the object at issue, there is no debate either. Contradiction, hence, is impossible, since each object has one and only one proper and true name by which it can be successfully called. Any other name simply does not hit the object. The sophist Prodicus is said to have justified this argument in the following way.

For if people speak in contradiction of one another, then they both speak.[4] But it is impossible that they both speak (truly) about the same object. For, he says, he who tells the truth, and reports subject matters as they are (*hôs ekhei ta pragmata*),[5] is the only one who is speaking; and the one who opposes him does not say anything at all about the object [...].

(Toura papyrus from the sixth century AD; commentary on
the *Book of Ecclesiastes*. For the text, see Binder and Liesenborghs 1966;
translation Denyer 1991: 26–27, slightly changed.)

To speak about an object means, not only, to say something true about it, but above all to *name* it correctly. This is why any discourse that does not correctly name the object under discussion simply is not a discourse at all and more resembles meaningless noise than speech, or is about some other object.[6] Note that the theme of the impossibility of contradiction is discussed here in terms of naming, and not in terms of making statements, for it would of course not be impossible to make different but true *statements* about one and the same thing. Moreover, statements can be negated, whereas names cannot be negated, or only in a very special way, as we shall see below. The winner of the debate is the one who gives to the object under discussion its correct name; the loser either names another object or does not name at all. If debating is seen as strife between rival ways of naming, the paradox of the impossibility of contradiction is even inevitable. The reason for this is quite obvious. If all the contents of knowledge are concentrated in the names, there is no room for knowledge outside these names. Moreover, the meaning of a name is

---

4   They say something *true* about the object.

5   For this expression, see also *Euthydemus* 284D1.

6   See *Cratylus* 429E to 430A.

supposed to be the same for all. Since naming is equated with saying what a thing is, the person who names an object correctly then also says something true about it – more precisely, even, speaks *the* truth about it. If there is only one possible way to name an object correctly, everybody who speaks truly about this object must say the same about it, since he must use the same name. Since speech is necessarily cast into names, it follows from there that it is impossible for two interlocutors to speak about the same object by using different names. Expressed in modern terms, we might say that meaning and reference are not separated. Moreover, names here also appear to have a propositional value.[7] Contradictions, then, are only apparent, and can always be explained away by insufficient knowledge of the meaning and reference of names. If two interlocutors believe themselves to be speaking about the same object while using different names, one of them, or even both, does not know the proper meaning of the names he uses.

In ancient China, we find a brief mention of a similar theory in the writings of the Later Mohists, a group of scholars that had tried to reconstruct, *more geometrico* the basic principles of the philosophy of Master Mo (*Mozi*[a]). In the *Mojing*,[b] the *Mohist Canon*, there is a short criticism of the axiom of the impossibility of contradiction.

> To say that there is no winner in disputation necessarily does not fit the fact. Explained by: disputation.
>   What something is called, is either the same or different. In a case where it is the same, one man calls it 'whelp' and the other 'dog'. In a case where it is different, one man calls it 'ox' and the other 'horse'. Neither wins the debate, because this is a case of not engaging in disputation. In disputation, the one calls it as it is, the other one, not. The one who fits the fact wins the debate.
>
> (*Mohist Canon*, B 35; Graham 1978: 402–403; translation slightly changed)[8]

For the Mohists, a debate can only take place if both interlocutors 'contradict' each other, that is, if they make contradictory assertions about one and the same object. As a preliminary, two cases of 'apparent debate' are ruled out: both interlocutors make identical assertions about one and the same object, but without being aware of it, since they use different – but equivalent – names, like 'whelp' and 'dog'; or both believe that they speak about the same thing, but in truth speak about two different things, and so debate is not even engaged.[9] The cases of apparent debate mentioned here belong to the same

---

7   Lorentz and Mittelstrass 1967.
8   References to the *Mohist Canon* are taken from the magisterial edition of A.C. Graham, *Later Mohist Logic, Ethics and Science*, London: School of Oriental and African Studies; Hong Kong: Chinese University Press, 1978 (= Graham 1978).
9   Debating, in this perspective, is above all a symptom of ignorance about the proper meaning of names. For who knows the names also knows the objects these names apply to. Cf. Plato, *Cratylus* 435E and 393D. The names, in other words, are descriptively transparent. See Guthrie 1978: 18.

paradigm as the one delineated by the Greek sophists, because debate is again conceived as strife between names.

There is another, much more subtle text on the impossibility of contradiction in the second chapter of the book *Zhuangzi*.

> Let us suppose that you and I argue. If you beat me, and not I you, are you in the end right and I wrong? If I beat you and not you me, am I then in the end right and you wrong? Or is one of us right, and the other wrong? Or are we both right or both wrong? If you and I cannot together decide about it, then other men too will be in the dark about it. Who shall I employ as arbiter between us? If I employ someone who takes your view to decide, how can he arbitrate between us, since he already sides with you? If I employ someone who takes my view to decide, how can he arbitrate between us, since he already sides with me? If I employ someone who differs with both of us, how can he arbitrate between us, since he differs from both? If I employ someone who agrees with both of us, how can he arbitrate between us, since he already agrees with both? But if you and I and the arbiter cannot decide about it, should we depend on someone still different?
>
> *(Zhuangzi*, ch. 2, p. 17, *Zhuzi jicheng* edition)

This time, the problem is envisaged from another angle, namely from the one of the decidability of the debate. Zhuangzi intends to show that a debate cannot be engaged at all, since the logically possible situations of contradiction cannot even be recognized as such, because this would necessitate that the truth be already known before the debate and independently of it. For who knows for sure that the two names 'whelp' and 'dog' apply to one and the same object? And who decides whether some name rightly applies to a given object or not? At first sight, Zhuangzi's arguments do not seem to fit quite straightforwardly into the paradigm of the special theory of naming outlined above. What distinguishes Zhuangzi from the Later Mohists is that the latter maintain that each name has an objective cognitive content. For Zhuangzi, on the contrary, names are arbitrary, and always depend on the person who utters them.

> What is It is also Other, what is Other is also It. There they say 'That's it, that's not' from one point of view, here we say 'That's it, that's not' from another point of view. Are there really It and Other? Or really no It and Other? Where neither It nor Other finds its opposite is called the axis of the Way.
>
> *(Zhuangzi*, ch. 2, p. 10, *Zhuzi jicheng* edition;
> translation Graham 1981: 53)

Names, for Zhuangzi, function like demonstratives. This difference does not appear to influence the general theory of naming that underlies these arguments, because there is still the presupposition of the one-to-one correspondence between names and things: if my 'this' becomes your 'that', my 'that' also becomes your 'this'. Zhuangzi, however, also rules out the notion of contradiction, because 'this' is properly contradicted only by 'not-this', and not by 'that'. 'This' and 'that' function like names, the only difference being that these names do not have an objective content.[10] Names, under these circumstances, are always private names and hence differ from person to person. Contradiction, or debate in the Mohist sense, simply never can happen.

The sophists have often been accused of having invented the paradox of the impossibility of contradiction only to avoid being contradicted themselves.[11] This is a superficial accusation, because the epistemological presuppositions of these arguments can only be made clear if we go back to the special theory of naming on which they are grounded. Its principle is simple: every thing in the world has one and only one 'correct' name. This name is not only a kind of etiquette that we stick on it, but it is also a telling name. If we name the object, we say at the same time also what it is. If we say that X is a dog, we say that X guards the house well or that it properly retrieves game, because we give the name only to an animal that properly fulfils its dog functions.

The paradigm that accounts for this curious theory of the impossibility of contradiction derives from some kind of proto-philosophical myth whose origins lie in the primitive belief that every thing has received, 'in the beginning', its name, its correct and unique appellation. The set of names and the set of things then correspond to each other in a one-to-one relation, because they were born at the same time. It is also natural and logical to give only one name to each thing. Avatars of such archaic theories of a natural correctness of names can be found in many different cultures.

In ancient China, the origin of names is shortly described at the beginning of one of the treatises, the *Jingfa*, discovered in Mawangdui.

> The only method to clearly know the Dao is to go back to the state wherein it was still completely empty. As soon as something as minute as an autumn-down springs from this complete emptiness, it must have a form and a name. If name and form are established, black and white can be separated.
>
> (*Jingfa*, ch. *Daofa*; Yu Mingguang 1993: 4;
> Chang and Feng 1998: 101)

If we go back to the origin of the world, we understand that things were named only *at the very moment* they came into being, and that only at this time did each thing receive its proper name. A nearly identical theory is also to be found in the Derveni papyrus, where Greek philosophers from the Orphic tradition try to demonstrate that the process of the origin and shaping of the world can be known through the inspection of the names. The order of the birth of the Gods can be reconstructed through the etymological examination of their names. These names, as they are supposed to be a true picture of what

---

10   From Zhuangzi's point of view the Later Mohists have only managed to fill the names with the contents of the Mohist philosophy. Their definitions only offer a rational reconstruction of the Mohist philosophy. If a Legalist or a Confucianist had tried to do the same, his definitions would have been quite different from those of the Mohists.

11   It is, as Plato says, an argument that presents 'a wonderful way of upsetting not merely other views but itself also' (*Euthydemus* 286C).

happened 'in the beginning', are indeed telling names.[12] This whole process implies, of course, that the sphere of names and that of things are of the same complexity. These considerations suggest that the principle of the one-to-one correspondence between names and things reaches down to pre-philosophical or even to mythological layers, and is not the result of philosophical theories. It is, simply, the first implicit theory of language that the first Greek and Chinese philosophers encounter.

In the *Cratylus*, Plato had tried to explore the meaning of natural names. Though his etymological reconstructions look at times convincing, his own conclusion was negative: names that are naturally, by virtue of their content and appearance, right, cannot exist. They could only exist if the divine name giver had had before his mind ideal models of the things to shape the name after them. But if such a model – Plato's ideas – existed, the function of natural and correct names would be superfluous, because they would then only be mirror images of these models.

In ancient China, there are no theories trying to prove the natural origin of names by etymological considerations. The only exception is the *Shuowen*, where we sometimes find attempts at etymological explanations of characters, as for example *ming*, 'name'.[13]

> The character 'ming'[c] comes from 'mouth'[d] and 'dark'.[e] The dark is obscurity. In obscurity, one cannot see one another. Therefore one names oneself with the help of one's mouth.

There is one early example in the *Hanfeizi*, where the meaning of the character *gong*[f] 'common' is explained in the manner of a *rebus*: the first element, *ba*,[g] normally means 'eight', but it can also be pronounced *bei*[h] and it then means 'to turn the back on'; the second element, *si*[i] means 'private'. The total therefore expresses the idea that the common good is the result of turning the back to one's private interests.[14]

Generally, however, the conventional origin of names is recognized by virtually every Chinese philosopher of the classical period.[15] Early Confucianism was the only school to adhere to the conception of naturally correct names, if the theme of the correction of names (*zheng ming*[j]) is early and authentic.[16] We should not forget, however, that the problem of the conventional or the

---

12   For the Derveni papyrus (4th century BC), see West 1983: 90f.; Burkert 1970; Laks and Most 1997.

13   See Yu, A.C. 2002: 238.

14   *Hanfeizi*, ch. 49, p. 345, *Zhuzi jicheng* edition. This explanation is later also to be found in the *Shuowen*.

15   See, for example, ch. 22 ('On the correction of names') of the book *Xunzi*. The conventionalist position of the Later Mohists is quite obvious; cf. Graham 1978: 32–33. See also Hansen 1983: 57–65; and Makeham, who uses the expression 'nominalist theories of meaning' (Makeham 1991).

16   See Gassmann 1988; Reding 1985: 248f. The concept of naturally correct names emerges, in ancient China, at a much later date, at the end of the Warring States period and at the beginning of the Han; see Makeham 1991.

natural origin of names is not the main theoretical postulate. What matters most is the principle of the one-to-one correspondence between names and things. Even if names apply to things conventionally, this by no means disturbs the principle of the one-to-one correspondence.

The comparison of Greece and China shows that the art of debating, when grounded on the principle of the one-to-one correspondence between names and things, is, in truth, an art of naming correctly, a technique of attributing the right names to the right things, no matter if these names are conventional or natural. A theory of the natural origin of names has the ancillary function of showing why a certain name applies properly to a certain thing. If each thing has its proper name, there must be a good reason for it, and this reason is to be found in the cognitive content of the name.

The theme of the 'correction of names' in ancient China is based upon the experience of changing political and social circumstances, where, for example, the king ceases to be a true king, or the father a true father. That these changing circumstances are perceived primarily as a disorder thrown into the names stems from the early conviction that names have a fixed and immutable cognitive content. Changes are therefore perceived as an *exchange* of names.[17] Moreover, Chinese philosophers frequently use a technique of argumentation grounded in the redefinition of terms, or the redescription of a situation.[18] This attitude is only possible with the belief in the principle of the one-to-one correspondence between names and things as its counterfoil.

In ancient Greece, a very revealing document, in this respect, can be found in the fragments of Democritus. He is said to have refuted the theory that names are correct by nature by showing that there is no one-to-one correspondence between names and things. For Democritus, language, in its present state, is imperfect, because it is hampered by irregularities such as polysemy, homonymy, change of name or absence of name. Democritus, thereby, allows us to reconstruct the ideal language he had in mind.

The ideal case is the one where we have one name applied to one thing. We have, thereafter, several deviant cases:

1 Homonymy, or *polusêmon* 'one word meaning different things', as Democritus himself calls it;
2 Polyonymy, or *isorropon* 'equivalent'. In this case, different names apply to one and the same thing;
3 Change of names, or *metônumon*. Plato's name, for example, was originally Aristocles;
4 Absence of name, or *nônumon*.[19]

(Democritus, fragment B 26; Diels 1951–1952 (= DK))

---

17 See Reding 1985: 251.
18 Defoort 1997: 135f.; Defoort 1998; Gassmann 1988 (for the *Zuozhuan*).
19 This is, although it is not recognized as such by Democritus, the typical case with metaphors: there is, for example, a word to designate the action of troubling water, but we lack a corresponding term to refer to the action of disturbing ('troubling') the mind.

These deviant cases are the proofs put forth by Democritus to show that language is not 'naturally' correct. The interesting facet about this argument is that the criterion of a natural name is here reduced to its most basic and essential element: a one-to-one correspondence between names and things.

The philosophical weakness of this theory is its incapacity to deal with the notion of contradiction, as defined by Aristotle, namely that it is impossible for the same thing to hold good and not to hold good simultaneously for the same thing and in the same respect (*Metaphysics* 1005b18f.). Contradiction defined in an Aristotelian way is an event that simply never can happen in the sophistic paradigm. The reason why these arguments on the impossibility of contradiction appear strange to us is that the possibility of a middle way is not taken into account. The hypothesis that both interlocutors might be partially right or partially wrong is not even evoked. It is clear that, on the level of names, there can never be a compromise in a debate: 'temperate' is not a compromise between 'hot' and 'cold', but something that is different from both.

The nature of this theory is easily understood, however, if we remember that it is grounded upon signifying, referring and asserting *names*. There are, simply, no *contradictory* names. This is, ultimately, the reason why there is no room for contradiction within the sophistic paradigm, which is grounded upon names, and not upon statements.

Like Plato and Aristotle, the Later Mohists had tried to rule out such cases as presented by the Greek sophists Prodicus and Euthydemus to salvage the notion of contradiction, but they were the only philosophers in ancient China to do so. If there is a debate between two persons, the Later Mohists observe, we have first to make sure that the debate really takes place. The condition for a correct debate is that one calls the object 'X', the other 'non-X'. Debate can only take place if the two claims are, as the Later Mohists say, the 'converse' of each other. This notion had been coined by the Later Mohists, and they had even invented a special character for it: *fan*.[k][20]

> *Fan* (being the converse of each other): it is impossible that both sides are inadmissible.[21]
> All oxen, and non-oxen marked off as a group, are the two sides. To lack what distinguishes an ox is to be a non-ox (*fei niu*[l]).
>
> (*Mohist Canon*, A 73; translation Graham 1978: 317–18; slightly changed)

---

20   Graham 1978: 184–85.
21   Aristotle has formulated his famous principle of non-contradiction in a positive way: 'For the same thing to hold good and not hold good simultaneously of the same thing and in the same respect is impossible' (*Metaphysics* Γ 3; 1005b18f.; translation Kirwan 1980: 7). It is curious to note that the Later Mohists express this same insight in a 'negative' way.

Bian[m] (disputation) is contending over claims which are the converse of each other. Winning in disputation is fitting the fact.

One calling it 'ox' and the other 'non-ox' is 'contending over claims which are the converse of each other'. Such being the case they do not both fit the fact; and if they do not both fit, necessarily one of them does not fit. (Not like fitting 'dog'.)[22]

(Mohist Canon, A 74; translation Graham 1978: 318)

The clause 'Not like fitting "dog"' rules out the case where two interlocutors point to the same object by using different names, like 'whelp' and 'dog'. The two names 'whelp' (*gou*[n]) and 'dog' (*quan*[o]) are a typical example adduced by the Later Mohists to illustrate cases where one and the same object is referred to by two different names. The solution invented by the Later Mohists raises a number of very delicate problems. First of all, it is not made clear if the arguments are located within the framework of a theory of naming, or whether the notion of the 'converse' coined by the Later Mohists should more properly find its place within a propositional context. The problem with this notion is that it leads to a special variety of names, which we might call 'anti-names': 'non-ox', 'non-horse'. In short, it is not clear if the 'converse' is the logical equivalent of the *name* 'non-ox' or of the *proposition* 'this is not an ox'. In my opinion, the notion of 'non-horse' or 'non-ox' clearly functions as a name. But it is a name with only a negative meaning.[23] Therefore, we may have doubts as to the coherence of the proposed solution, for the Later Mohists consider the case where one person calls the object 'ox' and the other 'horse' as an instance of not engaging in disputation. On a stricter analysis, however, must we not concede that 'horse' is also an instance of 'non-ox'? For this reason, the Later Mohists' attitude either aligns with the same paradigm as that delineated by the Greek sophists and Democritus, or else is inconsistent, unless we are ready to accept the concepts of *feiniu*[p] 'non-ox' or *feima*[q] 'non-horse' as a special concept that is neither a name nor a proposition.[24] Strictly speaking, 'non-horse' is but an abbreviation for every other possible *name* except 'horse'.

The Later Mohists were confronted with a problem that was familiar also to Plato: what does the one who loses the debate *say*? The loser cannot say anything about the object at issue, for then he would say something true about it. The Later Mohists do not try, like the Greek sophists, to explain away the problem by simply admitting that he who does not say something true fails to say anything at all. For them, there is only one issue: the loser talks about some *other* object.[25] This other object is a 'non-X', as the prefixed negative

---

22   See Graham 1978: 218–19.
23   Aristotle had clearly seen this problem in the *De Interpretatione* 2; 16a29, where he says that expressions like 'non-man' are not real names, but indefinite names that are neither a phrase nor a negation.
24   Note also that the notion of *feima* 'non-horse' is thoroughly exploited by the sophist Gongsun Long in his famous treatise.
25   This solution, however, is also proposed by Hermogenes in the *Cratylus* 429B–C.

fei[r] indicates. One cannot fail to notice how close in one way the Later
Mohists' solution is to Plato's, for Plato too explains negation, in the *Sophist*,
in terms of 'otherness'.[26] Not to be a horse, or not to be Socrates does not mean
a kind of 'anti-horse' or 'anti-Socrates', or a non-existing horse or a non-
existing Socrates, but simply something – and potentially everything – that is
not a horse or that is *not* Socrates. However, the Later Mohists had not tried to
shift the problem from the level of names to the one of *proposition*.[27]

From a comparative point of view, the most important element to notice is
that the paradoxical nature of contradiction had also been perceived by the
Mohists, and that they had sought a solution to it by defining the nature of
contradiction. The problem that arises, then, seems to be the following: given
that the prerequisites for developing and understanding the notion of contradiction were present in China as well as in Greece, how can we explain the
fact that the track opened by the Later Mohists had not been followed by other
Chinese philosophers? This is, however, only one side of the question,
because we also find, in ancient China, a notion of contradiction that has been
left unexplored by the first Greek philosophers: contradictory actions.

Every student of Chinese knows that the modern Chinese word for
contradiction, *maodun*,[s] derives from a well-known anecdote in the *Hanfeizi*:

> In Chu, there was a man who sold shields (*dun*) and spears (*mao*). When he adver-
> tised them he said: 'My shields are so hard that nothing can pierce them.' But he
> also advertised his spears, saying: 'My spears are so sharp that there is nothing they
> cannot pierce.' Someone asked: 'What would happen if your spears meet with
> your shields?'
>
> (*Hanfeizi*, ch. 36, p. 265, *Zhuzi jicheng* edition)

This rather amusing story tells us much more about the Chinese attitude to
logic than one first expects. Even if the contradiction is plain, the merchant
has good reasons to act as he does. The contradiction, indeed, does not manifest itself unless someone intends to buy both spear and shield at the same
place. If two different merchants had made separate advertisements for spears
and shields in exactly the same terms, there would only have been sound
competition. The real contradiction therefore lies in the fact that the merchant
is not consistent with his *own* interests and engagements, for a test of the
material in his case *necessarily* proves him wrong, whereas a test with the
material of two different merchants can only show that their pretensions are
factually wrong, not logically impossible.

The concept of *maodun* 'contradiction' therefore does not seem to refer to
logical principles that are independent of any human speaker, but to the 'illogical' behaviour of a person. It is indeed remarkable that in the writings of

---

26   *Sophist*, 257B9–257C3.
27   The Later Mohists discover the notion of the proposition only later, but did not get back to
     the problem of contradiction. See Graham 1978: 480–83. Hansen (1985: 517) disagrees
     with Graham on this point.

many early philosophers, such as Mozi and Mencius, the principle of non-contradiction is always illustrated by means of analogies showing inconsistent human behaviour.

> Gongmengzi said: 'There are neither ghosts nor spirits.' But he also maintained: 'The gentleman must study the sacrificial rites.' Mozi commented: 'Study the sacrificial rites while affirming that there are no spirits, this is like studying the ceremonials of hospitality where there are no guests; this is like knotting nets while there are no fish.'
>
> (*Mozi*, ch. 48, p. 276, *Zhuzi jicheng* edition)

Similar examples can be found in many other early Chinese texts.[28] We can even say that nearly every argument that draws the attention of the interlocutor to a contradiction is cast in terms of inconsistent human behaviour.[29] In spite of this, the discovery of the logical importance of the notion of contradiction did not take place in ancient China. The conceptualization of logical principles in ancient China proceeds from examples and situations related to human action and behaviour.

Moreover, the Chinese expression for pointing out a contradiction in the discourse of someone is *bei*,[1] which means, properly speaking 'self-contradictory'.[30] It is interesting to note that Gongsun Long's paradoxes, when a third party reports them, are transposed into the mode of human action, as for example in the first chapter of the book *Gongsunlongzi*, where we find an anonymous pastiche of the *White Horse Treatise*.

> Gongsun Long met Kong Chuan in the palace of Lord Ping Yuan from Zhao. Kong Chuan said: 'I have long heard of your high reputation. For a long time, I have wished to become your disciple. However, I cannot accept your doctrine that a white horse is not a horse. If you could agree to abandon this technique, then I can willingly become your pupil.'
>
> Gongsun Long said: 'Your words are *self-contradictory*. What I am famous for is precisely the doctrine of the white horse. But if you make me abandon it, then I will have nothing to teach anymore. Moreover, you would like that he who teaches be inferior in knowledge to the one who learns. If you want me to abandon my doctrine, you would be my teacher before being my pupil. To teach somebody before having him as one's master is *self-contradictory*.'
>
> (*Gongsunlongzi*, ch. 1; *Daozang* edition)

Gongsun Long points out the contradiction by showing that Kong Chuan *acts* in an inconsistent way. The argument is simply recast into the mould of human action, where the inconsistency of the discourse is mirrored in the

---

28 See Leslie 1964.

29 On this problem, see the essay 'The Origin of Logic in China' in this volume.

30 *Bei* 'self-contradictory' or 'self-falsifying' seems to have been one of the favourite expressions of Gongsun Long, and the strategy of nearly all the pieces that can be attributed to him rests upon the technique of proving that his opponent contradicts himself. *Bei* is also a key term in the *Mohist Canon* (Graham 1978: 199–200).

inconsistency of the action. In ancient Chinese philosophical literature, Gongsun Long's reputation is not solely grounded upon his famous *White Horse Treatise*, where the sophist tries to prove that a white horse is not a horse. He had also established a reputation for himself as a diplomat.[31] In the *Lüshichunqiu* we find several anecdotes illustrating Gongsun Long's method. There is one recurring theme behind all the stories: Gongsun Long, in an almost Socratic manner, shows that his interlocutor is not consistent with himself and that his behaviour is self-contradictory.

> King Hui of Zhao said to Gongsun Long: 'I have tried to stop war for over ten years. If I have not succeeded until now, does that mean that it is impossible to stop war?' Gongsun Long replied: 'The idea of pacifism is at the core of the doctrine of universal love. Pacifism, however, should not be an idle word; the deeds must follow. Recently, after Qin had taken away two provinces, Lan and Lishi, you were in deep mourning. If you, on the contrary, have conquered a city from Qi in the East, you organize a big feast. If Qin wins land, you are in deep mourning, but if Qi loses a city, you organize a big feast. This is not consistent with the principles of universal love. This is the reason why you cannot achieve pacifism.'
>
> (*Lüshichunqiu*, ch. 18.1; see also ch. 18.7)

Two political principles are prominent in this text: the idea of pacifism ('stop war', *yan bing*[u]) and that of universal love (*jian ai*[v]). Both are Mohist principles.[32] But the most important aspect is that Gongsun Long here only shows that the King is not consistent with himself. The same technique is used also in another text.

> When Qin attacked Zhao, the Lord of Ping Yuan searched for help in the State of Wei. The Lord of Xin Ling thereupon sent troops to the city-walls of Han Tan and Qin was obliged to retreat. A counsellor, Yu Qing, proposed to the King of Zhao to give land to the Lord of Ping Yuan as a compensation for his good offices: 'That the affair between both states has been arranged without war and injury is due, above all, to the Lord of Ping Yuan. It would be unsuitable, however, to rely upon the influence of somebody without rewarding him afterwards.'
>
> 'You are right,' answered the King, and he gave land to Ping Yuan.
>
> When Gongsun Long heard of it, he asked for an audience with the Lord of Ping Yuan: 'You have received the city of Dong Wu as an apanage, without having defeated an army and without having killed a general. In the State of Zhao, there are many men greatly superior to you in virtue. The charge of chief minister has been bestowed upon you only because of your noble lineage. You have received the city of Dong Wu as an apanage, without achieving anything whereby you would have merited it, and you did not refuse it. You have received the rank of a prime minister without having achieved anything proving that you were worthy of it, and you did not refuse. Now, however, after the first service you have rendered to the State, you agree to accept new territories. In the first place, you accept a fief

---

31   Reding 1985: 426–34.
32   Gongsun Long has perhaps been a Mohist student, for he uses, in his dialectical treatises, also the technical terms of the Later Mohists.

because of your noble lineage; thereafter, you agree to accept land as a salary for your good offices. In your place, I would not accept.'

'I shall faithfully follow your advice,' said Ping Yuan. He refused the fief.

> (*Zhanguoce*, p. 699, Shanghai, *Gujie chubanshe chuban* edition, 1978 =
> *Shiji*, ch. 76, pp. 2369–70, *Zhonghua shuju* edition)

Gongsun Long here points to an inconsistency in the behaviour of Lord Ping Yuan: he has received land only because of his noble position and should not, therefore, accept land also now because of his merits.

These examples show that Gongsun Long applies systematically a dialectical method of his own. It is a kind of political 'psychoanalysis': Gongsun Long shows to his patient that he follows, apparently in an unconscious way, principles that are in contradiction with his overt, public behaviour. This method has some resemblance to the Socratic method, because Gongsun Long, not unlike Socrates, does not bring his own philosophical or political convictions into the debate. He is satisfied to show that his interlocutor is not consistent with himself in the first place.[33] Gongsun Long must therefore have had a clear notion of the principle of contradiction, even if he did not try to spell it out, like Aristotle or Plato, in an abstract way.

An unexpected 'by-product' of the Chinese approach to the problem of contradiction is that the proof of the principle of non-contradiction is available without difficulties by placing the debate on the level of practical human discourse.

> To claim that all saying contradicts itself is self-contradictory. Explained by: what he says himself.
>
> To be self-contradictory is to be inadmissible. If what this man says is admissible, there is saying which he recognises as admissible (and so not self-contradictory). If what this man says is inadmissible, to suppose that it fits the fact is necessarily ill-considered.
>
> (*Mohist Canon*, B 71; translation Graham 1978: 445)

The Later Mohists envisage the problem from the point of view of what is said. If the man claims that all sayings are self-contradictory, the very proposition he utters must then also be self-contradictory. So if he presents his saying as true, he has issued at least one sentence he does not think self-contradictory, and *acts* thus in an inconsistent way. If he presents his saying himself as false – or even barely as self-contradictory – he cannot establish his claim.

It is curious to note that the Later Mohists do not pay attention to the dilemma that nearly every Western logician finds behind this paradox. When we ask the question: is the sentence 'every sentence is self-contradictory' self-contradictory or not?, we are driven to give two equally inconsistent answers. If the sentence is self-contradictory, then it is false, and so its opposite is true, namely that there are sentences that are not self-contradictory. But this goes against the initial hypothesis. If the sentence is not self-contradictory, then it says that the proposition that

---

33   Cf. Plato, *Sophist* 230B–C.

every sentence is self-contradictory is true, and hence also contradicts the initial hypothesis. Whatever the answer, there is a contradiction.

The reason why the Later Mohists do not see the dilemma is because they imagine the practical situation where someone actually *says* that everything he says is self-contradictory. We see, therefore, that even the writings of the Later Mohist, the most logical-minded thinkers in ancient China, presuppose a notion of contradiction – more precisely, as we have seen, self-contradiction – that is tied to human behaviour, speech and action, and not to immutable logical or metaphysical principles. No effort is made to relate this notion of self-contradiction in behaviour to the notion of *fan*w 'the converse'.

The Later Mohists were thus the only thinkers in ancient China that could have discovered the notion of contradiction in its Aristotelian acceptation. But Aristotle, on the other hand, also presents us with a typically Chinese argument. Aristotle had declared, in book Γ 4 of the *Metaphysics*,[34] that the law of non-contradiction could not be proved. He asserts, however, that it is possible to prove the principle, as he says, by 'way of refutation', if only the opponent agrees to say something. The important thing here is the remark that the interlocutor must open his mouth and *say* something to be refuted.[35] If he remains silent, he cannot be refuted, but is then, as Aristotle observes, in no way different from a vegetable.[36]

Aristotle concedes a few lines later that this kind of proof by 'way of refutation' is of another type than the standard proof. This 'other type', I would say, clearly is the Chinese way: the very act of saying that everything one says is self-contradictory is impossible as such. This, again, is a path that was not further explored by the early Greek philosophers.

I hope to have shown, through this short comparative analysis of the development of the notion of contradiction in early Greek and Chinese philosophy, that we do not move in two totally different and incommensurable philosophical universes, but that the theories proposed are the result of choosing one solution rather than another within one and the same pool of possibilities. In ancient Greece, the notion of contradiction had been discovered within the framework of epistemology and ontology,[37] whereas the notion had been conceptualized from a quite different direction, namely from the one of human action, in ancient China. Traces of the discarded solutions, however, remain as scattered elements in each culture and faintly recall unexplored possibilities.

---

34 *Metaphysics* Γ; 1006a3–a9: '[…] we have just accepted that it is impossible to be and not be simultaneously, and we have shown by means of this that it is the firmest of all principles. Some, owing to lack of training, actually ask that it be demonstrated: for it is lack of training not to recognize of which things demonstration ought to be sought, and of which not. For in general it is impossible that there should be demonstration of everything, since it would go on to infinity […].' (Translation Kirwan 1980: 8)

35 On this type of proof, often labelled *ad hominem*, see Dancy 1975: 14f.; Cassin and Narcy 1989.

36 *Metaphysics* Γ; 1006a11–a15.

37 See Thom 1999; Gourinat 2001.

Chapter 2

The Origin of Logic in China

The first remark that unerringly turns up when Oriental modes of thinking are compared to Western is that ancient China lacks, unlike Greece and India, a science of logic.[1] Two reasons have mainly been invoked to explain the absence of logic in ancient China: either the Chinese mind was judged to be illogical in itself[2] or the Chinese language was incapable of formulating the laws of logic. Considered from the point of view of the evolution of Western logic, these statements could mean no more than that the Chinese, in the beginning, were incapable of reasoning by syllogisms.[3] The first reaction to these claims was a desperate search for syllogisms in the corpus of early Chinese philosophical literature[4] forgetting, though, that the syllogistic form of reasoning is only a logical decision procedure, applied in very special circumstances, and only to arguments that may be cast into a normal form, which comprises a major premise, a minor premise and a conclusion. The degree of advancement of a science of logic in ancient China cannot be measured simply by counting the number of syllogisms occurring in argumentative texts. If the syllogistic mode of reasoning appears more natural to us, this perhaps only means that this form of reasoning is better adapted to our, Indo-European, modes of linguistic expression. There have also been attempts to show that Chinese reasoning comes closer to predicate logic or class logic[5] but few efforts have been made to study typically Chinese ways of reasoning.

Judging the logical achievements of the first Chinese philosophers by comparing them to Western standards of reasoning has proved, in the end, quite unsuccessful. These Western standards 'met with little success, but even if they had been more successful, it would still be interesting to find out how the ancient Chinese themselves looked at reasoning'.[6] If we truly want to discover how Chinese logic operates, we will have to study, as Chao Yuanren has put it, 'how logic operates in Chinese'.[7]

---

1   Bronckhorst 2001.
2   Forke 1901–1902: 5; Granet 1934: 37 and 337; Liou Kia-Hway 1965. See also Bao Zhiming 1987.
3   Granet 1934: 336.
4   Masson-Oursel (1913) tried to sort out 'sorites' (a kind of polysyllogism). For an example of a Chinese syllogism, see *Lüshichunqiu*, ch. 18.4. On syllogisms in Chinese, see also Harbsmeier 1998: 278–80.
5   Cikoski 1975: 325; Chmielewski 1962–1969.
6   Lau 1952–1953: 189.
7   Chao Yuanren 1959: 1; Chmielewski 1979.

Logic, in these contexts, has two different, though related, meanings. We have, on the one hand, the *logica utens*, the laws of logical reasoning such as they are used unconsciously and informally in natural languages. On the other hand, we have the *logica docens*, the explicit formulation of a system of all valid logical inferences.[8] The formation of a *logica docens* is linked to the existence, in a natural language, of zones of logical perturbation, that is, of instances where there is a conflict between the structures of language and those of logic. The instinctive reaction, in such problematic cases, is to look for a set of sure and indisputable cases that can serve as guidelines to correct reasoning. The search for systems of formal logic *outside* language is the typical Western choice, whereas the search for logical structures *within* language is the option taken by the Chinese.

The notion of a *logica docens* within language is hard to conceive at first sight. Nevertheless, the claim made in this essay is precisely that analogical reasoning is the typically Chinese way of representing logical structures within language. The present investigation thus focuses mainly on the logical processes governing the analogical mode of arguing used by the first Chinese philosophers.[9]

Analogical *reasoning*, I suggest, is the typically Chinese answer to the problem of logical reasoning. Analogical reasoning, as it will be defined in this essay, is extremely rare in early Greek philosophical literature.[10] We find there, instead, mostly in connection with cosmological speculation, another type of analogy, which I shall term 'heuristic analogy'.[11] Here is a typical example:

> Some of them say that when the earth is heated by the sun, the sea comes into being like sweat – which is also the reason why it is salty, for sweat is salty.
> (Empedocles, fragment A 25 DK = 371 KRS)[12]

This basic contrast between ancient Greek and ancient Chinese intellectual history is intriguing enough to deserve a more thoroughgoing exploration.

Also, the problems analogical reasoning had to face in ancient China are far more complex than has hitherto been assumed, because they force the Western philosopher to look far beyond syllogisms and even resort to mathematical logic and formal syntax to get an accurate understanding of the goals the first Chinese logicians had set themselves. I do not claim, though, that the Chinese had anticipated mathematical logic.

---

8   Hansen (1983: 17–23) draws a similar distinction between explicit and implicit logic.
9   Lau 1963; Cikoski 1975; Graham 1986a; Volkov 1992.
10   See Barnes 1982: 55. Modern discussions of analogical reasoning also do not seem to take into account the logical feature; see, for example, Helman 1988. There is a doctrine of analogical inference in Stoic philosophy, especially in Philodemus. But this theory deals with what we would now call induction.
11   For examples, see Lloyd 1966: 384–420.
12   Quotations of the fragments of the Presocratics refer to Diels, H. (1951–1952), *Die Fragmente der Vorsokratiker*, ed. W. Kranz, 3 vols, sixth edn, Berlin: Weidmann (= DK) and to Kirk, G. S., Raven, J. E. and Schofield, M. (1983), *The Presocratic Philosophers: a Critical History with a Selection of Texts*, second edn, Cambridge: Cambridge University Press (= KRS).

In order to render my own approach to this problem more explicit, I would like to present first my model of analogical reasoning. An argumentative analogy consists of two parts, the *exposition* and the *application*. The exposition comprises the narrative element, generally a story or a parable; the application, that is the concrete case at issue that is to be exemplified, is not overtly expressed, though all the elements the hearer needs to reconstruct it can be guessed from the context.[13] Analogical reasoning, to put it roughly, is a representation of logical structures through narrative elements, as we can see in the following story.

> Ch'un-yü K'un [Chunyu Kun] said, 'Is it prescribed by the rites that, in giving and receiving, man and woman do not touch each other?'
> 'It is,' said Mencius.
> 'When one's sister-in-law is drowning, does one stretch out a hand to help her?'
> 'Not to help a sister-in-law who is drowning is to be a brute. It is prescribed by the rites that, in giving and receiving, man and woman should not touch each other, but in stretching out a helping hand to the drowning sister-in-law one uses one's discretion.'
> 'Now the Empire is drowning. Why do you not help it?'
> 'When the Empire is drowning, one helps it with the way; when a sister-in-law is drowning, one helps her with one's hand. Would you have me help the Empire with my hand?'
>
> (*Mencius*, IV,A,17; translation Lau 1983: 124–25)

In order to show the purely logical elements of this story, I shall first develop a technique of analysis. The constituents of the exposition are its *terms*. By term, I understand an element of the exposition that has a corresponding explicit or implicit counterpart in the application (for example, the sister-in-law is drowning – the Empire is drowning). The logical relations holding between the terms of the exposition determine the *logical structure* of the exposition or its *premises*.

The terms of the exposition and their corresponding counterparts in the application are, according to my analysis, the following:

Exposition	Terms	Application
the rites	P	the Way
a constitutive principle of the rites (man and woman should not touch each other while giving and receiving)	Q	a constitutive principle of the Way (not making a compromise, for example)
the sister-in-law is drowning	R	the Empire is 'drowning'
the sister-in-law is rescued	S	the Empire is saved
to be a brute	T	to be a brute
to use one's discretion i.e. resort to weighing relative benefit and harm	U	to resort to weighing

---

13   The distinction between what I have termed exposition and application is parallel to many similar distinctions made by linguists, semanticists and philosophers, especially where the domain of metaphor is concerned, as for example tenor and vehicle (cf. Richards 1936) or focus and frame (cf. Black 1981).

The logical structure of this analogy can be expressed as follows:

1   If the rites prevail, man and woman do not touch while giving and receiving.
2   If your sister-in-law is drowning and you do not rescue her, then you are a brute.
3   Your sister-in-law is rescued if and only if you seize her hand.
4   If you seize the hand of your sister-in-law to rescue her, then you resort to weighing (of relative benefit and harm).

The logical properties of this piece of analogical reasoning follow from the inferences that can be drawn from these four premises.[14] It can be shown, for example, that the proposition 'if the rites are observed, then the sister-in-law is not rescued when drowning', i.e. $P \supset (R \supset \neg S)$, logically follows from premises 1 and 3.

Chunyu Kun, the opponent of Mencius, claims that the logical properties of the exposition are transposable *salva veritate* on to the application of this analogy. The whole argument can then be rewritten by simply replacing the terms of the exposition by those of the application, as the table given above readily shows. Chunyu Kun's conclusion is that 'if the Empire is drowning and you do not resort to weighing (deviate from your moral principles and make a compromise), then you are a brute' (formalized: $(R \& \neg U) \supset T$). This conclusion follows logically (truth-functionally) from the four premises established before.[15]

Chunyu Kun's argumentative analogy then is formally valid. The reason why Mencius nevertheless does not accept it cannot therefore depend on its formal aspects. Once the formal element in argumentative analogies is recognized, we can inquire into the kind of logical relations that may be expressed in analogies. It appears at once that Chinese thinkers are especially fond of one very well defined type of argumentation, namely of analogies by contradiction.[16] The distinctive feature of this type of argument is that its logical structure contains a contradiction. Here are two examples of this kind of argument.

---

14   Here is a formal representation of the argument:
    1   $P \supset Q$
    2   $(R \& \neg S) \supset T$
    3   $S \equiv \neg Q$
    4   $(\neg Q \& S) \supset U$
15   The direct proof of this conclusion would be long. Indirect proof is simpler in this case. Take the conjunction of premises 1, 2, 3 and 4 as the antecedent, and the conclusion $(R \& \neg U) \supset T$ as the consequent of an implication. Suppose then, *per absurdum*, that this implication is false. It is false, if and only if, U and T have negative truth-values and R has a positive truth-value. But if you admit this same distribution of truth-values also for the antecedent, it becomes inconsistent, which is contrary to the hypothesis. Therefore, it is impossible for $(R \& \neg U) \supset T$ not to follow from premises 1 to 4.
16   For this type of analogy, see Leslie 1964.

Gongmengzi said: 'Poverty or wealth, old age or premature death, all are determined by Heaven and cannot be changed.' But he also said: 'The gentleman must study.' Mozi commented: 'To be in favour of fatalism and yet maintain that men should study, this is like telling somebody to cover his hair while removing his hat.'

(*Mozi*, ch. 48, p. 275, *Zhuzi jicheng* edition)

Gongmengzi said: 'There are neither ghosts nor spirits.' But he also maintained: 'The gentleman must study the sacrificial rites.' Mozi commented: 'Study the sacrificial rites while affirming that there are no spirits, this is like studying the ceremonials of hospitality where there are no guests; this is like knotting nets while there are no fish.'

(*Mozi*, ch. 48, p. 276, *Zhuzi jicheng* edition)

The terms of the last of these two analogies are easy to state:

Exposition	Terms	Application
knot nets	P	study sacrificial rites
there are fish	Q	there are spirits

The logical structure of the analogy can be represented by means of the following two premises:

1   You knot nets if and only if there are fish.
2   Gongmengzi knots nets while there are no fish.

The logical property[17] of this analogy is a special case, for it expresses a contradiction: the inference $Q \& \neg Q$ logically follows from the two preceding premises. Mozi wants to stigmatize Gongmengzi's illogical and inconsistent behaviour; hence the contradiction in both analogies. It is obvious that premises 1 and 2 cannot both be true. Gongmengzi either has to abandon the study of sacrificial rites, or he has to believe in the existence of spirits, if he wants to be consistent with himself.

Analogies do not only illustrate situations where a contradiction is expressed, but can also be made to represent other types of reasoning, such as for example the principle of a necessary condition. Take the following text from the second chapter of the book *Zhuangzi*.

For there to be 'that's it, that's not' before they are formed in the heart would be to go to Yue today and have arrived yesterday.

(*Zhuangzi*, ch. 2, p. 9, *Zhuzi jicheng* edition; translation Graham 1981: 51)

---

17   Here is a normalization of this structure: 1 $P \equiv Q$; 2 $P \& \neg Q$

The idea of a necessary condition is implied in the second part of the text: 'you can arrive at Yue if and only if you have previously set out to get there.' This statement is analogous to Zhuangzi's (unexpressed) premise: 'there can be judging of alternatives if and only if the contents of these alternatives previously exist in one's mind', implying thereby that each judgement is relative to the position of the person who utters it and that it does not refer to objective and immutable features existing independently in the outer world.[18]

The logical principle here expressed is the one of a necessary condition. The mind of a human person is the condition of there being alternatives, since nothing definite corresponds to these alternatives in the outer world. In logically less refined texts, this principle of a necessary condition is often expressed by the following formula: 'Who can hold something hot and not cool his hand first with water?'[19]

The early Mohists were even able to distinguish quite neatly between a necessary and a sufficient condition, as the following two examples show. Here is the first one.

> Master Mozi was ill. Die Bi entered his room and asked: 'Master, you said that ghosts and spirits are omniscient, that they have the power to send blessing and misfortune, and that they reward the good and punish the evil. However, you are a sage. How can it be that you are ill? Is it that these teachings of yours are incorrect, or is it that the ghosts and spirits lack omniscience?' Master Mozi replied: 'Even if I am ill, how could the spirit's lack of omniscience be held responsible for it? Diseases can be contracted in many ways. Some diseases are caused by excessive cold or heat; others are caused by excessive work or hardship. If there are one hundred gates and you shut only one of them, how can you prevent the burglar from getting in?'
>
> (*Mozi*, ch. 48, p. 280, *Zhuzi jicheng* edition)

Sickness is, for the Mohists, the typical example of an event that may have more than one cause.[20] Mozi here enumerates several causes: climate, exhaustion, evil conduct and possibly many more. By adopting virtuous conduct, as Master Mozi certainly does, only one out of many different possible causes for illness, namely punishment by omniscient spirits for evil conduct, is eliminated. He 'shuts only one gate'.

Consider now another, quite complementary, analogy from chapter 8 of the book *Mozi*.

> Superiors employ inferiors by appealing to only one criterion: [select the worthy, employ the able]. Inferiors serve their superiors by means of only one skill [be able, be worthy]. Compare this situation to the rich man who builds a high wall around his splendid palace and who, after the completion of the wall, pierces only

---

18   On these matters, Zhuangzi sharply disagrees with the Later Mohists. See theorem A 74 of the *Mohist Canon*, Graham 1978: 318.
19   See, for example, *Mencius* IV,A,7; *Mozi*, ch. 9, p. 30, *Zhuzi jicheng* edition.
20   For an example in the writings of the Later Mohists, see Graham 1978: 226.

one gate. If there is a burglar getting in, the rich man shuts the gate through which the burglar has come in, and then searches for him. The burglar cannot get out by another way [he has to come back to the gate]. And then, the rich man can get hold of him. Why? – Because the rich man occupies the strategic point.

(*Mozi*, ch. 8, p. 26, *Zhuzi jicheng* edition)

Mozi's goal is to show that the principle of employing the worthy is a necessary condition for good government. For him, there is only one condition (gate) to it, and it is called 'employ the worthy'.[21] This last analogy, the 'one-gate-analogy', symbolizes an event that can have only one cause; the foregoing analogy, the 'one-hundred-gates-analogy', is supposed to show that one and the same event may be brought about by many different causes.[22]

My claim then is that every argumentative analogy embodies a rule of inference.[23] Analysing another analogy from the Mencius can bring out this principle very clearly.

[Mencius said to King Xuan of Qi:]
'Should someone say to you "I am strong enough to lift a hundred chün but not a feather; I have eyes that can see the tip of a fine hair but not a cartload of firewood", would you accept the truth of such a statement?'
'No,' said the King.
'Why should it be different in your case? Your bounty is sufficient to reach the animals, yet the benefits of your government fail to reach the people. That a feather is not lifted is because one fails to make an effort; that a cartload of firewood is not seen is because one fails to use one's eyes. Similarly, that peace is not brought to the people is because you fail to practice kindness.'

(*Mencius*, I,A,7; translation Lau 1983: 56)

This analogy provides us with two different expositions (a and b), as the following table shows.

Exposition	Terms	Application
a) strong enough to lift a heavy load b) eyes that can see the tip of a fine hair	P	compassion is sufficient to reach the animals
a) strong enough to lift a feather b) able to see a cartload of firewood	Q	compassion is sufficient to reach the common people
a) use one's strength b) use one's power to see	R	use one's compassion

---

21 The analogy of the gate seems to have been quite common. It is to be found in *Lunyu* 6.17; in the *Shangjunshu*, ch. 5, p. 11; the *Xunzi*, ch. 17, p. 213 and also in the *Huainanzi*, ch. 18, p. 320, *Zhuzi jicheng* edition.
22 For a more rigorous formulation of these two principles in the *Mohist Canon*, see theorem A 1, Graham 1978: 263–65.
23 Sacksteder 1974: 236.

The logical structure of this analogy may be represented as follows:

1   $(P \& \neg Q) \neg \supset R$
2   P
Conclusion: $R \supset Q$

Mencius wants to prove to King Xuan of Qi that, if he resorts to compassion (*en*[a]), the benefits will reach the common people (in formalized language, $R \supset Q$). To prove the validity of this analogy, we need only to show that the proposition $R \supset Q$ logically follows from the premise $(P \& \neg Q) \supset \neg R$. It does, if we supply a second premise, namely (2) P, in the application of the argument. This condition is fulfilled, since the text of the *Mencius* itself provides us with the missing premise: the King had indeed once shown compassion for an animal.[24] Our analogical argument is, then, logically sound.[25] The fact that we have to deploy the tools of mathematical logic to make sure of it only shows that our logical intuition is, compared to the one of the first Chinese philosophers, less powerful.

Argumentative analogies are a purely formal device. Background information is useful only insofar as it contributes to an adequate understanding of the logical properties of the analogy.[26] The formal riguru of these analogies often escapes the Western mind, not prepared to look for logical principles in seemingly anecdotal or narrative material.[27]

Argumentative analogies are also a widespread phenomenon in philosophical texts other than the *Mencius* or the *Mozi*. In the *Lüshichunqiu*, for example, the sophist Hui Shi always resorts to argumentative analogies when debating with Bai Gui, Kuang Zhang, or King Hui of Wei.[28] Each one of these debates invariably adopts the form of an analogy followed by a counter-analogy. Gongsun Long's *White Horse Treatise* also follows this same model.[29] Take the following argument.

---

24   See *Mencius*, I,A,7; Lau 1983: 55.
25   Proof:
    1   $(P \& \neg Q) \supset \neg R$ (premise)
    2   P (premise)
       $R \supset Q$ (conclusion)
    (i) $R \supset \neg (P \& \neg Q)$ 1; contraposition
    (ii) $R \supset (\neg P \vee Q)$ (i); De Morgan
    (iii) $R \supset (P \supset Q)$ (ii); def. implication
    (iv) $P \supset (R \supset Q)$ (iii); permut. antec.
    (v) $R \supset Q$ (iv); 2; mod. ponens.
26   On this point, I diverge from Lau 1963: 173.
27   I totally disagree with Bodde 1967: 228, who writes: 'Chinese philosophy, because of this special emphasis upon analogy, is rarely written in the form of logically developed essays, but usually consists of a series of picturesque metaphors, parables, and anecdotes strung together to illustrate certain main ideas. Once more the result is to make Chinese philosophy poetic rather than logical. It tries to bring emotional rather than intellectual conviction and its main appeal is to the heart rather than to the mind.'
28   *Lüshichunqiu*, ch. 18.6; ch. 18.7; ch. 21.5.
29   See Reding 1985: 411–13; Harbsmeier 1989.

Someone who looks for a horse will be just as satisfied with a yellow or a black horse. Someone who looks for a white horse will not be satisfied with a yellow or a black horse. Supposing that 'white horse' was nothing other than 'horse', he would have been looking for the same thing in both cases. And if he had been looking for the same thing in both cases, a white horse would not have been different from a horse. If he was not seeking something different, why is it then that such horses as the yellow and the black were admissible in one case but not in the other? Admissible and inadmissible are plainly contradictory. Therefore yellow and black horses have the peculiarity that one may produce them in answer to 'is there a horse?', but not in answer to 'is there a white horse?'. This is conclusive proof that 'white horse' is not 'horse'.

(*Gongsunlongzi*, ch. 2, *Daozang* edition)

Gongsun Long here wants to show that the terms 'white horse' and 'horse' cannot be exchanged *salva veritate* in every context. The phrase *baima fei ma*[b] hence should not be translated as 'A white horse is not a horse', but rather '"white horse" *is not the same as* "horse"'. There are many cases in which this statement proves to be true: if I want to have many horses, this does not imply that I want to have many white horses, or if I sell many horses, this does not imply that I sell many white horses. The real importance of Gongsun Long's dialogue appears if we view it as a model-treatise, as a kind of empty form with the possibility, for example, to replace the terms 'white' and 'horse' by other, philosophically much more important terms such as 'criminal' and 'man' and rewrite the whole treatise as a proof that 'criminal man is not the same as man', to show that killing a criminal man is not the same as killing a man. The Later Mohists, as we shall see below, had indeed tried to prove that 'killing a criminal man is not the same as killing a man', but they had started from the proposition 'A criminal man is a man'.

Analogical reasoning then comes astonishingly close to formal reasoning. In one sense at least, analogical reasoning appears to operate in the same way as does formal logic, namely with variables. Terms such as 'horse', 'white', 'lift a feather', occupy what we would now call empty predicate places. The main role of the exposition of an analogical argument is to make sure that the proposed structure is formally correct, and hence rationally acceptable to the opponent. The crucial dialectical move with analogical reasoning is, then, the replacement of the terms of the exposition by those of the application. Are white horses really of the same kind as criminal men? Is the capacity to lift a feather really of the same type as the capacity to feel compassion for animals? Indeed, the opponent might well agree that the exposition is formally correct, but refuse to extend it to the intended application.

This observation gives us a clue for analysing the *dénouement* of one of our preceding analogies (*Mencius*, I,A,7).

---

29   See Reding 1985: 411–13; Harbsmeier 1989.

[Mencius to King Xuan of Qi]

'Hence your failure to become a true King is due to a refusal to act, not to an inability to act.'

'What is the difference in form between refusal to act and inability to act?'

'If you say to someone, "I am unable to do it", when the task is one of striding over the North Sea with Mount T'ai under your arm, then this is a genuine case of inability to act. But if you say "I am unable to do it", when it is one of massaging an elder's joints for him, then this is a case of refusal to act, not of inability. Hence your failure to become a true King is not the same in kind [*lei^c*] as "striding over the North Sea with Mount T'ai under your arm", but the same as "massaging an elder's joints for him".'

(Mencius, I,A,7; translation Lau 1983: 56)

King Xuan's question allows us to infer that he did not range 'compassion' (*en^d*) in the same category as 'clear-sightedness' (*ming^e*) or 'strength' (*li^f*). He probably considered compassion as a charismatic endowment rather than as a dispositional state. Mencius, on the other hand, is eager to prove that compassion is of the same kind (*lei^g*) as strength and clear-sightedness, and therefore attempts to prove that compassion expresses, like strength and clear-sightedness, a dispositional state, that is, a quality one can have without presently displaying it and a quality one can possess to a larger or to a smaller extent. King Xuan agrees with Mencius on the logical properties of the analogy. The point, then, on which he is not willing to give in is the category, the kind (*lei*), of the key-term 'compassion'. The same remark applies to the analogy Chunyu Kun had tried to enforce upon Mencius.[30] As this analogy is logically sound, Mencius' disagreement can only arise from the substitution of the corresponding terms Chunyu Kun intends to make in the basic model.

For Chunyu Kun, 'Way' and 'rites' belong to the same 'category' (*lei*). Mencius, by his final response, 'would you have me help the Empire with my hand?' points to the fundamental difference that exists between 'the Way' and 'the rites'. If you violate a constitutive principle of the rites, you do so in order to obey the imperatives of a still higher principle, namely humanity, which requires a drowning person to be rescued. The Way however has not got above it any higher principle. Hence, the very possibility of 'weighing' (*quan^h*) is ruled out in this case. The constitutive principles of the Way cannot therefore be violated to settle a conflict between moral rules and worldly needs.

In order to be correct, all analogical reasoning has to fulfil two conditions. First, it has to comply with the formal standards of logical reasoning; second, the terms of the application must be of the same kind, or category, as those of the exposition. One would expect to find both of these aspects equally represented in the logical discussions of the first Chinese philosophers. The formal aspects of analogical reasoning (their *logica docens*) have received surprisingly little attention in the face of the remarkable logical achievements recorded in the *Mencius* and in the *Mozi*. The only explanation for this intriguing phenomenon seems to

---

30   Cf. *Mencius*, IV,A,17; see above.

me to admit that the first Chinese philosophers possess a spontaneous and intuitive capacity of reasoning (a *logica utens*), which proceeds as yet unhampered by the fetters of speculative grammar and metaphysics.[31] But if one may say that the formal aspects of analogical reasoning do not put any serious problems before these philosophers, the same is not true of the second condition, that is, the problem of the similarity of the terms.

The problem of the validity of argumentative analogies amounts to finding out which structure-preserving substitutions of basic terms can be made in the exposition of an analogy in order to yield also in the application a valid piece of reasoning. This means that we now have to search for a criterion likely to guide these structure-preserving substitutions. Such a criterion is easily formulated: the corresponding terms in the exposition and in the application must be of the same kind. The concept of kind (*lei*[i]) is the most important in analogical reasoning. If we look for a technical vocabulary stating the rules of the 'art of debating' (*bian*[j]), we regularly fall back upon statements describing or regulating the use of analogies. These discussions are usually concerned with the category to which the terms of the analogy belong. Refusal of a proposed analogy is often expressed by saying that the terms of its exposition are 'of a different kind' (*yi lei*[k]) than the terms of the intended application. The expression 'ignoring the category' (*bu zhi lei*[l]) is very frequent in these contexts.[32] The isolated example of an 'overlooked category' (*yi lei*[m]) is worth noting.[33] Finally, there is also the expression *lin lei*[n] 'neighbouring category'.[34]

Further evidence for the logical importance of the notion of kind (category, *lei*) can be derived from the fact that an anti-rationalist like Zhuangzi starts his attack on rationality by undermining precisely that concept. For him, the category to which an object belongs can never be fixed. Every object may, after all, be considered similar to any other object. This is the position Zhuangzi adopts in the second chapter of the book named after him, and again at the beginning of the fifth chapter. Depicting the attitude of the sage, Zhuangzi writes:

> Death and life are mighty indeed, but he refuses to alter with them; though heaven were to collapse and earth subside he would not be lost with them. He is aware of the flawless and is not displaced with other things; he does his own naming of the transformations of things and holds fast to their Ancestor. [...] If you look at them from the viewpoint of their differences, from liver to gall is as far as from Ch'u to Yüeh; if you look at them from the viewpoint of their sameness, the myriad things are all one.
>
> (*Zhuangzi*, ch. 5, p. 31, *Zhuzi jicheng* edition;
> translation Graham 1981: 76–77)

---

31 'But logic as a discipline will develop only with consciousness of thinking illogically.' (Graham 1989: 403)
32 See, for example, *Mozi*, ch. 50, p. 294, *Zhuzi jicheng* edition; *Mencius*, VI,A,12 (with *Hanshi waizhuan*, 4.27); *Lüshichunqiu*, ch. 13.4 (likely to be of Mohist origin).
33 See *Zhuangzi*, ch. 24, p. 159, *Zhuzi jicheng* edition.
34 See *Lüshichunqiu*, ch. 10.3. For further examples, see Harbsmeier 1998: 223–28.

Zhuangzi here identifies the activity of categorizing with the activity of naming, except that naming, for him, is an entirely subjective, and hence arbitrary, activity.

> What is It is also Other, what is Other is also It. There they say 'That's it, that's not' from one point of view, here we say 'That's it, that's not' from another point of view. Are there really It and Other? Or really no It and Other? Where neither It nor Other finds its opposite is called the axis of the Way.
>
> (*Zhuangzi*, ch. 2, p. 10, *Zhuzi jicheng* edition;
> translation Graham 1981: 53)

Zhuangzi's philosophy expresses a deep concern for the notion of category (*lei*) and its role in the art of debating. When he attempts to show, in chapter 2, that disputation is impossible, he starts precisely by deconstructing the concept of category.[35] For Zhuangzi, disputation had come to a dead end, and he tried to show that no suitable criterion for fixing the kind could be found. His criticism holds as long as the classification of things, events and processes into their corresponding kinds rests upon the vague classes established by common knowledge. There are lists of this type, established by the philosophers dedicated to correlative thinking, but these had not been established primarily for argumentative purposes, but rather for cosmological reasons. Chapter 17 of the *Huainanzi*, and chapter 25.2 of the *Lüshichunqiu* bear the significant title *Bie lei*° 'distinguishing between kinds'.[36] Moreover, the logical problems raised by the concept of category cannot be solved by a classification of things into their corresponding natural kinds.

One of the Later Mohists' central concerns is to point out that Zhuangzi fundamentally misunderstood the logic that backs up the activity of naming. They had noticed, as Graham has pointed out, that 'the whole art of disputation is discredited if, as Zhuangzi maintains, the distinctions marked by "that" and "this" are unreal. The Mohist answer is that the relativity of the demonstratives has no bearing on the reality of the distinctions.'[37] The Later Mohists do not say that naming is not categorizing; they only point out that naming, and hence categorizing, obeys rules that their technique of debating (*bian*) is able to spell out.

The Later Mohists believe that consistent description is intimately connected with the activity of naming correctly, that is, of naming the similar similarly and the different differently. Under this aspect, the Later Mohists' conception of 'category' (*lei*) comes close to the development of a general method of finding categories of naming. In their treatise on *Names and*

---

35   See *Zhuangzi*, ch. 2, p. 12, *Zhuzi jicheng* edition.
36   For a study of how correlative thinking interlocks with language structure, see Graham 1986a: 16–24.
37   Graham 1978: 441; see also theorem B 68, *ibid.*, pp. 440–41.

objects,[38] they point out the difference in category that exists between 'white' and 'big'.

> If this stone is white, when you break up this stone all of it is the same as the white thing; but although this stone is big, it is not the same as the big thing. In all cases of naming otherwise than by reference to number or measure, when you break up the object, all of it is the thing in question.
>
> (*Names and objects*, fragment 1 (= NO 1);
> translation Graham 1978: 470–71)

Every part of a white stone is white, but not every part of a big stone is also big. 'Big' and 'white' then must belong to different categories of naming. Whereas this first fragment from *Names and objects* introduces a difference between naming by reference to number or measure and naming by shape or characteristics, the next fragment moves to naming on the basis of residence and migration.[39] The expressions 'white horse' (*bai ma*^{p}) and 'Qin horse' (*Qin ma*^{q}) behave syntactically in exactly the same way, but the kind of knowledge they provide is not the same. If we know that a horse is white, we know something definite about it, but not if we only know that it comes from the State of Qin.

The relevance of categories of naming to analogical reasoning appears very clearly also in the following example. Somebody objects to the Mohist doctrine of universal love (*jian ai*^{r}) that it is impossible to love each single man, since the number of men is potentially infinite. The Later Mohists observe that the logical functioning of the predicate 'to love' (*ai*^{s}) is the same as the predicate 'to ask' (*wen*^{t}). If it is possible to ask about an infinite number of men, then it must also be possible to love an infinite number of men.[40] The Later Mohists' method is grounded in the possibility that different predicates (to love, to ask) behave in a logically similar way, and that the logical rules governing some of these predicates are easier to grasp than those governing the more obscure cases.

What hinders the progress of the Later Mohists is the fact that there is no systematic heuristic device to discover all the rules of analogical reasoning at once. There is no system of axioms from where each and every valid rule of reasoning could be deduced. The logical clarification of an argument then amounts to matching a logically obscure predicate with a limpid one.

The more difficult cases, especially the predicate 'to love', may need more than one logical matching. The Later Mohists' opponent may concede that it is not necessary to love an infinite number of men, but he then launches an attack from the other side. He argues that Mohist universal love only requires that we love some men, not all of them, and that this case is similar to the

---

38   Reconstructed by Graham (1978: 469–94).
39   *Names and objects*, fragment 2 (= NO 2); Graham 1978: 470–71.
40   This argument is developed in theorem B 74; Graham 1978: 449–50.

riding of horses: one is said to ride horses already if one rides only some horses, not all of them.

> A white horse is a horse. To ride a white horse is to ride horses. A black horse is a horse. To ride a black horse is to ride horses. Jack is a person. To love Jack is to love people ('persons'). Jill is a person. To love Jill is to love people […].
>
> (*Names and objects*, fragment 14 (= NO 14);
> translation Graham 1978: 485)

At first sight the grammatically similar expressions 'to love people' and 'to ride horses' seem to be also of the same logical type. The Later Mohists observe that the logical and syntactical parallelism holding between 'to ride horses' and 'to love people' breaks down when the reference shifts from 'some horses' to 'all horses' and from 'some man' to 'all men'.

> 'He loves people' requires him to love all people without exception, only then is he deemed to love people. 'He does not love people' does not require that he loves no people at all; he does not love all without exception, and by this criterion is deemed not to love people. 'He rides horses' does not require him to ride all horses without exception before being deemed to ride horses; he rides some horses, and by this criterion is deemed to ride horses. On the other hand, 'he does not ride horses' does require that he rides no horse at all; only then is he deemed not to ride horses.
>
> (*Names and objects*, fragment 17 (= NO 17);
> translation Graham 1978: 491)

This argument shows clearly the logical difference there is between the predicates 'to love people' and 'to ride horses': not to ride horses does mean that one rides no horse at all; but one can be deemed not to love people if one's love does not extend to everyone without exception. If quantification may bring to the surface, as in this example, the fundamental logical differences that exist between syntactically similar expressions, the more so are negation and epistemic or intensional contexts, not to speak of a combined influence of both, as in the following example.

> Robbers are people, but abounding in robbers is not abounding in people, being without robbers is not being without people. How shall we make this clear? Disliking the abundance of robbers is not disliking the abundance of people, desiring to be without robbers is not desiring to be without people. The whole world agrees that these are right; but if such is the case, there is no longer any difficulty in allowing that, although robbers are people, loving robbers is not loving people, not loving robbers is not not loving people, killing robbers is not killing people. The latter claims are the same in kind (*tong lei*[u]) as the former; the world does not think itself wrong to hold the former, yet thinks the Mohist wrong to hold the latter […].
>
> (*Names and objects*, fragment 15 (= NO 15);
> translation Graham 1978: 487–88)

Xunzi quotes 'killing robbers is not killing people' as a sophism.[41] We do not know to what kind of logical standard Xunzi appeals. The Later Mohists, however, are sensitive to his criticism, and simply reply by showing that the type of argument they propose in favour of the killing of robbers (without abandoning their main tenet of universal love) is valid if considered against the background of the natural logic of the Chinese language.

Although a robber is a man, these two terms cannot be exchanged, *salva veritate*, in every context: if I wish an abundant population for my country, this does not mean that I also want many robbers. The Later Mohists thus shift the argument from the level of formal validity or invalidity to the level of its practical applicability. It would be rash to interpret the Later Mohists' method of parallel predicates as an attempt at establishing the outlines of a system of formal logic. The specific problem of these first Chinese logicians is to find out how logic operates in a natural language. The only kind of Western logic that could have been useful to the Later Mohists would have been logical or formal syntax.

The method used by the first Chinese philosophers seems to be the following. They try to clear up the logically obscure sectors of their language with the help of the logically more transparent ones. These logically more transparent sectors assume, in fact, the role of a formal system of logic, in providing standards of valid reasoning. But these operate still *within* language, not in a system of formal logic that is detached from it and that has to be matched to language.[42]

This attitude has far-reaching consequences upon the very style of arguing in Chinese. Let us consider again an example taken from the *Mencius*. Accused by the philosopher of letting the population of his country starve to death, King Hui of Liang argues in the following way.

> *Fei wo ye, sui ye.*^v
> It is none of my doing. It is the fault of the harvest.
>
> (*Mencius*, I,A,3; translation Lau 1983: 52)

To counter this argument, Mencius offers the syntactically similar (but unacceptable) reply of a person having stabbed somebody to death but not willing to assume the responsibility of his forfeit.

> *Fei wo ye, bing ye.*^w
> It is none of my doing. It is the fault of the weapon.
>
> (*Mencius*, I,A,3; translation Lau 1983: 52)

---

41   Cf. *Xunzi*, ch. 22, p. 279, *Zhuzi jicheng* edition.
42   There is also the problem of *translating* the logical arguments of natural languages into the language of symbolic logic. On this aspect, see the remarks of Wardy (2000: 35).

Mencius' counter-argument is based on a logico-syntactical parallelism whose principle is easy to state: if a piece of reasoning leads to a grammatically odd sentence, its underlying logic must also be false.

Now we begin to notice why it is important to make logical differences of this type in argumentative contexts. The obvious distinctions (the knife and 'me') are used as a test, to drive out the real meaning of the opponent's claim. Killing by famine and killing by stabbing to death are, for Mencius, of the same logical type, that is, both presuppose the responsibility of an agent, for the king is believed to have control over the causes of a famine. The syntactical structure of both expressions (*fei wo ye, sui/bing ye*) is the same. Mencius wins the debate at the very moment King Hui of Liang acknowledges the logical identity of both structures. The decisive step is to show that the sentences 'It is none of my doing. It is the fault of the weapon' when pronounced by somebody stabbing to death another person are grammatically odd because they are logically odd. It clearly is a case where the violation of a grammatical rule is at the same time a logical mistake. The *Mohist Canon* uses the following stock-example to make a similar point:

> *Ju dou, bu ju er.*
> *Bai ma duo bai, miao ma bu duo miao.*[x]
> They both fight; they are not both two.
> Most of a white horse is white; most of a blind horse is not blind.
> (*Mohist Canon*, B 3; Graham 1978: 354)

The Later Mohists here use only intuitively clear examples to make their point. But the goal behind these introductory moves to the complex game of dialectics is to attract our attention to possible dangers of analogical reasoning. As soon as we leave the ground of intuitively clear cases, our logical capacities dwindle away. It is highly interesting, however, to notice that the first Chinese philosophers, when confronted with difficult arguments, instinctively react by trying to find a structurally similar but logically more transparent case. What is at stake, always, is the kind, the type of one of the substitutable terms, such as 'ask' and 'love'; 'ride horses' and 'love men'; 'the rites' and 'the Way' and so on. The Later Mohists start from the standard logical value of a given syntactical structure and then go on replacing some elements of this structure by other elements ('blind' for 'big'; 'two for 'fight'). If the substitution leads to unacceptable and logically false sentences, the replaced terms ('big'; 'fight') cannot be of the same type as the original term ('blind'; 'two').

Some of the proto-logical experiments of the Later Mohists can be summarized for convenience in the following synoptic table. Consider the schematization of an argument of the Later Mohists that we have already examined.[43]

---

43   See above; (*Names and objects*, fragment 15 (= NO 15); translation Graham 1978: 487–88).

	I	II	III	IV	V	VI	neg.	I	II	III	IV	V	VI	
1				duo	dao	ren	fei				duo		ren	ye[y]
2				wu	dao	ren	fei				wu		ren	ye[z]
3		wu		duo	dao	ren	fei		wu		duo		ren	ye[aa]
4		yu		wu	dao	ren	fei		yu		wu		ren	ye[ab]
5		ai			dao	ren	fei		ai				ren	ye[ac]
6	bu	ai			dao	ren	fei	bu	ai				ren	ye[ad]
7			sha		dao	ren	fei			sha			ren	ye[ae]

1 Many robbers is not the same as many people.
2 There being no robbers does not mean that there are no people.
3 To hate there being many robbers is not to hate there being many people.
4 To desire that there be no robbers is not to desire that there be no men.
5 To love robbers is not the same as to love people.
6 Not to love robbers is not the same as not to love men.
7 To kill robbers is not the same as to kill people.

The table shows that the logically important operators always hold the same positions in a syntactically invariant grid.

I   negation
II   modalities or epistemic operators
III   actions (transitive verbs)
IV   quantifiers
V   adjectives
VI   basic terms (nouns)

The equivalence between sentence-halves is invariably negated by *fei*[af] The table above also shows that logical syntax was indeed the only form of logic possible in ancient China. It should be obvious therefore that class logic, especially under its syllogistic aspect, is totally inadequate to express and translate the logical insights of the Later Mohists or Mencius. The Later Mohists draw attention to the fact that even if robbers are men (*dao ren ren ye*[ag]), the expression 'robber' cannot be replaced *salva veritate* by the expression 'men' or 'people' in every context. The Later Mohists are well aware of the fact that criminal men belong to the human kind. Their problem, rather, is that class logic seems to be invalid in a number of contexts. For their purposes, the laws of class logic even represented an obstacle to correct reasoning.

The moral and political problems the logic of the Later Mohists was supposed to solve would have required a much more developed form of logic than class logic. Class logic has grown in ancient Greece as an offspring of the first investigations into natural science. Later Mohist logic, on the contrary, was created to deal with social and political problems. But it would be wrong, here, to qualify both as different forms or different kinds of logic. This feature again supports my claim that one of the main differences between Greek and Chinese philosophy is due to a difference in the starting-point.[44]

These examples taken from classical Chinese philosophy reveal that logical problems can be mastered, up to a certain degree, without developing a system of formal logic. Although the first Chinese philosophers do not come to recognize logic and grammar as two independent intellectual activities, they discover the principles of logical syntax, that is, the rules that tell us how to relate grammatical structures to logically correct or logically false expressions, well before Carnap, Wittgenstein and Russell.[45]

One of the consequences of the Later Mohists' approach then also is that they miss, unlike their Greek contemporaries, not only the discovery of formal logic but the discovery of grammar as well, because they only consider instances where they notice a divergence between logic and grammar. What interests them is the divergence, not logical or grammatical rules as such, probably because Chinese is, as has been observed, 'logically more transparent' that Indo-European languages.[46]

The first Greek philosophers, on the other hand, have to fight against a language that seems to be much more hostile to logical reasoning than classical Chinese and that, as a consequence, also needs much stronger and much more explicit 'correctives' than classical Chinese. Nevertheless, there is no need to postulate the existence of an exotic Chinese logic to explain the observed differences. Logical reasoning, here, is like a river that flows straight when there is no obstacle and that meanders only where it is forced to espouse a different linguistic substratum. Even if the meanders look different at a distance, the flow takes nonetheless always the shortest possible line.

---

44   See the *Introduction*.
45   Scharfstein and Daor (1978: 173–76) also note this correlation.
46   See Harbsmeier 1998: 8; Graham 1989: 403.

Chapter 3

Philosophy and Geometry in Early China

It is important for our understanding of Chinese culture to learn that it is not only based on Daoist mysticism or Confucian morality, but that it also had, even at its beginnings, a rational ingredient. The internal logic of Western rationalism, however, puts before us a dilemma: either Chinese rationalism is of the same type as Western rationalism, and hence inferior to it, because less well developed, or Chinese rationalism represents a different kind of rationalism, which seems impossible. Chinese rationality, therefore, is either not rational at all, or is less rational than Western rationalism. The best way to get out of this dilemma is to investigate the behaviour of both of these forms of rationalism when they are confronted with similar tasks, and under comparable circumstances.[1]

The opportunity for undertaking a comparative analysis of this scope does not present itself very often. The purpose of this study is to show that the Later Mohists had succeeded in developing the framework of the axiomatic method in geometry and in philosophy. The *Mohist Canon* (*Mojing*[a]) is the most rational document ever produced in ancient China.[2] This text, written by a group of scholars in the third century BC, is in fact built up like a geometrical treatise, the bulk of the text being divided into theorems (*jing*[b]) and demonstrations, or explanations (*shuo*[c]). Keeping in mind the overwhelming influence mathematics and geometry have had upon Platonic and Aristotelian philosophy, and later upon Descartes, Spinoza and Hume,[3] we have to seize this unique opportunity to compare the interactions of geometry and philosophy in two civilizations that had evolved in total independence.

It has often been pointed out that Chinese philosophy lacks one of the major attributes of Western philosophy, namely the ability to organize a body of knowledge into a coherent system of thought.[4] This opinion derives from the literary style of the philosophical writings of the classical period. The *Lunyu* are a collection of sayings and aphorisms; the *Zhuangzi* presents itself as a collection of dialogues, anecdotes and analogies. The early Mohist School states its main points in the form of a manifesto, the famous 'ten theses':

---

1 See Biderman and Scharfstein 1989. Caveing (1993: 578) even uses the bold formula of an anthropology of forms of rationalism: 'une anthropologie des formes de rationalité, sans que soit donné d'avance un paradigme de la raison.' See also Gloy 1999.
2 For an edition and translation of these texts, see Graham 1978.
3 See Hume's biography in Aubrey 1962: 230.
4 Cf. Feng Youlan 1952: 4.

49

1 Elevating the worthy
2 Conforming to superiors
3 Universal love
4 Rejecting aggression
5 Economy in expenditure
6 Economy in funerals
7 The Will of Heaven
8 Serving the spirits
9 Rejecting music
10 Rejecting destiny

(Mozi, ch. 8–37; Graham 1978: 241)

The rather haphazard style of this collection is obvious, although one may feel the deep logical unity of the underlying thought. In the third century BC, the Later Mohists undertook the formidable task of reconstructing *more geometrico* these ten theses. This project had been conceived to provide a solution to a major philosophical crisis in ancient Chinese philosophy.[5] It is a well-known fact that many philosophers had grounded their ethical views on the concept of human nature (*xing*^{d}). According to Mencius, human nature is basically good; for his opponent, Gaozi, it is indifferent. For Xunzi, human nature, if it remains uncultivated, will be evil. The Later Mohists had clearly recognized that these philosophical debates could never come to an end so long as the concept of human nature was considered to be basic, because it is all too obvious that each philosopher assigns to human nature the properties *they* find suitable. Finally, there is no way to decide between all these conflicting opinions.

The Later Mohists' innovation is to show that the very concept of human nature is not a unitary one. It may indeed be further seperated out into its basic properties, namely desire (*yu*^{e}) and aversion (*e*^{f}). It is worthwhile noticing that 'desire' and 'aversion' are ethically neutral, neither good nor evil. These two concepts are the starting-point of the Later Mohists' ethical philosophy. With the help of these, the notions of benefit (*li*^{g}) and harm (*hai*^{h}) are then defined in theorems A 26 and A 27.

> Harm is what one dislikes getting.
> Benefit is what one is pleased to get.
>
> (Mohist Canon, A 26, A 27; Graham 1978: 282–83)

At first sight, this seems to outline an individualistic or egoistic ethical system, close to hedonism. The Later Mohists, however, do not profess a philosophy of *carpe diem*. They are well aware of the fact that an immediate pleasure may lead to future evil.[6]

---

5 On this problem, see Graham 1978: 15–22.
6 A fruitful comparison is to be drawn here with Cicero, *De finibus*, § 30, where a reconstruction of Epicureanism is offered. The §§ 37 and 38 are also worth reading in parallel.

The Later Mohists' ethical philosophy is individualistic only insofar as it reacts against Confucianism, which grounds its moral philosophy on the family, and on the social group rather than on the individual. After the preliminary definitions of benefit and harm, the Later Mohists go over to the definition of the cardinal virtues of ancient Chinese moral philosophy, namely humanity (*ren*[i]), justice (*yi*[j]), filial piety (*xiao*[k]). The plan of the Later Mohists is to show that all these virtues are ultimately grounded in the concepts of desire and aversion. Their purpose is to put an end to the crisis outlined above by showing that human nature cannot be qualified any more by global predicates such as goodness, badness or moral indifference. The task of ethics is now to show how the virtues of justice, humanity and filial piety arise out of the interaction of desire and aversion in human nature.

Let us briefly examine these basic ethical concepts. The notion of *yi* 'justice' is directly built upon the freshly defined notion of *li* 'benefit'.

> To be *yi* (righteous/dutiful/moral) is to benefit.
> In intent, he takes the whole world as his field; in ability, he is able to benefit it. He is not necessarily employed.
>
> (*Mohist Canon*, A 8; Graham 1978: 270–71)

Filial piety (*xiao*) is also based upon the notion of benefit.

> To be *xiao* (filial) is to benefit one's parents.
> In intent, he takes his parents as his field; in ability, he is able to benefit them. He does not necessarily succeed.
>
> (*Mohist Canon*, A 13; Graham 1978: 274–75)

One of the main notions of the Later Mohists' ethical system is love (*ai*[l]).[7] The definition of this term is unfortunately lost. Graham has offered a plausible reconstruction: loving somebody means to desire benefit for him and dislike harm for him, for his own sake, for the man he is, and not for the social position he has, or because he is a relative. Graham proposes: *Ai, ti li ye.*[m] 'Love is to benefit individually.'[8] This reconstruction, however, is not entirely satisfactory, because the notions of desire and aversion are rather used for describing the results of actions on individuals, not their mental attitude. I would propose, therefore, to reconstruct the definition of 'love' (*ai*) with the help of another key notion, namely 'intention' (*zhi*[n]):

> <*Ai, zhi li ye.*>[o]
> To love is to have the intention of benefiting others (and keep off harm from them).

---

7   The Chinese concept *ai* has little to do with Christian love or even love in the modern, Western, sense. Its core meaning is 'to spare' (see, for example, *Mencius* I,A,7). The Mohist definition of *ai* is indeed easily understood in the light of the meaning 'to spare'. The Mohist formula *jian ai* is probably better translated as 'mutual sparing' than as 'universal love'.

8   See Graham 1978: 48–49.

The intent to benefit expresses a fundamentally positive attitude, much in tune with the 'good will' of Kant. This is a recurring theme in the ethical system of the Later Mohists. The definition of *zhi* is, unfortunately, also lost. The definition of humanity brings in the notion of love.

> To be *ren*[p] (benevolent/humane/kind) is to love individually.
> Love of oneself is not for the sake of making oneself useful. Not like loving a horse.
>
> *(Mohist Canon*, A 7; Graham 1978: 270)

The concept of humanity is defined in terms of another, already defined concept, namely *ai* 'love' and with the help of the expression *ti*[q] 'individually'. This term is defined in theorem A 2.

> A *ti* (unit/individual/part) is a portion in a *jian*[r] (total/collection)/whole).
> For example, one of two, or the starting-point of a measured length.
>
> *(Mohist Canon*, A 2; Graham 1978: 265)

This approach of proceeding from the simple to the complex, and from the undefined to the defined, pervades the whole texture of the *Mohist Canon*, and is not unique to the rational reconstruction of the ethical system. One cannot fail to notice that there must be a consistent method operating behind the Later Mohists' ethical derivations. Let us try to spell it out.

Ethical concepts are divided into two groups: complex concepts and simple concepts. The former are defined, the latter remain undefined. Complex concepts are defined in terms of simple concepts, or other, already defined, complex concepts. The exposition of this ethical system proceeds steadily from the simple to the more complex notions. What is the origin of this method? Where is its homeland?

The Later Mohists consider their ethical system as being independent of experience, or, as a Western philosopher might say, *a priori*. The Mohists do in fact possess a notion that comes quite close to the Western *a priori*: it is the notion of *xian zhi*[s] 'know beforehand'. Theorem A 93 gives the following definition:

> When we 'jump the wall', the circular stays fixed. By the things which follow from each other or exclude each other, we may know *a priori* what it is.
>
> *(Mohist Canon*, A 93; Graham 1978: 342–43)

The Later Mohists define here a kind of conceptual and semantic *a priori*, an *a priori* that has to do with the implicit cognitive content of linguistic expressions. To illustrate this type of knowledge, the Later Mohists refer to the example of the wall. They imagine an object placed behind a wall and ask what we can know about this object when we only know its name. If this object is a horse, we can know *a priori* that it has hoofs and a mane, but we do not know whether it is black or white. In this case, jumping over the wall to investigate the properties of this object adds something to our knowledge about it. In the case of a circle, however, we know its basic properties without having to investigate them: they are *a priori*. Hence the knowledge we may have of the circle is the most typical example of *a priori* knowledge.[9] From this example it appears that the notion of 'cognitive content' does not appeal to mental imagery or verbal connotations. It is grounded, rather, on a special kind of knowledge, termed by the Later Mohists 'knowledge by explanation' (*shuo*[1]) in theorem A 80:

> Knowing that something square will not rotate is by explanation.
> *(Mohist Canon*, A 80; Graham 1978: 327–28)

Knowledge by explanation is one of the three main types of knowledge recognized by the Later Mohists, along with knowledge by hearsay or tradition and knowledge by acquaintance or experience. They focus on knowledge by explanation, the only one capable of providing *a priori* knowledge. The reason why the Later Mohists are interested in this type of knowledge is that they believe that moral knowledge also belongs to this kind. For them, it is possible to know *a priori* how one should act in a given situation.

After this outline of the Later Mohists' epistemological methodology, we can now approach the problem of its origin. This origin, I believe, is geometrical. First of all, the type of knowledge termed 'knowledge by explanation' is, as we have seen, twice illustrated by geometrical examples in theorems A 80 and A 93. In addition, the *Mohist Canon* also lists well over a dozen purely geometrical propositions. To these we shall now turn, in order to determine their underlying methodological principles and their overall organization.

The first question to be raised in this context concerns the status these geometrical propositions are supposed to hold in the *Mohist Canon*. Graham assigns to geometry simply the place of one science among other branches of knowledge, such as optics or mechanics.[10] The geometrical propositions (that is, theorems A 52 to A 69), however, cannot be considered as a summa of the geometrical knowledge acquired in the third century BC, the time of the compilation of the Later Mohists' writings, because the scientific level of ancient Chinese geometry was already quite elevated, probably due to the advances made in geometrical astronomy.[11] The geometrical propositions of the *Mohist Canon* are not likely, therefore, to be a summary of the geometrical knowledge accumulated at that time in ancient China.

It should be no less obvious that the geometrical definitions of the Mohists also have nothing to do with land surveying. In the Western world, as we know, the origin of geometry is sometimes traced back to ancient Egypt, where the flooding of the Nile is said to have rendered necessary the annual re-measurement of the fields and had thus favoured the development of

---

9   See also Graham 1975.
10   Followed by Martzloff 1988: 257.
11   On this problem, see Cullen 1976; Sivin 1969; Graham 1978: 369–71; Ho Peng Yoke 1985; Cullen 1995.

geometry. The geometrical fragment we find in the *Mohist Canon* would have been wholly useless for practical purposes.[12]

These geometrical propositions are quite elementary in nature. We find definitions of the circle, the square, the line, and the point, organized according to a method that we can qualify without hesitating as axiomatic. Note that Euclid's *Elements* also had the function of providing an epistemological foundation to an already constituted body of geometrical knowledge.[13] In what follows, I shall try to recover the real purpose of the Later Mohists' geometrical corpus and show through a careful analysis of its underlying logical principles that its function had also been epistemological. I shall start my analysis by examining the Later Mohists' definition of the circle (*yuan^u*) in theorem A 58.

> *Yuan* (circular) is having the same lengths from one centre.[14]
> The compass draws it *in the rough*?
> > (*Mohist Canon*, A 58; Graham 1978: 307–309)

The primitive concepts used in this definition are those of the 'centre' (*zhong^v*) and 'of the same length' (*tong chang^w*). These two concepts are in turn defined in theorems A 53 and A 54. Theorem A 54 states:

> The centre is [the place from which?] they are the same in length.
> > (*Mohist Canon*, A 54; Graham 1978: 305)

The concept of the centre (or middle) in turn is built itself on the concepts of geometrical point (implicit in the 'that from which') and 'of the same length'. Let us examine first the notion of geometrical point (*duan^x*). It has to be noted, however, that the Chinese *duan* is not exactly the equivalent of our geometrical point. The correct translation of *duan* rather is 'starting-point' or 'end point'.[15] Theorem A 61 states:

> The *duan* (starting-point) is the unit without dimension which precedes all others.
> > (*Mohist Canon*, A 61; Graham 1978: 310)

This definition further refers to the notion of 'dimension' (*you hou^y*). Dimension (*hou*) is defined in the following way in theorem A 55:

> *Hou* (having bulk/thickness/dimension) is having something than which it is bigger.
> > (*Mohist Canon*, A 55; Graham 1978: 305–306)

---

12   The excellent account of Martzloff (1988) seems to be wrong on this point. After having noted that true geometry is a deductive discipline (p. 256), he fails to see (pp. 257–58) that this must have been the goal of the Mohists too.
13   See von Fritz 1955: 90–91; Lloyd 1979: 110; Szabo 2000: 233.
14   See also Plato's definition of the circle in *Letter VII* 342B7–8 and in the *Parmenides* (137E2–3).
15   The Later Mohists' definition comes close to the one devised by Aristotle: 'the point is what limits the line' (*Metaphysics* 1060b12–16; *Physics* 220a9–11).

For the purpose of this study, however, I shall treat *duan* (starting-point) as a basic geometrical term. As far as the extant textual material goes, nothing permits us to infer that the Later Mohists had sharply distinguished mathematical objects from physical objects. Mathematical objects rather seem to be geometrical properties of physical objects.[16]

Another important function of this notion of a 'starting-point' had perhaps been the elimination of paradoxes originating from overlapping lines, as theorem A 60 shows.[17] The starting-point intervenes here to explain that the two rulers (or lines) touch each other at an ideal point, the *duan*, where there is neither overlapping nor any extra space, however small, between the two rulers. It is clear, then, that the centre of a circle must also be a 'starting-point'.

After having defined the first concept entering into the definition of the centre, namely the starting-point, we shall turn now to the notion of 'the same in length' defined in theorem A 53:

> *Tong chang* (of the same length) is each when laid straight (*zheng*[z]) exhausting (*jin*[aa]) the other. The same lengths of door-bar and doorframe are straight.
>
> (*Mohist Canon*, A 53; Graham 1978: 304–305)

To illustrate this theorem, the Later Mohists use the example of the door-bar and the doorframe that 'exhaust each other'. This is a typically mathematical argument, as can also be seen from the way in which Liu Hui proves Pythagoras' theorem in his commentary to chapter 9.3 of the *Jiuzhang suanshu*.

But here we reach, as it seems, the very foundations of the Later Mohists' geometrical system. The notion of *tong chang* (of the same length) contains two quite fundamental geometrical concepts, namely the idea of congruence (by exhaustion)[18] and the idea of a straight line *zheng*. The latter concept (here *zhi*[ab]) is defined in theorem A 57:

> *Zhi* (straight/on a straight course) is in alignment (*can*[ac]).
>
> (*Mohist Canon*, A 57; Graham 1978: 306–307)

The concept of *can* (alignment) is not further defined. It is, as Graham has noted, 'the standard term in Chinese astronomy for the aligning of two gnomons with the observed heavenly body.'[19]

---

16   This statement seems to hold for ancient Chinese mathematics in general. See Martzloff 1988: 258 ('Dans la tradition chinoise [...] les figures sont de véritables objets matériels et ce sont ces objets eux-mêmes qui, manipulés de manière adéquate, permettent de rendre visibles certaines propriétés mathématiques.')

17   Graham 1978: 309–10.

18   The method of congruence (*epharmozein*) is also very important in Euclid's *Elements* and even before him (von Fritz 1955; Szabo 2000: 245).

19   Graham 1978: 307. See also theorem B 38, *ibid.*, p. 405. The key text is *Lüshichunqiu*, ch. 13.1, where the astronomical sense of *can* is plain, as Tan Jiefu (1964: 138–39) has shown. See also Cullen 1976: 110.

It is worth noticing that the Later Mohists' definition of the straight line is at least formally equivalent to Euclid's first two postulates, expounded at the very beginning of the *Elements*. The first postulate claims that it is always possible to link two points to each other by means of a straight line; the second, that a finite straight line can always be continued in a straight way in the same direction. From there it appears that the notion of alignment requires the presence of at least three points. This idea appears very clearly in the famous definition of the straight line given by Plato in the *Parmenides*:

> Straight is when the centre screens off either of the two end points.
>
> (Plato, *Parmenides* 137E4)

We have to imagine three points arranged in such a way that the sight from one end point to the other is obstructed by the point in the middle. It is possible to show, by means of etymological considerations, that the meaning of the Chinese *can* is grounded in this very same intuition. The original graph of *can*, according to the *Shuowen*, the oldest Chinese dictionary, had three stars in its upper part. Written like this, the graph is in fact pronounced *shen*[ad] and is used to name the constellation of Orion.[20] The three stars of the graph *shen* (which survive in *can*, 'align') refer to the three aligned stars of the constellation of Orion. Several astronomical instruments exploit the alignment of these three stars. Note also that in the manuscripts found in Mawangdui the graph *san*[ae] 'three' is generally replaced by *can*.[af]

These considerations have shown that Chinese geometrical intuition, with the discovery of the notions of alignment (*can*) and congruence by exhaustion (*jin*), has hit upon the same elementary geometrical concepts as Euclid and his predecessors in ancient Greece. The Later Mohists' definition of the circle may now be represented in such a way as to show the conceptual lineage of each term:

1   *can* (alignment)   2 *jin* (congruence)   3 *duan* (starting-point)
4   *zheng* (straight line)
5   *tong chang* (of the same length)
6   *zhong* (centre)
7   *yuan* (circle)

The first three notions (1, 2 and 3) are elementary notions. The straight line (4) is defined with the help of the concept of alignment (1). Of the same length (5) relies upon the notions of congruence (2), straight line (4) and starting-point (3). The centre (6) is built upon the concepts of starting-point (3) and of the same length (5). The notions of centre (6) and of the same length (5), finally, define the circle (7).

---

20   See B. Karlgren, *Grammata serica recensa*, series no. 647 (Karlgren 1957: 172). On the ethnoastronomic importance of this constellation, see Lévi-Strauss 1990: 222–45.

There can hardly be any doubt about the fact that the Later Mohists used one and the same method in their ethical and in their geometrical derivation of concepts. Their method may aptly be described as axiomatic; that is, the whole body of knowledge of some branch of science is deduced from a very limited number of elementary propositions or notions. This, finally, is the reason why moral knowledge is comparable to geometry: just as the basic properties of the circle can be known by inspecting its definition, the content of the standard moral terms can also be known by breaking down these terms into their basic components. There is no room, of course, for the conceptions of other schools. The Later Mohists do not even feel the need to refute rival definitions of humanity and justice. The most challenging aspect of this doctrine is that, in the Mohist perspective, the correct definition of the basic moral terms shows these to be in accord with the fundamental Mohist principles. The Later Mohists are convinced that their doctrine is unconditionally true.

> Even if there were no men in the world, master Mozi's words would still stand.
> (*Mozi*, EC 2; Graham 1978: 247)

One difficulty, however, remains. As the Later Mohists have applied their axiomatic method with equal success to geometry and ethics, we would like to know where this method actually originated. It seems that geometry is the obvious candidate. More plausible, however, is the hypothesis of a mutual influence between geometry and philosophy. It is easy to imagine philosophers looking for an immaculate model of rationality outside the sphere of philosophy itself. Philosophers know only too well that their reasoning and their deductions are likely to be secretly influenced and distorted, especially in areas where uncontrolled subjective factors are at work. Hence the need for a model and a standard of rationality. The axiomatic reconstruction of geometry is probably the work, not of geometricians, but of philosophers eager to develop a perfect model of rationality, to serve as a guideline for their future philosophical and ethical deductions. Without the model of geometry, philosophy could not have formulated rigorous standards of rationality; without the rational needs of philosophy, the model of rationality inherent in geometry would perhaps not have been brought to light.[21]

The interdependence of axiomatic geometry and rational philosophy had thus been recognized at a very early stage in China as well as in Greece. The nature of this relationship, however, is unclear. As far as ancient Greece is concerned, we are confronted with four basic options.

Lloyd writes: 'So far as the fifth century goes, we have little reason to suppose that philosophical influences were at work on the development of an explicit conception of the axiomatic foundations of mathematics.'[22] Szabo, on the other hand, traces the origin of the axiomatic method back to

---

21   See also Menn 2002: 196.
22   Lloyd 1979: 112; cf. p. 115.

Eleaticism.[23] Knorr thinks rather that philosophy is indebted to mathematics. He is ready to concede that mathematics and philosophy may have developed similar methods in a similar 'intellectual climate'.[24] Lloyd has later adopted a more sceptical attitude to this problem, and opts for some kind of independence of philosophy and mathematics.[25] Kahn takes a different option again, and claims that since astronomy, mathematics, geometry and philosophy had been in the hands of the same people – Thales and Pythagoras are as well known for their philosophical achievements as for their mathematical and astronomical discoveries – we will have to focus our attention on the specific method these thinkers used coherently in domains that now appear separated to us, but had not been so for the first Greek philosophers.[26] Kahn's remark gives us an important clue to the situation in China. Astronomical knowledge, in ancient China, could not be separated from calendar science, but calendar science had not been exclusively in the hands of the philosophers, and had not gone very far anyway until the end of the second century BC.[27] There are, of course, the famous *Yueling*ᵃᵍ chapters, which tend to establish a strict correspondence between astronomy and human affairs, but the kind of astronomy found there is not the same as Greek astronomy.[28] More interestingly, though, it has also to be noted that mathematical (but not astronomical) and philosophical knowledge had been concentrated in the hands of the Later Mohists, whose origin lies, as we know, in the class of the craftsmen and engineers.[29] The situation described by Kahn for ancient Greece is comparable to the case of the Later Mohists, but clearly not for the way astronomy and calendar science had been practised in ancient China. The Chinese case therefore is only partially comparable to the situation as it presented itself in ancient Greece, where mathematical, astronomical and philosophical knowledge was concentrated in one and the same group of persons.[30] Nevertheless, there is, between the Greek and the Chinese tradition, one fundamental point of agreement, and it sets Greece and China apart from Indian and Mesopotamian traditions: the Later Mohists as well as the Greek

23   Szabo 1977: 239. Szabo 2000: 248f. Szabo argues convincingly against the traditional view that credits Plato with a decisive influence on Euclid's axiomatic method. He shows that Plato's arguments in the *Theaetetus*, the *Meno* and the *Cratylus* proceed rather from an already constituted body of mathematical knowledge and techniques.

24   Knorr 1981: 145–86. On this problem, see also Knorr 1982: 112–45.

25   Lloyd 1990: 82f. See also Caveing 1993.

26   See Kahn 1991: 6: '[...] in the beginning the philosophers and the mathematicians will often have been the same people [...].'

27   Sivin 1969. During the period of the Warring States (475–221 BC), local courts generally had their own astronomers; see *Lüshichunqiu*, ch. 6.4.

28   See Sivin 1995b: 33: '[...] cosmology and astrology have implications for the state in China, for the individual in Greece.'

29   Graham 1978: 6–7.

30   Kahn's claims (Kahn 1991) have been criticized by Curd (1998: 5): 'In any case, it is doubtful that even if Thales had provided arguments for his mathematical and geometrical measurements, he would have transferred the method used there to his philosophical claims.' Szabo goes even further and maintains that the rise of early Greek mathematics is inseparable from the development of astronomical theories (Szabo 2000).

mathematicians and philosophers consider geometrical knowledge as a special kind of knowledge, namely knowledge that is '*a priori*'.[31]

This kind of knowledge is special insofar as it requires a procedure of justification, or a proof. There is thus an important concept that ties together mathematical and philosophical demonstrations, namely proof. But here again, there is much disagreement about the issue, at least from the comparative perspective. Needham is rather optimistic and thinks that the Later Mohists had been close to Euclid's achievements.[32] Graham writes: 'It is remarkable that the Mohist seems to have the idea of geometrical proof, for the absence of strict proofs in geometry is perhaps the most obvious weakness in Chinese as compared with Greek science',[33] and again: '[...] although he [the Mohist] certainly has the idea of the geometrically demonstrable [...] he probably did not develop true proofs in the manner of Euclid [...].'[34] Later, Graham declares: 'There is no evidence however that the Mohists formulated geometrical proofs, the absence of which is one of the crucial gaps in Chinese as compared with Greek thought.'[35] Lloyd writes: '[...] certain features of that concept of demonstration – notably its axiomatic basis – are peculiarly Greek and have no counterpart in the notions of proof developed in classical Chinese thought, whether in mathematics or elsewhere.'[36]

Among the hypotheses proposed to explain the absence of the notion of proof in ancient China, we find, of course, the linguistic argument. Proofs, especially the type of proof called *reductio ad absurdum*, rely essentially on disjunction. This proof is Euclid's favourite and is considered, already in Plato's time, to be the type of proof characteristic of the mathematicians in general.[37] Here is an example.

> Zeno argues as follows: what moves, moves either in the place in which it is, or in the place in which it is not; and it does not move either in the place in which it is or in the place in which it is not; nothing therefore moves.
>
> (Epiphanius, *Adv. Haer.*, III,11; quoted after the edition of H.D.P. Lee, *Zeno of Elea*, London, 1936, fragment 18, pp. 42–43)

---

31 Caveing 1993: 577 ('Rappelons qu'un des aspects spécifiques de la mathématique grecque, c'est sa fonction de la connaissance des propriétés 'immuables' des figures, susceptible d'être appliquée à l'intellection d'un cosmos géométrisé dans la forme de la sphère, et qu'un autre aspect, lié au premier, c'est la formation d'un discours technique logiquement nommé, maîtrisant des méthodes de preuve irréfutables et garantissant contre l'erreur éventuelle. Or ces deux composantes renvoient elles-mêmes à une seule et même structure organisatrice de la culture grecque.')

32 Needham 1959: 94.
33 Graham 1978: 56.
34 Graham 1978: 435.
35 Graham 1989: 160; see also Scharfstein 1998: 28.
36 Lloyd 1996: 75.
37 Lasserre 1964; Szabo 1977: 237, note 1.

The logical and philosophical importance of this type of proof, however, never came to the mind of the first Chinese philosophers. Classical Chinese, as Chmielewski rightly notes,[38] does not express disjunctives directly, by means of a single linguistic device. Instead of the formula 'either P or Q', classical Chinese resorts to the formula 'if not P, then Q' (*fei* P *ze* Q[ah]), which is, in fact, the perfect logical equivalent of 'either P or Q'.[39]

We seem to be led to the conclusion that classical Chinese had obstructed the way towards the discovery of this notion of proof, whereas ancient Greek, with its great facility for expressing disjunction, had, on the contrary, helped to sharpen the first Greek philosophers' eyes for techniques of rational proof, above all for the proof by *reductio ad absurdum*.

The Greek language marks the disjunctive sentence-structure in a quite ostentatious manner, and has thereby greatly facilitated the discovery of the structure and the mechanism of indirect proofs in ancient Greek philosophy. The importance of disjunctive sentence-structures must have been recognized as early as the first Eleatic speculations on being, and perhaps still earlier. To my mind, this Whorfian hypothesis of a direct influence of language upon the structures of thought seems to be too simplistic to gain credence.[40] First, it has to be noted that disjunctives had also been, in ancient Greece, an inexhaustible source of paradoxes.[41] Many proofs relying on disjunction turned out to be fallacious, a feature that shows up especially through the number of paradoxes resulting from this type of argumentation.[42] Next, we must concede that even if the structures of the Chinese language are less propitious to the formulation of disjunctive sentence-structures than classical Greek, the *reductio ad absurdum* is not unknown in ancient Chinese philosophical literature, as the following passage from the *Guanzi* shows.

> There is something that spans out Heaven; there is something that holds up Earth. If nothing spanned out Heaven, it would collapse. If nothing held up Earth, it

---

38   Chmielewski 1963: 104–105; Chmielewski 1966: pp. 39–40.

39   The problem of the expression of disjunctive sentence-structures in classical Chinese is further discussed in Chmielewski 1966: 39–40; Chmielewski 1963: 104–105; Graham 1964: 39, note. For examples of disjunctive structures in classical Chinese see, for example, theorem B 35 of the *Mohist Canon*, or chapters 20.4 and 19.3 of the *Lüshichunqiu*. The initial discovery of the fact that 'P or Q' is expressed in Chinese by its logical equivalent 'not P then Q' must be attributed to Chao Yuanren 1959: 6–7. Harbsmeier 1981: 25, qualifies the *fei* in the expression '*fei* P *ze* Q' as a 'conditional *fei*'.

40   Chmielewski's views are rather crude. He writes: 'I should like to point out that some of the shortcomings of Chinese propositional logic are of linguistic origin. Specifically, I mean that some of the binary operations (that is to say, operations involving more than one proposition), common not only in the modern calculus but also in Greek and Indian logic, must have escaped the Chinese thinkers because of the very lack of clear and adequate linguistic means for their expression in Chinese.' (Chmielewski 1963: 103)

41   On paradoxes related to disjunction, see particularly Aristotle, *Physics* 191b13–17; 191a28; *De Generatione et Corruptione* 317b1f.; Plato, *Euthydemus* 275D.

42   Zeno's paradoxes, Plato's *Euthydemus* and Aristotle's *Sophistical Refutations* are the most conspicuous examples of this tendency.

would sink down. Since Heaven has not collapsed and Earth has not sunk down, there must be something spanning out Heaven and holding up Earth.

(*Guanzi*, ch. 38, pp. 25–26, *Zhuzi jicheng* edition)

Furthermore, even without disjunctive sentence-structures, rational proofs are not impossible in Chinese. The sentence-structure of the Chinese language does not favour any specific type of proof. The overwhelming part of what we would now call 'logical reasoning' takes place, in early Chinese philosophical texts, in cognitive metaphors and 'argumentative analogies'.[43] Logic, therefore, operates in a more spontaneous and in a more disseminated way in the Chinese language, but not therefore, it has to be emphasized, in a faulty manner. As a result of this habit, logic could not develop, in ancient China, as an independent discipline, but came out, eventually, as a kind of logical syntax in the Later Mohists' writings.

Even if the notion of proof did not emerge as a clear concept in ancient China, there was a kind of implicit use of it in several different domains. Caveing has introduced the concept of 'implicit knowledge' to explain the absence of the notion of proof in Egyptian and Babylonian mathematics, comparable in this respect to Chinese mathematics. It would be wrong indeed, as Caveing rightly notes, to try to divide ancient mathematical knowledge into deductive and empirical knowledge.[44]

The most important result of our investigations at this point, however, is that the linguistic differences between both cultures are by no means sufficient to explain the observed philosophical differences. We should rather note the remarkable convergence of the intellectual methods. The Later Mohists' conceptual derivations may already be considered as proofs, if but to a limited extent. Even if their method is open to the suspicion that there might be a confusion between definition and demonstration, we should not ignore the fact that the axiomatic reconstruction of geometry comprises two aspects that should be sharply distinguished from one another: the axiomatic system and the choice of the starting-points, or of the axioms. We have thus, on the one hand, the conception of a homogeneous system of interrelated concepts as well as the techniques of proof, which enable us to proceed from axiom to theorem and from one theorem to another, and here, we find that both civilizations are in agreement; on the other hand, we have the concept of an unshakeable starting-point and there, we find the differences.[45]

Note that there is even agreement on the importance of the starting-point in both cultures. The Presocratic notion of *arkhê* need hardly be recalled at this point. Diogenes of Apollonia, for example, begins his book by saying that the starting-point of any inquiry must be indisputable.[46] The starting-point, however, cannot itself be

---

43   See the essay 'The Origin of Logic in China' in this volume.
44   Caveing 1993: 547–53. On the notion of proof in a comparative context, see also Joseph 1991: 126–28.
45   On this problem, see Lloyd 1979: 118.
46   See fragment 64 B1 DK = 596 KRS.

demonstrated, it must be self-evident. The conception of a unique, firm and self-evident starting-point is also at the heart of most, if not all, philosophical schools in ancient China. Remember Mencius' arguments for an originally good human nature or the Legalists' argument for a greedy and egoistic human nature that runs where the profit is:

> Men run after profit just like water flows downwards without choosing between the four directions.
>
> *(Shangjunshu,* ch. 23, p. 38, *Zhuzi jicheng* edition)

In both cases and in many other schools of thought in ancient China as well, the fundamental properties of human nature are the starting-point. As far as the problem of the importance of the starting-point is concerned, there is not much difference between Greece and China. In the case of geometry, as we have seen, both cultures even seem to agree on the basic concepts of geometry.

There are, however, two major points of divergence: the nature of the starting-point itself and the problem of its conceptual clarification. As I have already proposed in the Introduction, both cultures do not land at the same places on the continent of philosophy: the Chinese philosophers begin their explorations starting from the domain of politics and economics, the Greeks, on the other hand, from natural philosophy, cosmology and theology.

The starting-points chosen by the first Chinese philosophers therefore fall within the range of politics and economics, like the notion of *xing*[ai] 'human nature', or of *yu,*[aj] the basic desires or impulses. The Presocratic philosophers and Plato, on the other hand, appeal not only to concepts whose origins are to be found in quite different domains, but also to concepts that are foremost the creations of the philosophers themselves, like Anaximander's *apeiron* or Democritus' atoms. This move is inevitably preceded by a critique of the commonly used terms. The Later Mohists' method of conceptual analysis, on the contrary, does not start with a preliminary critique of the ordinary use of terms such as justice or humanity. Conceptual analysis is a basic theme only in Western philosophy.[47] Its fundamental assumption is that the expressions used by natural languages are not sufficiently clarified and have, therefore, to be replaced by a conceptual language whose terms are logically more consistent. Science, for example, uses the notion of 'temperature', not the subjective terms 'hot' and 'cold'. This view presupposes, therefore, that there can be a set of 'perfect concepts', imperfectly expressed in natural language, an assumption never shared by the first Chinese philosophers. No need was felt to develop a special group of abstract concepts in ancient China, whereas the

---

47   Flew 1979; Scharfstein and Daor (1979) have discussed the origin of the method of conceptual analysis in Western philosophy in a comparative perspective. Hansen (1987) has tried to show that classical Chinese philosophy is in its very essence linguistic philosophy. See also Mou 2001. Even if language is an important topic in early Chinese philosophy, this does not imply that this kind of philosophy is linguistic philosophy in the Western sense of the term.

proliferation of such concepts in Greece clearly bears the stamp of philosophical innovation. Abstract concepts like 'size', 'quantity', 'existence' are very often expressed by the juxtaposition of the two relevant antonyms in Chinese: *daxiao*[ak] ('size', lit. 'large-small'), *duoshao*[al] ('quantity', lit. 'many-few'), *youwu*[am] ('existence'),[48] but never with the help of newly created terms, understandable only by the philosopher.

There is one crucial point that has to be noticed: the definitions proposed by the Later Mohists are not definitions in the Western sense of the term, in that they indicate the meaning of a word or a concept, but are already proofs, because they purport to be the only possible meaning of a concept. The axiomatic system of ethics that the Later Mohists propose is, according to their view, already present in the ordinary meanings of the ethical vocabulary. The Later Mohists, as they understand themselves, purport to extract the content of the Mohist philosophy from the basic Chinese moral terms. Their method is not preceded, as in ancient Greece, by a preliminary critique of the common use of these terms. They do not think that the moral terms are false or inadequate and they do not intend to replace the common content of these terms by new, Mohist principles; they rather think that the common content of these moral terms already embodies the Mohist principles. The very possibility of an understanding of these common moral terms in a Mohist sense is already sufficient proof. The fact that they fit in a perfect system of interrelated concepts only underlines this view.

One notices easily that demonstrations, in this context, are not really needed. The very possibility of the definition is already the demonstration, because all the terms are tied together within a unified system, where each single name is bound to find its place. The only difference that can be observed between both civilizations in this respect is a terminological one. The first Chinese philosophers tend to use the same terms as their intellectual rivals, for the simple reason that they believe that their views also reflect the correct way of using the language that is common to all.[49] The first Greek philosophers, on the other hand, prove to be extremely inventive as far as their basic philosophical concepts are concerned.

The development of philosophy, in ancient Greece, is inextricably linked to the creation of a special kind of language. Western languages have always been deeply influenced and transformed by the 'idiolects' created by philosophers.[50] There is thus also a sharp contrast in the way terminological innovations are handled by the first Greek and the first Chinese philosophers. Every Greek philosopher coins his own stock of technical terms, many of which were and have remained *hapax legomena* (that is, one occurrence only in the

---

48   Lit. 'there is-there is not'; cf. *Mozi*, ch. 31, p. 139, *Zhuzi jicheng* edition.
49   It is difficult to estimate, however, to what extent the later standardization of writing during the Han dynasty may have obliterated terminological innovations of the philosophers. I am indebted to Bobby Gassmann for this remark.
50   Modern Chinese, however, seems now also to be on its way to adopting the Western way of terminological proliferation. See Lackner 1993 and Trauzettel 1970.

whole body of ancient Greek literature).[51] Chinese philosophers, on the contrary, tend to use a rather restricted stock of shared expressions, like *ren*,[an] *yi*,[ao] *dao*,[ap] *xing*[aq] and so on which they then fill with different contents.[52]

This difference then also sheds light on the problem of the relationship between definition and demonstration in ancient Chinese thought. The Western tradition distinguishes sharply between definition and demonstration. Viewed from this angle, it seems as if the Later Mohists never made the decisive step from definition to demonstration. Nevertheless, we must not forget that the accurate distinction between demonstration and definition is Aristotle's achievement, and cannot therefore be used without caution as a standard of comparison between early Greek and early Chinese thought. One can also observe, in this context, that there is already an element of proof in Plato's attempts at establishing definitions in the *Sophist*. If we start from the way in which the fisherman is defined in the *Sophist* (218Ef.), it is obvious that Plato searches for a real definition grounded in the nature of things. The final terms of his successive dichotomies reveal, in the end, necessarily, the proper nature of the defined object (*Sophist* 264D).[53] This procedure must therefore also count as an attempt to prove the correctness of these definitions. The system that ultimately derives from these procedures is a system of interrelated *names*: names are derived from other names, just as theorems are derived from other theorems or axioms.

---

51   The *Wortindex* of the third volume of the edition of the fragments of the Presocratics by Diels and Kranz comprises no fewer than 488 pages, with a huge list of *hapax legomena*. See also Luther 1966: 28 and von Fritz 1966: 10.

52   'A feature of the classical [Chinese] vocabulary is that a shared terminology is often used by rival schools to articulate significantly different conceptual content.' (Ames and Hall 1987: 42) See also Ames 1988: 265.

53   Aristotle holds strong to the principle of division, especially in his biological research work, even if the Platonic method of division by dichotomies is severely criticized; see Balme 1975; Lloyd 1962. For a comparison and a discussion between Plato's and Aristotle's approach to the problem of division, see Pellegrin 1991.

Chapter 4

Greek and Chinese Categories

Aristotle's categories have come under the fire of two leading European Sinologists. Gernet, who sees in the peculiarities of the Greek language and its implicit metaphysics the chief culprit of the Western missionaries' failure to convert the Chinese mind to the delights of Scholastic philosophy, calls in Aristotle's categories as his main witness.[1] Graham, in an experimental paper,[2] asks himself the question what Aristotle's categories would have looked like had they been elaborated in classical Chinese rather than in Greek. He then attempts to play the part of a Chinese Aristotle in order to construct a table of the Chinese categories. Despite this difference in purpose, both Gernet's and Graham's approaches rely upon a common basis, namely, Benveniste's celebrated study of Aristotle's categories,[3] which they, rather uncritically,[4] accept as their starting-point. Benveniste had tried to show that the Aristotelian categories ultimately derive from linguistic features characteristic of the Greek language and suggested that, had there been an African Aristotle, his final result would inevitably have been different.[5]

At the time Benveniste wrote his article (1958), there was indeed a study in African ontology available to him, namely Kagame's *La philosophie bantu-rwandaise de l'être* (Kagame 1956). In this book, Kagame tries to lay bare the hidden ontological assumptions and the categories of the Kinyarwanda language. Ironically enough, he compares his project in scope to Aristotle's, and lists four categories with their Aristotelian equivalents, not noticing, however, that the very possibility of this Neo-humboldtian reading of Aristotle ruined at the same time the foundations of Aristotelian philosophy, for it suggests that Aristotle had also extracted his categories out of the Greek language.[6]

This aspect of Kagame's investigations had been fully grasped by Benveniste.[7] Each of the ten categories, Benveniste noticed, has a neat linguistic counterpart. *Ousia*, 'substance', corresponds to the grammatical category of nouns; *poson*, 'how many?', and *poion*, 'of what sort?', correspond to

---

1 Gernet 1991: 322–33.
2 Graham 1986e; the problem of the Chinese categories is again treated, without much change, in Graham 1989: 415–16.
3 Benveniste 1966c.
4 Both start from the assumption that Benveniste has 'demonstrated' the linguistic origin of Aristotle's categories. See Gernet 1991: 324. Graham (1986e) argues in a similar way.
5 Benveniste 1966c: 71–73; Trendelenburg 1846.
6 This is nicely pointed out by Hountondji 1982.
7 Benveniste does not refer to Kagame's work (Kagame 1956) that appeared two years before his article on the categories. Benveniste could well have been acquainted with it, however, inasmuch as he also quotes examples from African languages.

adjectives derived from pronouns. *Pros ti*, 'relative to what?', refers to adjectives which are implicitly comparative, like 'double', 'half', and so forth. *Pou*, 'where?', and *pote*, 'when?', designate adverbs of time and place. *Keisthai*, 'being in a position', refers to verbs in the middle voice; *ekhein*, 'having', to the perfect tense. *Poiein*, 'doing', represents the active voice; *paskhein*, 'suffering', the passive voice.[8] As these linguistic features – or at least their distribution – are unique to the Greek language, Benveniste feels himself entitled to conclude that, since no two languages are alike in structure, a list of categories constructed in a language different from Greek must, *a priori*, be different from Aristotle's.[9] Moreover, this difference will be all the more striking if a list of categories is elaborated, not in another Indo-European language close to Greek, but in Chinese, in American Indian or in African languages.[10] Whereas Benveniste was satisfied with this *a priori* conclusion, unconditionally accepted by Gernet, Graham went a step further and actually worked out a list of Chinese categories (which I shall consider later), much larger than Aristotle's and sometimes different from it. Graham's results follow neatly from his premises (that is, his interpretation of what Aristotelian categories are), and his project is carried out with much elegance and economy. However, before examining Graham's conclusions and Benveniste's theory, I want first to raise a few methodological questions.

How can we make sure that a list of categories is relative to a language? What are our means of testing such a claim? There seems to be a straightforward answer to that question: all we really need to do is to take a list of categories (let us say Aristotle's) and relate it to the Greek language; then take another language (let us say Chinese), and perform on that language exactly the same operations as Aristotle had to perform on the Greek language in order to arrive at his list of categories. If the two lists of categories show among them differences that are analogous or even identical to characteristic differences between Greek and Chinese, we may then with certainty conclude that categories are relative to language, and we shall also know how a list of categories is in fact built up.

But we are faced here with two different problems that have to be kept separated. There is, on the one hand, the problem of the origin of the Aristotelian categories; on the other, the problem of the relation between categories and language in general. We must keep well in mind that the thesis of the linguistic origin of Aristotle's categories is only one among a number of rival explanations. And not only this: we must even assume that Benveniste's way of relating Aristotle's categories to the Greek language is not the only one possible; indeed, Ryle, although not himself a spokesman for linguistic

---

8   Benveniste 1966c: 66–70.
9   *ibid.*, p. 73.
10   Mauthner had probably anticipated Benveniste's thesis: 'Die ganze Logik des Aristoteles ist nichts als eine Betrachtung der griechischen Grammatik von einem interessanten Standpunkte aus. Hätte Aristoteles Chinesisch oder Dakotaisch gesprochen, er hätte zu einer ganz andern Logik gelangen müssen.' (Mauthner 1902: 4)

relativism, has actually propounded another one which I shall consider in due course. However, even if we assume, let alone prove, that Aristotle's categories are relative to language, we have not yet ascertained thereby that any list of categories is relative to a language. It will not do to say, right from the outset, that every list of categories is relative to a language, and then try to see how that list of categories is related to the relevant language, for this, clearly, would beg the question at issue. We have to realize that there are here two logically different claims. We could, for example, argue that only Aristotle's thinking got entangled in the meshes of the Greek language, whereas the African and the 'Chinese Aristotle' might shake off the fetters of their native tongues and get along without categories. We might even say that a list of categories makes sense only in relation to the Greek language, and take the absence of any historically documented table of Chinese or African categories as positive evidence for that claim.[11]

Somebody might argue that there exists a list of Indian categories (*padartha*). Indeed, already in the *vaisesika-sutra*, a list of six categories is to be found:

1	substance	*dravya*
2	quality	*guna*
3	action	*karma*
4	generality	*samanya*
5	specificity	*visesa*
6	inherence	*samavaya*

A seventh category, namely, 'absence' (*abhava*), was added later. Annambhatta, in his *tarka-samgraha*,[12] argues against the admission of the notion of potentiality (*sakti*) into the list of the categories. A superficial comparison of this table with Aristotle's shows that the two lists are divergent rather than convergent; only four categories show up in both lists: substance, quality, relation and action. But we cannot state dogmatically, without having looked into the matter thoroughly, that *padartha* is equivalent or even comparable to the Greek *katêgoria* ('category'), or that Aristotle's intentions correspond to those of the Nyaya-Vaisesika school. My ignorance of Indian philosophy forces me to leave this question unanswered. Foucher's remarks on this subject are few and need revision.[13] Moreover, Sanskrit is, like Greek, an Indo-European language. It is even more strongly inflected than Greek and

---

11   The categories listed in Kagame 1956 are reconstructed artificially. Moreover, the author explicitly states that he wants to conduct Aristotle's experience again in an African language. Aristotle's category of substance corresponds to two African categories, namely *umuntu* (animated beings) and *ikintu* (inanimate beings); space and time are conflated in the unique category *ahantu* (space-time); the six remaining Aristotelian categories are summed up in the unique African category of *ukuntu* (modality).

12   Foucher 1949: 15–16.

13   Foucher 1949: 162–63.

thus likely to have provoked similar philosophical treatments.[14] This possibility rules out the case of the Indian categories for the present investigation, for which it is essential that the two languages and cultures under consideration be wholly independent of each other. For if Greek and Indian categories turned out to be relative to language, this would only prove that Indo-European languages are prone to produce categories, not that categories in general are relative to language, nor even that there are categories in every language. This is not to say that a comparison between Greek and Indian categories is altogether impossible. What I want to suggest is that we have to find out first what kind of influence language has or might have upon the shaping of philosophical thinking, before we can proceed to the comparison of systems of thought within the Indo-European tradition. Otherwise, the result of the comparison may always be vitiated by the immeasurable influence of language. This is the reason why, in my case, Greece and China offer themselves as the most suitable, and even unique, starting-point.[15]

Graham's and Gernet's way of handling the problem rests upon a conflation of two different approaches: they start from an assumption about what Aristotle's categories are and in what respect these categories are relative to the Greek language; then they carry over that interpretation into another language, relying upon the unwarranted premise that Aristotelian-type categories can be found in any language, even if their list could be different from Aristotle's. The approach I would like to suggest is somewhat different: my idea is to go back to the intention or to the motives that lay behind Aristotle's theory of the categories. In other words, I shall try to go back to the question to which the list of Aristotle's categories was supposed to be an answer. It is with this question in mind that I shall then turn to classical Chinese philosophy and see if any of the ancient Chinese philosophers did ask the same questions as Aristotle, and if so, what these answers were and what role, if any, linguistic considerations had played in giving these answers.

With these introductory remarks, I have set the scope and the limits of my own investigation. In a first, negative, part I shall discuss the foundations of Benveniste's study of the Aristotelian categories, check some of his results, and assess their consequences for Graham's approach. In a second, positive, part I shall make a fresh start. After a few methodological remarks, I shall outline a new experiment. Starting from the philosophical problems Aristotle has been struggling with, rather than from the bare list of categories, I shall turn to the philosophers of ancient China, to see whether any of them raised and answered problems similar to the concerns of Aristotle, and whether anything like a list of categories had been propounded to solve these problems.

'Aristotle, after having set out to tabulate the most general concepts – those precisely, which organize the field of our experience – is condemned finally

---

14   On this theme, see already Nietzsche [1885] 1930: 27–28 (§ 20).
15   See also the Introduction.

to give but a list of linguistic distinctions.' This is the radical conclusion Benveniste comes to after his examination of the Aristotelian categories.[16] The way in which Benveniste introduces the object of his study makes us believe that there is something empirical and scientific about the method he is using, and that his analysis of Aristotle's categories represents some kind of test, or experiment, related to an initial hypothesis. Upon closer inspection, however, it turns out that Benveniste had reached his conclusions before he even started to analyse the categories. Benveniste's problem seems to be this: 'even if we admit,' he says, 'that thought can only be shaped and expressed in language, do we still possess the means to point out the features which are peculiar to thought and which owe nothing to their expression in language?'[17] Abstract discussion, he goes on, is of no help in the rather vague disputes surrounding this difficult philosophical problem. We therefore shall have to turn to a concrete example, readily found in Aristotle's categories. Aristotle's categories are meant, according to Benveniste, to be categories of thought. If, then, the categories of Aristotle turn out to be merely categories of language, we shall have to conclude, after the failure of that exemplary project, that there are no such things as categories of thought, and that any attempt to establish such categories inevitably throws us back upon the strands of our native tongue. It is worthwhile taking a closer look at the two expressions 'categories of language' and 'categories of thought' Benveniste here uses. What he means by 'categories of language' can be gathered from other writings of his.[18] Linguistic or morphological categories are limited in number and can be integrated into a single, logically organized scheme. Each language makes use of only a limited number of these categories, and languages even differ from one another by the set of morphological categories they put to use. Gender, for example, is a linguistic category, subdivided by some languages into masculine, feminine and neuter, by others into masculine and feminine only; some languages appear to lack that category, whereas still others replace it by the distinction between animate and inanimate. Mental categories and laws of thought, Benveniste argues, only reflect the organization and the distribution of these categories of language. When we think, we think a universe already shaped by language.

The material I have been drawing upon for clarifying Benveniste's assumptions about categories partly antedates his study of the Aristotelian categories. Thus, it is not clear whether his study on Aristotle was meant to be an exemplification of his general thesis of the dependence of categories of thought upon categories of language, or if it was even meant to be a proof thereof. We may suspect that there is a vicious circle here, and that Benveniste builds the correctness of his interpretation of the Aristotelian categories on this general theory, and the latter on his views about the categories. Surely, Benveniste cannot mean that the categories are dependent upon the way in

---

16   Benveniste 1966c: 65.
17   *ibid.*, p. 64.
18   Benveniste 1974: 126–27. See also Benveniste 1966b: 6, and Benveniste: 1966e: 25.

which they are expressed in language. For then every linguistic form of a language would at the same time be a category of thought. What Benveniste wants to say, I believe, is that the categories are not an invention of Aristotle, but that Aristotle, while constructing his categories, draws upon a common stock of linguistic lore. Aristotle grasps something that is already there, though not overtly; he hits upon something that lies concealed in the structures of language. Thought, as an individual phenomenon transcending language, is therefore a false picture of our mental activities. Benveniste might thus even admit that different thinkers could hit upon different categories, as long as they stay within the structures forced upon them by their native language. A problem, however, arises here. Aristotle's categories, even if we grant that they are linguistic in nature, do represent only a small fraction of the whole range of available linguistic categories. Clearly, then, Aristotle must have made a choice.[19] What was his criterion? Why do some of the linguistic distinctions warrant categories, whereas others do not? Benveniste does offer us an answer: categories, for him, depend upon the concept of being, although he does not make it clear what exactly he thinks that relation to be.[20] There is an Aristotelian doctrine commonly expressed in the *Metaphysics* (see, for example Δ 7 and E 2), according to which there are as many ways of being as there are categories, and to which Benveniste seems to refer. However, it has to be noted that the concept of being to which the categories are related is, as we shall see, much narrower than the concept of being Benveniste describes, namely the 'is' of identity, the existential use ('there is') and the 'is' of predication. He rightly observes that the usage we make of the verb 'to be' is expressed in Ewe, an African language, by a variety of idioms, and that this is not the result of a different cutting-up of an otherwise homogeneous semantic field of being. The very way that 'to be' is used in Indo-European languages sets them and, according to Benveniste, their modes of thinking as well, apart from any other type of language which does not share in that pattern. We have thus uncovered a second premise of Benveniste's argument, namely, that Aristotle's categories are closely related to the concept of being. Benveniste's final argument rests upon a proportional analogy, which we can picture as follows:

$$\frac{\text{'to be' in Greek}}{\text{categories in Greek}} \quad = \quad \frac{\text{'to be' in Ewe}}{\text{categories in Ewe}}$$

Significantly enough, Benveniste does not give us the list of the categories in Ewe. They must, he says, be different *a priori*, since the concept of being is different from the Greek one. So here, clearly, Benveniste's proportional analogy breaks down, for he cannot infer the missing link from the other three terms. The reason for this failure is all too obvious: Benveniste cannot really

---

19   See also Vuillemin 1967: 76f.
20   Benveniste 1966c: 70.

tell us *how* Aristotle's categories, and *a fortiori* Ewe categories, are related to the concept of being. But let me pause here and see what I can do to relate the categories of Aristotle to the verb 'to be'.

The earliest text in which Aristotle tries to relate the categories to the verb 'to be' is probably the seventh chapter of book Δ of the *Metaphysics*.[21] This chapter, however, resorts to only one form of the verb 'to be', namely its usage as a copula. This appears from some of the examples Aristotle actually uses. He says, after introducing the accidental and the essential use of the copula (the categories being related to the essential use), that there is no difference between 'a man recovers' (*anthrôpos hugiainei*) and 'a man is recovering' (*anthrôpos hugiainôn estin*), or 'a man walks, cuts' (*anthrôpos badizei, temnei*) and 'a man is walking, cutting (*anthrôpos badizôn estin, temnôn estin*).[22] The 'is' of the copula, however, is empty. It is a mere sign of predication. The essential use of the copula (*kath' hauto*) Aristotle lists in *Metaphysics* Δ 7 is not subdivided into the ten (or sometimes only eight) categories. The essential use of 'is' consists in predicating between each other terms belonging to one and the same category (see *Topics* A 9; 103b35–39). This is the reason why Aristotle can say that there are as many essential uses of 'to be' as there are categories. The operation which the 'is' of the copula performs is to provide a verb in a sentence which otherwise would comprise only two nominal elements ('man' and 'recovering', for example) and would not be a sentence at all. 'Recovers' is a verbal form that requires only a subject ('man') to yield a complete sentence. 'Recovering', on the other hand, does not yield a sentence when coupled with 'man': we need a further element, a copula, to say 'a man *is* recovering'. That the verb 'to be' has come to be used as a copula in most Indo-European languages is, linguistically speaking, an accident.[23] Many other verbs, or particles, or other elements, could have performed the same function. Indeed, most, if not all, languages do have nominal sentences with a copula; only Indo-European languages appear to use the verb 'to be' in the function of a syntactic link tying together the nominal elements. Classical Chinese, with a rather high proportion of nominal sentences, uses a particle, *ye*,[a] or a negative copula, *fei*;[b] some Semitic languages use a demonstrative, as does Mandarin Chinese.[24] One can imagine that Indo-European languages did once possess

---

21   Book Δ, Aristotle's philosophical lexicon, was written before most, if not all, of the other books of the *Metaphysics*, as can be seen from the references to book Δ contained in the remaining books. Book Δ probably also antedates the *Nicomachean Ethics* and the *Eudemian Ethics*, which both also equate categories with forms of being, surely a later evolution of the Aristotelian doctrine of categories. In the *Categories* and in the *Topics*, Aristotle never introduces the categories as categories of being.

22   See *Metaphysics* Δ 7; 1017a27–30. See also *De Interpretatione* 10; 20a3f. and 12; 21a38f.

23   As Benveniste himself has noted (Benveniste 1966d: 189). This article is without doubt one of the most enlightening studies on the functions of the copula, except for the confusion between predication and identity, but which has no bearing on the outcome. What a pity Benveniste did not see the real connection, or rather the absence of any connection, between the copula and the categories.

pure nominal sentences without a copula (as Greek certainly has), and that this capacity has been lost at some time with the appearance of the copula to fill the gap.[25] If we compare the function of the Greek copula with the function of the two Chinese ones, we come to an unexpected result: both are ambiguous between, at least, the following three logical functions, namely, identity statements, class-inclusion and class-membership.[26] But the chief function of the copula seems to be predicating: 'one thing is said of another'; for example, 'animal' is said of 'man' in 'man is an animal'. Predication thus appears to be a means of creating logical ties between nominal elements, 'things'. Moreover, nominal sentences are normally tenseless, and tend to depict invariable relations between nominal elements, a property that foreshadows the logical career of the nominal sentence. Note however that most of our adjectives (colours, for example) are verbs in classical Chinese, and that a sentence like *ma bai*[c] 'the horse is white' is a verbal sentence. To be fair to Benveniste's African language, I should have to look at the way predication works in that language, and whether it has nominal sentences with a copula, as opposed to verbal ones. But I need not pursue this issue, for the concept of predication itself is, as I have already noted, entirely empty. There is no bridge between the bare notion of predication and the categories. So this attempt to improve on Benveniste's approach fails.

Predication is a uniform activity, not essentially linked to the verb 'to be', but to the presence of nominal elements which need syntactic coherence. This coherence may be provided by the verb 'to be', but there are, as we have noted, also other linguistic solutions. Whether there are different types of predication corresponding to categories cannot therefore appear solely from the method used to tie together nominal elements. The syntactic function of the copula is always the same, whatever the category.

Let me now look at the details of some of Benveniste's claims. His interpretation of the origin of Aristotle's categories will have to stand against, at least, the following three challenges:

(a) is his account of the origin of the categories satisfactory?
(b) is his theory consistent with all the other information we have concerning the philosophical theories of the early Aristotle?

---

24   The copula therefore has primarily a logical function. It may be interesting to investigate why the Greek verb *einai* has been chosen as a copula, rather than some other verb; but this problem, to my mind, is not essential, for the logical puzzles originated by the different uses of the copula turn up independently in other languages not using the same copula. Cordero (1984: 229–32) considers the Greek *einai* as 'gradually weakening' from a strong, existential sense, to a weaker, copulative, sense.

25   This is the standard theory. It goes back to Meillet (Meillet and Vendryès 1963). Kahn's theory, which claims that among all the different meanings of *einai* in Greek, the copulative sense is the most central, is not universally accepted (Kahn 1973a: 380). On this problem, see also the essay '"To Be" in Greece and China'.

26   Already noticed by Waley (1934: 63). See also Graham 1986d.

(c) can we point out, for at least some of the categories, a more plausible origin than the linguistic one offered by Benveniste?

As far as the first challenge is concerned, we must conclude that Benveniste fails to explain, as I have already indicated, why Aristotle chose but a few grammatical forms out of the vast array available to him. So here his theory proves too much. The examination of the second challenge is less easy. However, let us start from Benveniste's own words, and look at what Aristotle has to say about the same issue. 'In constructing his table of "categories",' Benveniste says, 'Aristotle had in mind the listing of all those predicates which mean something independently of their integration into a proposition. Aristotle took as his criterion, *unconsciously*, [my italics] the existence of different expressions for each of these predicates. He was thus condemned to fall back upon the distinctions embodied in the language itself, and without noticing it.'[27] This claim is disproved, I believe, if we can quote a text in which Aristotle states that a category can be referred to by two or more different expressions. Here are a few such cases. The category of relation (*pros ti*) counts among its members items such as 'knowledge', 'science', 'slave', 'double', 'half'.[28] Indeed, knowledge is always knowledge of something; a slave is someone's slave; double and half are double and half of some other number. It is easy to see that there is a logical tie holding together the members of this category. The category of relation provides a logical framework for all terms whose nature it is to be related to something else. If Aristotle introduces the category of relation by terms such as 'double' and 'half', he only uses uncontroversial and intuitively clear examples to make a logically very important point. Let us imagine, for a moment, that terms such as 'science' and 'slave' are, in some way, linguistically 'earmarked', so as to put them into the same semantic and syntactical category as 'double' and 'half'. Now if we know right from the start that 'slave' and 'science' are of the same type as 'double' and 'half', there is no need to tell us that there is a single category of relation embracing them. We need a category only if there is a possible confusion. But what we mix up are not linguistic expressions, but the logical properties that are hidden behind these linguistic expressions.

The terms of the Greek language may be divided into two large groups. The first group, which I shall name 'friends of the categories', consists of terms such as 'double' and 'half', which clearly and unambiguously exhibit the logical properties of the (logical) category they belong to. The other group, which I shall name 'foes of the categories', includes all those terms which, like 'slave' and 'science' do not mirror their logical properties, but rather purport to belong to a different category. 'Slave' could be mistaken for a

---

27 Benveniste 1966c: 70. On this point, Benveniste has been severely criticized. See Derrida 1981.

28 The members of the category of relation are called *ta pros ti*, that is, 'those in relation to something'. Aristotle only knows about *relata*, not about a concept of relation the way we use it.

member of the category of substance; 'knowledge' for a member of the category of quality. On another occasion,[29] Aristotle points out that *hugiainein*, 'to recover', despite its ending in *-ein* (which is the infinitive marker of most Greek verbs that depict an action, like *leg-ein*, 'to say', or *trekh-ein*, 'to run') does not belong to the category of action, but to the category *keisthai*, which signifies a state. Aristotle also shows that *aisthanesthai*, 'perceive', with its passive ending *-sthai* does not, like *temnesthai*, 'to be cut', and *kaiesthai*, 'to be burnt', belong to the category of *paskhein*, 'suffering', but to the category of relation. The criteria Aristotle uses to establish these differences must therefore be logical criteria. The reason why we need categories in Greek has by now become clear: there is a rift between logic and language, and it is the function of the theory of categories to bridge the gap.[30]

But could an unconditional supporter of Benveniste's views not now argue that the theory of the linguistic origin of the categories is after all correct? Could Aristotle not have set up his list simply by inspecting the Greek language for friends and foes of the categories? This is to put the cart before the horse. We need a formal definition, or at least an intuitive grasp of what a logical category is, before we can start to pin down the friends and foes of the categories. If categories can be discovered through a language, this does not mean that they are relative to that language; it only means that the categories mirror themselves, though imperfectly, in language. It would also be wrong to say that language channels our thinking: it rather floods it, and it is the philosopher's duty to mark the fordable places. We need more than a linguistic criterion to decide whether a given term belongs to the category of relation or to the category of action. Aristotle indeed does supply us with formal criteria for the identification of nearly all the categories. A characteristic of substances, for example, is that there is nothing contrary to them (see *Categories* 5; 3b24–25); it is the property of quantities to be called equal and unequal (see *Categories* 6; 6a26–27). Relatives have a correlative, and both are simultaneous by nature (see *Categories* 7; 7b15f.). Qualities may be called similar and dissimilar (see *Categories* 6; 6a30f.; 8; 11a15–16). The criteria for the other categories have not come down to us. It would be wrong to argue that Aristotle had set up these criteria only after having discovered the list of the categories, for it can be shown that some of Aristotle's categorial distinctions are inherited from his predecessors, still ignorant of the categories. The category of relation or, to be more precise, the logical underpinning of that category had already been known to Plato. Plato's *Parmenides* even uses the examples of 'slave' and 'knowledge' (see *Parmenides* 133A–134C), the same as those Aristotle uses in the *Categories*. The reason why Aristotle resorts to these particular examples is clear: they had already become stock-examples in the philosophical debates in the Academy. But this means in turn that Aristotle had not got his category of relation out of the Greek language, but rather

---

29   See *Sophistical Refutations* I, 22; 178a4–19.
30   On this problem, see also Frede 1981.

that he took it over as an already constituted piece of philosophical argument. If the evidence from the *Parmenides* is not convincing, I can quote the *Charmides*, an early Socratic dialogue. After having made clear that a science is always a science of something (*Charmides* 165Cf.), in other words, that 'science' is a relative term, Socrates brings in three illustrative examples: 'more than' (*meîzon* 168B4), 'double' (*diplasion* 168C2) and 'half' (*hêmisu* 168C4). When introducing the category of relation in the *Categories*, Aristotle adduces precisely these three examples (see *Categories* 4; 2a1). The same is also true of the other examples of the *Categories*: *kaiein*, 'to burn', and *temnein*, 'to cut' (4; 2a4) are already associated with action in the *Gorgias* (476Bf.) and even in the *Cratylus* (387A3 and 387B3). These cases may appear inconclusive, because we get the category and the example at the same time, without a possibility of deciding which of the two is the earlier. So let me take another example. The category of *ekhein*, 'having', is illustrated in the *Categories* by the two forms *hupodedetai*, 'he has his shoes on', and *hôplistai*, 'he has his armour on' (4; 2a3). Benveniste had focused on the grammatical form of these examples. Both are, as he rightly observes, perfect tenses with an aspectual value. That is not the point of these examples. The logical function of the category *ekhein* becomes immediately clear if we link it to a passage in Plato's *Theaetetus* (197A–D). Socrates, while discussing with Theaetetus the merits of a definition of knowing (*to epistasthai*) in terms of having knowledge (*hexis epistêmês*), introduces a distinction between having knowledge (*ekhein epistêmên*) and possessing knowledge (*kektêsthai epistêmên*). The example Plato then uses to make clear the distinction he wants to draw is directly relevant to our case. Socrates says:

> To me, having (*ekhein*) does not seem to be the same as possessing (*kektêsthai*, literally, 'having acquired'). For example, if someone has bought a coat and if he, though owning it, does not wear it, we would not say that he has (*ekhein*) it, but only that he possesses (*kektêsthai*) it.
>
> (Plato, *Theaetetus* 197B)

The distinction here drawn is vitally important for the subsequent discussion of the way in which somebody can have knowledge. Aristotle probably has in mind this passage of the *Theaetetus* when he is looking for examples to illustrate his category of *ekhein*, 'having'. We may even speculate that the category *keisthai*, *ekhein*'s twin, represents the contrasting category of possessing (without using). The logical distinction between these two categories is probably the one we would draw between a disposition (knowledge, for example) and a state (illness, for example). It is highly significant that Aristotle then uses the same 'wardrobe-examples' as Plato did in the *Theaetetus*. The key to the understanding of these examples is not their verbal form, but their association with things somebody wears, 'has on', as opposed to clothes he 'owns' but does not currently wear. Now it would be preposterous to say that Plato had been guided by perfective verbal forms (which do not appear in his examples) when drawing the distinction between having and possessing. What we have here is, rather, a logical distinction that is at the same time linguistic, that is, occasionally grammaticalized in the aspectual value of *hupodedetai* 'he has his shoes on' and *hôplistai*, 'he has his armour on'.

Aspects are a universal feature of language.[31] No language is entirely deprived of aspects, although the means for expressing aspects, either through lexicalization or through grammaticalization,[32] differ widely. Aspects, at least the more basic ones, as for example the perfective and the progressive aspects, are expressed in all known languages. It follows from there that the category of *ekhein*, 'having', could have been discovered in any language, provided, according to my line of argument, that the language under consideration has two different ways (one misleading thought, another guiding it) of representing that category. So, even if we admit with Benveniste that some (or all) of the categories of thought are categories of language, it does not follow, as Benveniste wants us to believe, that the categories of thought will vary from one language to another. The truth is that only those categories that are likely to be mixed up come to the consciousness of the philosopher. And if these are not the same in all languages, this proves only that different languages have different ways of misleading the philosopher's efforts for logical clarity. It does not show that categories are relative to language, but that language mirrors, in part, logical structures, and that different languages may mirror these structures in different ways. The hypothesis that the logical relationships between aspects differ from one language to another is not only unnecessary to explain the observable data, but also has undesirable epistemological consequences: we are misled into asking questions such as 'Is there a Chinese logic, distinct from Western logic?', 'Which is the better?' and so forth.[33]

---

31   Henry Rosemont, Jr. has pointed out to me that, since aspects are substantive linguistic universals, Whorf's and Benveniste's claims are vitiated right from the start. More precisely, it is the fact that there exist a certain number of logical relationships between aspects which has invalidated the claims of the relativists. On the logic of aspects, see Lyons 1977: 710, where an axiomatization of the different linguistic aspects is put forward. Galton (1984) takes up Lyon's hint and offers an extensive formalization of what is termed 'event logic'.

32   I use the terms 'lexicalized' and 'grammaticalized' after Lyons 1977: 705 and 679. A meaningful element in a language is said to be 'lexicalized' if it is expressed by means of a word: for example, if past tense is expressed only by a word whose equivalent is 'yesterday', 'last year', and so forth. An element is said to be 'grammaticalized' if language resorts to inflection or to some other syntactic or morphological device to bring forth the corresponding meaning. The comparative degree, for example, is grammaticalized in classical Greek, but lexicalized in classical Chinese. The notion of grammaticalization goes back to Meillet 1926.

33   The most thoroughgoing investigation that has been carried out in that respect is Chmielewski's impressive series of articles 'Notes on Early Chinese Logic I–VIII', in: *Rocznik Orientalistyczny* 26–32 (1962–1969). Interestingly enough, Chmielewski's general conclusion is that classical Chinese resembles in many ways a propositional calculus, and is thus even more logical than any Indo-European language. On the problem of Chinese logic in general, see, for example, Cheng Chung-Ying 1965; Cikoski 1975; Lau 1952–1953; Hansen 1983. Recently, however, Harbsmeier has shown that the Chinese language is as well equipped as any Western language to express the standard logical features and concepts (Harbsmeier 1998).

When we learn to speak a language, we learn a great amount of logic as well. We do not learn the rules of syntax separately from the rules of logic. If the native speaker of a language is satisfied with the inherited logical structure of its linguistic make-up, no problem will ever arise. If he is not satisfied with it, it will take him an enormous effort to segregate the logical from the grammatical rules. Aristotle, clearly, is someone who was dissatisfied with the logical make-up of the Greek language. Nevertheless, his attitude to language is fairly subtle. For one part, he accepts the teachings of language, and he often argues philosophical points by appealing to the forms of language.[34] But Aristotle is also well aware that language may lead the philosopher astray, and he actually claims that Plato's theory of ideas is the result of just such an error, as appears from *Categories* 5; 3b10 and *Sophistical Refutations* I,6; 169a33f. and 168a25f.

My approach forces me to go a step further. We have noticed, up to now, that the Greek language in general does not seem to be a 'friend of the categories', but rather one of its worst enemies. Time and again, its grammatical and syntactical features are found to lead astray even the most logically minded philosophers of ancient Greece. But we can perfectly well imagine that there may be languages which are logically better organized than Greek and, consequently, which show less of a rift between logical and linguistic functions and hence feel much less the need to establish lists of categories.[35]

The preceding remarks have shown that the problem of categories has linguistic as well as logical aspects. Ryle is one of the first modern philosophers after Aristotle to have tried to develop a theory of categories which takes into account both of these aspects. Ryle's approach to the problem of the origin of categories avoids, as we shall see, the shortcomings of Benveniste's and Gernet's, while maintaining the thesis of the linguistic origin of the categories. Ryle's option has yet another advantage over Benveniste's: it also reveals to us the 'principle of deduction' of Aristotle's categories. 'Aristotle's method, so far as he had one,' says Ryle, 'seems to have consisted in collecting the ordinary interrogatives of everyday speech.'[36] Ryle's Aristotelian categories thus turn out to be types of predicates: 'any two predicates, which satisfy the same interrogative are of the same category.'[37] Interrogative pronouns like 'who', 'what', and so on are more than purely linguistic entities; they have a logical importance as well. Ryle views interrogative pronouns as markers of empty places, 'arguments', in a propositional function. Instead of writing P (x), where P represents a predicate ('to be white', 'to be ill', and so forth) and (x) the arguments which, combined with this predicate, yield a proposition, we might just as well ask 'who is ill?' or 'what is white?' A propositional function, after all, 'is only "question" writ sophisticatedly.'[38] One can see that,

---

34   This is especially conspicuous in the *Physics* and in the *Nicomachean Ethics*.
35   I take 'categories' here in the sense that I have been using the term, namely, as a stopgap between linguistic expressions and logical functions.
36   Ryle 1971: 172. For the 'erotetic' aspect of the categories, see also Kahn 1978; Hintikka 1983.
37   Ryle 1971: 171; Ryle 1954: 9.
38   Ryle 1971: 172.

defined in this way, categories set up, at the same time, the logical rules governing the formation of propositions. Indeed, as is easily seen, the answers must go with the questions asked. It would be absurd to give 'Saturday is in bed' as an answer to the question 'who is in bed?' In other words, the days of the week are not in the same category as persons. Categories are, according to Ryle, logical types: 'The logical type or category to which a concept belongs is the set of ways in which it is logically legitimate to operate with.'[39]

I cannot here discuss the merits and defects of Ryle's general theory of categories.[40] Let me focus instead on the outcomes relevant to our problem. First, it has to be noted that not all Aristotelian categories correspond to interrogative pronouns. No interrogative pronouns can be related to the last four categories (doing, suffering, having, being in a state). On the other hand, not all interrogative pronouns possess a corresponding category. The Greek *pôs*, 'how?', and *pêi*, 'in what manner?', do not appear to have generated a corresponding category. The absence of *pôs*, 'how?', is especially conspicuous, because there is a grammatical category, namely the adverbs of manner ending in -*ôs*, which nobody keen on extracting categories from the Greek language could have overlooked. Even though Ryle cannot give us a watertight account of the origin of the categories, his definition of a category as a logical type comes very close to some of the usage Aristotle makes of his categories in the *Sophistical Refutations*, as we already have noticed. If Ryle's theory of the origin of Aristotle's categories has to be rejected, I shall keep, however, his insights into their logical functioning, especially his theory of 'category-mistakes'.

To someone acquainted with Ryle's account of the origin of Aristotle's categories, Graham's approach to the problem must come as a surprise.[41] Whereas Ryle admitted, presumably without having looked into the matter, that interrogative pronouns are the same in every language and that, accordingly, the categories must also be the same for every language and thus universally compelling,[42] Graham undermines this claim by showing that the list of interrogative substitutes in pre-Han classical Chinese is not the same as in Greek. However, and this too is very surprising, Graham does not therefore reject Ryle's interpretation of the nature of the categories, but accepts Ryle's 'principle of deduction' of the categories and reapplies it to classical Chinese.[43]

39   Ryle 1949: 8.
40   Smart 1953.
41   Graham 1986e.
42   Ryle 1971: 184 '[…] there are not English category-propositions as opposed to German ones, or Occidental opposed to Oriental […].'
43   The already mentioned work of Kagame (Kagame 1956) on the ontology of Kinyarwanda, an African language, is, in this respect, strangely similar to Graham's. Hountondji (Hountondji 1982: 399) rightly comments upon Kagame: '[…] son seul réflexe a été de faire comme Aristote, de reproduire, sur sa propre langue maternelle, l'opération que le Stagirite avait effectuée sur la sienne, et de croire que, ce faisant, il produisait à son tour une ontologie. Kagame n'a pas perçu que le sens du projet d'Aristote résidait, précisément, dans sa prétention à l'universalité, ni que la ruine de cette prétention devait conduire, en toute logique, à l'abandon du projet ontologique en général […].'

His result is, roughly, the following. There are three types of categories in classical Chinese. The first is generated by interrogatives whose function is to isolate things. The corresponding interrogative pronouns are:

shu[d] 'which?'
shui[e] 'who?'
he ruo[f] 'what is it like?'
he wei[g] 'what does he do?'
he shi[h] 'at what time?'
ji he[i] 'how many?'

The second type comprises interrogatives whose function it is to relate things to one another. The interrogative pronouns are:

he[j] 'what?' (asking for the kind of relation which exists between two things)
wu hu[k] 'whence?', 'where?', 'whither?'
he yi[l] 'by what means?'
he wei[m] 'for the sake of what?'

The third type of categories, which collects the interrogatives relating things to names, corresponds to the various forms the Aristotelian question *ti esti*, 'what is it?' takes in classical Chinese. It is noteworthy that this last group, perhaps as a consequence of the Chinese philosophers' nominalistic bias,[44] is totally independent of the other categories. The 'what is it?' question in classical Chinese may ask either for the identity of an object (*X he ye* 'what is X?'), or for the kind this object belongs to (*he X ye* 'what kind of X is it?'), or for what the essentials of that object are (*he wei X* 'what is it to be X?'). This means that when a Chinese philosopher asks the Aristotelian 'what is it?' question, he generally asks for the meaning of the name of a thing.

In a final table, Graham attempts to fit into the categorial framework he has worked out some of the traditional classes of ancient Chinese thought. The category *he shi*, 'at what time?', for example, is correlated to the four seasons and to the three dynasties; the categories *he ruo*, 'what is it like?', to the five colours or to the round and the square. But this system of correspondences is rather speculative in nature, because there is no direct link between these broad classes of things or events and the categories. Nevertheless, this aspect of Graham's work may without loss be left out of the present investigation.

One can say that, up to this point, Graham has faithfully carried out the task he has set himself. Much is to be learned from this manoeuvre, which hardly anybody else other than Graham could have undertaken. Especially noteworthy is the fact that the Chinese interrogative substitutes are integrated into syntactical surroundings entirely different from their Greek homologues.

---

44   Graham 1989: 141; Graham 1978: 29–30.

Whereas Greek relies upon the distinction between parts of speech, the grammaticalization of tense, aspect (sometimes) and voice, the case and the gender of the noun, classical Chinese, a wholly uninflected language, generates meaning almost exclusively through the positioning of its monosyllabic words in extremely rigid syntactical patterns. I am conscious that this is an oversimplification of the matter. My point is that rigidity of syntax is the general 'drift' of classical Chinese grammar, which generates meaning through different ways of arranging morphologically unchanging elements. This is also the reason why this kind of syntactical organization is best described by grammars of the slot-filler type, as Graham's table shows.[45] Extreme rigidity of syntax is simply the result which is to be expected when philosophers, keen on creating a tool adequate to the expression of the strictness of their logical thinking, have to write in classical Chinese.[46] Whereas Greek interrogatives tend to pick out parts of speech (whose syntactic positions are generally not as rigidly fixed as their Chinese counterparts) as their correlated substitutes, Chinese interrogatives rather guide our attention to classes of words filling out the same position in a syntactical sequence. In classical Chinese, for example, temporal indications are expressed at the beginning of a sentence, generally after the initial particle;[47] frequencies, on the other hand, tend to come at the end. This is, in my opinion, the fundamental difference between classical Chinese and ancient Greek. Graham, on the contrary, writes: 'Classical Chinese differs radically from Greek or English in dispensing with a copulative verb, and in the profound structural divergence between the nominal and the verbal sentence. Aristotle's thinking starts from questions depending on that Indo-European idiosyncrasy the verb "to be", which combines the copulative function with the existential function which in Chinese belongs to the verb *you*,[n] "there is"; and for him a sentence with "is" is not merely like any other sentence, it is the characteristic kind of sentence. We may anticipate that the sorts of categorial distinctions that he draws will appear in Chinese only in the verbal sentence.'[48] However, Aristotle's categories have nothing to do with this peculiarity of the Indo-European languages. The kind of 'being' on which the categories focus is, as I have already argued, the one expressed by the copula.[49] The 'is' of the copula, however, only fulfils the function of

---

45   Graham 1986e: 370.
46   'The Later Mohists, more than any other Chinese philosophical school, were concerned with logical precision, to which grammatical precision is an essential means. We should therefore expect in principle a grammar of exceptional strictness, the study of which might be relevant to the whole question of the possibilities and limitations of the Chinese language as an instrument of analytic thought. But this general consideration hardly prepares us for the precision and consistency of the grammatical system as we actually find it.' (Graham 1978: 111) On this problem, see also Ames and Hall 1987: 261–304, and Graham 1989: 389–428.
47   Graham 1986e: 370.
48   Graham 1986e: 373.
49   The concept of existence in ancient Greece is perhaps less problematical than has hitherto been assumed; cf. Kahn 1976.

predication. The difference between nominal and verbal sentences is not as radical as Graham wants us to admit: after all, as we have seen, Greek has the possibility of transforming verbal sentences into nominal ones. Aristotle even argues that every sentence which expresses an act of predication may be rewritten in the form: A *esti* B. Thus *anthrôpos badizei*, 'the man walks', is, according to Aristotle (see *Metaphysics* Δ 7 and *De Interpretatione* 20a3f. and 21b9–10) equivalent to *anthrôpos badizôn estin*, 'the man is walking' (literally: 'is a walking one'). Classical Chinese lacks this periphrastic possibility. The fundamental difference between Greek and Chinese thus consists in the basic organization of their syntactic structures, and the possibilities of generating meaning which derive from it. There are other profound differences between Greek (and Western inflected languages in general) and classical Chinese: in Chinese, the context is very important for interpreting a sentence structure. As a result, Chinese expressions may often seem to be semantically overloaded.[50] Rosemont observes rightly that 'a peculiar – and seemingly ignored – ramification of that importance (importance of the context) is that syntactically correct but semantically anomalous passages like the famous "colourless green ideas sleep furiously" cannot be communicated in classical Chinese, for the lack of coherent semantic reading for such sentences would block the (explicit or intuitive) assignment of syntactic categories to the constituents of any proffered translation.'[51] Taking Rosemont's remark even further, one could say that thoroughly inflected languages are syntactically overloaded. The fact, for example, that adjectives in Greek agree in gender and number with the noun they are applied to does not convey to us any new information. The device, nevertheless, is useful in many cases, for it may help us in correctly interpreting sentences which otherwise would be vague or ambiguous. Syntactic and semantic overload may thus be considered as two different but complementary aspects in the general process of generating meaning.[52]

The tabulation of the interrogative pronouns and the corresponding syntactic counterparts of a language do not necessarily unveil to us the categories of that language. By stressing the logical import of Aristotle's categories and by showing that the Greek language only has an influence on how these categories are expressed, I want to prepare the reader for a different interpretation of the linguistic facts uncovered by Graham. The only road that can lead us to the Chinese categories is a study of how logical distinctions can be distorted by the syntax of classical Chinese. Graham's analysis increases our knowledge of Chinese syntax, but is uninformative on the problem of distortion.

A last point is to be made concerning Graham's approach. Graham has acted as though the Chinese philosophers had 'forgotten' to establish a list of their categories. This is contrary to the evidence we have. Our evidence tells us that Greek philosophy had a list of categories and that Chinese philosophy

---

50 Rosemont Jr. 1974: 83.
51 Rosemont Jr. 1974: 82, note 15.
52 On this problem see also Ames and Rosemont Jr. 1998.

did not. The question, which is to be answered, is the following: why did only Aristotle feel the need to draw a list of categories? There are two answers to that question. Either we can assume that categories appear at the more 'advanced' stages of philosophical development and argumentative sophistication, and that these stages simply had not been reached by the philosophers of ancient China, or we can view the very idea of constructing categories as a symptom of the downfall of Western philosophy, and even congratulate the Chinese philosophers for not having indulged in that kind of conceptual prolixity. Both attitudes are linked to a general, preconceived, opinion of the relationship between Western and Chinese philosophy. This problem is not my concern. All I shall have to do in the present context is try to discover if somebody among the ancient pre-Han philosophers did ask questions similar to the ones raised by Aristotle. I do not yet want to know who gave the better answers; I only want to know if the structure of language has had an influence in the shaping of these answers.

The value of a comparative analysis in philosophy stands and falls with the value and the accuracy of the method it uses. First, we must not confuse the activity of comparing with the application of the comparative method. Whereas the former is an intellectual activity, the latter is a piece of scientific methodology. Philosophy is not the homeland of the comparative method.[53] Philosophy has 'borrowed' that method, like so many others (think of geometry), from disciplines such as comparative philology (historical linguistics), comparative mythology, and other comparative sciences that became fashionable in the nineteenth century. The comparative method is used in all those disciplines where an experimental confirmation or refutation of hypotheses cannot be carried out because of the historical nature of their main data. Historical phenomena are unique; they cannot be repeated. Therefore, no experiments can be made in these disciplines. Nevertheless, that does not mean that there are no predictable (or retrodictable) events in those disciplines. The ideal conditions for testing the hypothesis of the influence of language on the shaping of a table of categories would be the following: first, to reconstruct the situation Aristotle was confronted with in all its details, then to change the experimental conditions and replace Greek by Chinese, and look at the final outcome. However, we are not, like the physicist, in a position where we can manipulate or create the kind of data that would be required. Nevertheless, the data we need can become available to us, if only they exist in recorded history. We do not really need another Aristotle. It would be enough, for our purpose, to find somebody who has asked the same questions as Aristotle, and who did so in cultural surroundings entirely different from and independent of Aristotle's. We are fortunate enough to have such data in the writings of the Later Mohists, a pre-Han philosophical school. We shall have the opportunity to review their achievements.

---

53   On the problems posed by the methodology of comparative philosophy, see the Introduction to these essays in this volume.

There is another path of enquiry, followed consciously by Wardy and unconsciously by the translators of Aristotle's *Categories* into Chinese.[54] It is the project to dissect the first translation of Aristotle's treatise into literary Chinese, carried out by a small group of Western missionaries and Chinese Christians in the middle of the seventeenth century, and to look for characteristic interferences in the Chinese language by Western idioms. The force of this witness, however, is weaker than Wardy would be ready to concede.[55] Even if we gloss over the fact that the translation had been made after an expunged Latin version, we cannot ignore that this translation is, in many respects, an artificial text and not really a primary document in literary Chinese. The Western, and especially the Greek style of philosophizing, is characterized by the incessant creation of new words and expressions, as I have already indicated in the preceding essay, and obliges the Chinese translator to find an equal amount of Chinese equivalent neologisms.[56] We end up with the Greek version of the categories translated into another language. The result of this procedure is inevitably the creation of a hermeneutically misconceived text, because the problems to which the theory of categories pretended to be an answer had to be introduced as an artificial product into the Chinese language at the same time.[57]

From my point of view, there is a transcultural problem of 'categories' that surfaces under different aspects in Greek, Chinese or in other languages. The Greek theory of categories developed by Aristotle and variously used also by other Greek philosophers, such as Plato, for example, is not the standard by which to compare other possible forms of categorial theories. Aptitude or inaptitude to translate the *Categories* is not the touchstone for checking the validity of the hypothesis of linguistic relativism.

Wardy is right, however, in insisting against Graham that the translation of complicated Greek philosophical texts into Chinese does not necessarily produce ungrammatical Chinese, but only a new Chinese idiom that may lack an appropriated linguistic community. A translated work acts on an intellectual community in the same way as a work newly created in and for this community. To be understandable, this work needs a receptive public that shares with it a certain amount of presuppositions.

A comparison which starts off from the bare list of Aristotle's categories exposes itself to one of the fatal dangers threatening any comparative analysis, namely, that of mistaking a superficial resemblance for a deep structural

---

54 Wardy 2000.

55 'I answer with a historical fact which, if not massive, is at least intriguing: Aristotle's *Categories* was translated into literary Chinese, so disputants in the "guidance and constraint" debate can appeal to an actual text in support of their claims, rather than making up hypothetical competitors to Aristotle.' (Wardy 2000: 70)

56 This is also acknowledged by Wardy: 'But what this trivially entails is that the book would be little better than gibberish, at least *in extenso*, for learned Chinese unschooled in the newly created philosophical jargon.' (Wardy 2000: 86)

57 In the end, it would have been easier for the Chinese to learn Latin or Greek than to read a Chinese translation of Aristotle translated into Latin, as Wardy ironically notes (Wardy 2000: 86–87).

affinity. There is, to give a crude example, a Chinese concept of immortality in later Taoist writings; but it would be an unthinking attempt to try to relate that concept to early Christian ideas of immortality. The only measure we can take against this risk in our case is to go back to the question, to the philosophical problem, to which Aristotle's table of categories has been the answer. This means, in turn, that I now have to sketch the outlines of the general theory in which the doctrine of categories is embedded.

There is evidence that the theory of categories has undergone some changes between its early appearance in the *Topics* and in the *Categories*, and its later developments in the *Physics* and in the *Metaphysics*. To be fair to the theory of a linguistic origin of the categories, my investigation will have to focus on the earliest available version of that doctrine, namely, the one contained in the *Topics*, the *Sophistical Refutations*, and the *Categories*. The full list of the categories is only stated twice, once in the *Topics*, an early work on dialectics (that is, a codified search for definitions between two partners), and once in the *Categories*. The version presented in the *Categories* runs as follows:

> Of things said without any combination, each signifies either substance (*ousia*) or quantity or qualification or a relative or where or when or being-in-a-position [a state] or having or doing or being-affected. To give a rough idea, examples of substance are man, horse; of quantity: four-foot, five-foot; of qualification: white, grammatical; of a relative: double, half, larger; of where: in the Lyceum, in the market-place; of when: yesterday, last year; of being-in-a-position: is-lying, is-sitting; of having: has-shoes-on, has-armour-on; of doing: cutting, burning; of being affected: being-cut, being-burnt. None of the above is said just by itself in any affirmation, but by the combination of these with one another an affirmation is produced. For every affirmation, it seems, is either true or false; but of things said without any combination, none is either true or false (e.g. 'man', 'white', 'runs', 'wins').
>
> (*Categories* 4; 1b25f.; translation Ackrill 1979)

To contrast, here is the version of the *Topics*.

> Next, we must define the kinds of predication (*ta genê tôn katêgoriôn*) into which the four above-mentioned predicates [that is, the four predicables, namely definition, proprium, genus and accident] fall.
>   They are ten in number: what is it, how many, how much, in relation to what, when, where, state, having, doing, suffering.
>
> (*Topics* A,9; 103b20f.)

The attentive reader will have noticed a slight difference in the presentation of the two lists: the first category in the *Categories* is called substance (*ousia*), whereas the *Topics* give 'what is it' (*ti esti*). There is another, much more marked contrast in the way both lists of categories are introduced. In the *Categories*, we have items 'said without any combination'; in the *Topics*, on the other hand, we have 'kinds of predication'. The Greek *katêgoria* simply means 'predication' or 'predicate', and is thus not the equivalent of our 'category'. Moreover, *katêgoria* is never used in the *Categories* to designate one of the categories!

But the difference between the two lists of categories is easily explained if we stick to the very way both are introduced: the list of the *Categories* deals with terms (types of predicates), whereas the list of the *Topics* deals with kinds of predication, that is, different ways of predicating these terms of one another. Terms and kinds of predication are but two aspects of a single theory. The kinds of predications fall into two basic types, one regular, the other irregular. We have irregular predication when terms not belonging to the same type (category) are predicated among each other, regular predication when the terms belong to the same category. 'Man is an animal' would be an example of regular predication, 'man is white' of irregular predication. Why is the latter form of predication irregular? What is the norm in comparison to which it is defective? The answer is that regular predication, as we shall see, is an operation vitally important for the task of establishing definitions. The search for definitions starts in Greece with the activity of Socrates, who asks questions such as 'what is courage?', 'what is virtue?', 'what is justice?' This preoccupation is constantly being refined by Plato in his middle and late dialogues, and eventually under Aristotle reaches a high degree of accuracy.

Definition is basically an act of predication. One of the main criteria for correct or regular predication is that the predicate, which purports to be a definition, belongs to the same category as its subject. This is the reason why terms not belonging to the same category predicated of one another are instances of irregular predication. Irregular predication is sometimes termed by Aristotle 'accidental predication', that is, as a kind of predication which can yield a true proposition, but does not necessarily do so. The proposition 'man is white' is not essentially true, for the colour white does not belong to man as such. Normally, then, a definition consists of a *genus* and its *differentia* or *differentiae*, and the term that is defined is a species. The species 'man', for example, is defined as a rational, bipedal, featherless animal. Animal is the *genus*; rational, bipedal, featherless are the *differentiae*. The main difficulty in constructing definitions resides in the problem of how to find the correct *genus*, and how to devise methods for eliminating terms which are only apparently of the same category as the subject of which they are predicated. Intuition, it has to be said, is of no great help for ruling out irregular predication. Different people may have different intuitions, and the dispute cannot be settled unless a criterion of decision is found. What is needed is a method that tells us, independently of the intuition we may have, whether two given terms belong to the same category or not. Now we begin to see the importance of the logical criteria for defining categories we have already met above, for they will eventually enable us to tell one category from another. Let me take an example. Somebody defines the soul as a harmony. If we want to overthrow this definition, all we have to do is to show that the terms 'soul' and 'harmony' do not belong to the same category. This is precisely what Aristotle does:

> Harmony has a contrary, he says, namely, disharmony. The soul has no contrary; therefore, the soul cannot be a harmony.
>
> (Aristotle, *Eudemus* (lost); fragment 7, Ross 1955: 18)

The grammatical form under which the terms 'soul' and 'harmony' appear seems to give an indication of the category they belong to: both are nouns and hence present themselves as a substance. However, this appearance is, as Aristotle shows, deceptive, since the logical functioning of both concepts is different: hence the necessity of logical criteria or tests to find out the category a given term belongs to. These tests can take two different forms, depending on whether we try to set up a definition or overthrow it. For overthrowing a definition, it is enough, as we have seen, to show that one logical criterion ('having a contrary', for example) does not apply to both terms. It is much more difficult to construct a definition. In this case, we shall have to determine first the category of the term we want to define, which means that we shall have to go through the logical criteria characteristic of each category and see which of these criteria fits. The result, in this case, will be that the soul is a substance, whereas harmony is a relative. The exact function of the doctrine of categories in Aristotle's early writings can now be stated. A definition must, as I have shown, bring together terms belonging to one and the same logical type. If the left-hand term is an *ousia*, an essence, for example, 'man', the right-hand term of the definition (A is B) must be an essence too, for example, 'animal'. This is, however, only a preliminary condition to correct definition; the next step, if the sameness in category is secured, is to find the correct *genus*, that is, the *genus proximum* of the term to be defined. But this problem falls outside the scope of this essay.

Aristotle's method looks easy. Its application, however, meets a number of difficulties. The most urgent of these difficulties is doubtless the phenomenon of homonymy, that is, words having several meanings. There are two basic forms of homonymy in Aristotle: chance homonymy and real homonymy. If a word is homonymous by chance, there is no steady semantic connection between the multiple meanings this word may have (the word 'bank', for example). But real homonymy affects words such as 'good', 'being', 'one', 'healthy', 'friendship'. Predicated of God, 'good' means a good thing; predicated of the soul, it means a good quality; of time, the appropriate or the right time; and so forth. Good can be predicated essentially ('regularly') in as many ways as there are categories. This means, in turn, that there are really ten different terms all of which are labelled 'good' and, therefore, that we shall be in trouble in determining whether or not an expression of the form 'A is good', even if we know the category that A belongs to, is a case of legitimate ('regular') predication. This curious situation, however, has an explanation. There is a link between all these different categorial meanings of 'good'. The nature of this link has been described as 'focal meaning'.[58] There is one basic sense of

---

58   Compare Owen 1979a: 17.

'good', namely, the one attached to the first term in the series (good as an *ousia* 'essence' = God) towards which the meanings of the other nine (or fewer) terms tend to converge.

Let me now sum up the main points of my short review of Aristotle's early doctrine of categories. Aristotle starts from the insight that categories are easily confused in Greek, hence the necessity to draw a list of categories and to provide criteria independent of language to identify them. Two major sources of confusion have been recognized. On the grammatical level, the Greek language can mislead the philosopher, but can also guide him. Some expressions are 'friends of the categories' while others are 'foes of the categories', as we have seen above. On the semantic level, we have hit upon the phenomenon of 'focal meaning'. We have seen the ways in which the Greek language could lead astray the philosopher in search of definitions, and some of the means invented by Aristotle to keep the philosopher's thinking out of these blind alleys.

It is time now to turn to the achievements of the philosophers of ancient, pre-Han China. Our material comes from a philosophical school known as the Later Mohists,[59] which flourished in ancient China at around 300 BC. They were a group of scholars who undertook the formidable task of rebuilding, rationally and *more geometrico*, the philosophy of Mozi, the founder of the school, who lived in the fifth century BC. By the middle of the fourth century, a philosopher named Yang Zhu had entered the philosophical scene and provoked, in the camps of the Mohists and the Confucians (the only important philosophical schools existing at that time), a major philosophical crisis.[60] Yang Zhu starts from the concept of human nature *xing*,° and declares that its basic tendency is aspiration towards longevity and pleasure, and that the world is well governed only if nobody has to make sacrifices, however small, to the common good of society. This clearly undermines the Mohists' claim that heavenly providence and a society organized after Mohist standards is the panacea to heal the current worldly disorder. The Later Mohists' reaction, far from being apologetic, was actually to take up Yang Zhu's challenge, and they showed that if thinking really takes the fundamental aspirations of human nature as its starting-point, it will unerringly rediscover the main principles of Mohist philosophy. One of the most interesting facets of the Later Mohists' undertakings, which at once bring them nearer to classical Greek philosophy, is their fondness of dialectic. The goal of the Later Mohists' dialectic *bian*[p] is the correct description and definition of basic terms, chiefly of those belonging to the domain of ethics. Dialectical debate is conceived by them as a struggle between two names, each of which purports to be the correct description of one moral, or other, concept. A definition, for them, is thus simply an equivalence between two names or group of names. The

---

59   For a reconstruction, edition and translation of the writings of the Later Mohists see Graham 1978.

60   Graham 1978: 15f.

distinctive feature of names is their having an implicit cognitive content. The Later Mohists use a very suggestive illustration to make this idea plain: they imagine an object placed at the other side of a wall and then ask what we can tell about that object when only knowing its name. This type of knowledge, which is, according to them, 'knowledge in advance' *xian zhi*,[q] receives the name of *shuo*,[r] that is, 'knowledge by explanation'. Knowledge by explanation is twice illustrated by geometrical propositions in the Later Mohists' unfortunately badly mutilated summa on dialectics, a fact which suggests that the geometrical method had come to be recognized as the model for any demonstrative science.[61] The term *shuo* has, interestingly enough, both the meaning of 'explanation' and of 'proof'.[62] This, perhaps, is the reason why definition and demonstration are seen, by the Later Mohists (but not by Aristotle!), as one and the same activity. Let me now step into the conceptual construction of the Later Mohists and have a brief look at their rational reconstruction of Mozi's moral philosophy. The cornerstone of the Later Mohists' ethical system is a pair of definitions:

> Benefit *li*[s] is what one is pleased to get. (A 26)
> Harm *hai*[t] is what one dislikes getting. (A 27)
> (*Mohist Canon*, A 26, A 27; Graham 1978: 282–83)

These definitions do not obey the strict Aristotelian pattern of a *genus* followed by a *differentia*. Nevertheless, they are true definitions in the sense, namely, that the *definiens* states what the *definiendum* essentially is. Desire (*yu*[u]) and aversion (*e*[v]) are the basic, and therefore undefined, terms of the Later Mohists' ethical system, and all the other ethical concepts are defined in terms of them or in terms defined by means of them.[63] The gist of the Later Mohists' answer to Yang Zhu is that human nature (*xing*[w]) is a concept which can be further analysed and broken down into desire and aversion. The key concept of the Later Mohists' ethical system however is love (*ai*[x]). The definition of this term is lost, but we can reconstruct it: 'To love is to have the intention of benefiting others (and keep off harm from them).'[64] Duty (*yi*[y]) and humanity (*ren*[z]) are defined in terms of love and benefit, and so is filial piety (*xiao*[aa]).[65] The Later Mohists do not only give definitions in the field of ethics, but they also define mental faculties, the relations between leader and follower and between subject and ruler, different forms of change, the concept of necessity, and so forth. The way the Later Mohists proceed leaves the impression that these thinkers did not stumble on any of the serious difficulties encountered by Aristotle. Note, incidentally, that Aristotle's investigations in the *Topics* closely resemble the Later Mohists' project. Aristotle's

---

61   On this problem, see the essay 'Philosophy and Geometry in Early China' in this volume.
62   Graham 1978: 216 and 317.
63   Compare Graham 1978: 47ff.
64   See the essay 'Philosophy and Geometry in Early China' in this volume.
65   Graham 1978: 270 (theorems A 7 and A 8); p. 275 (theorem, A 13).

writings, however, are mostly lecture notes, whereas the Later Mohists' summa is the result and the final product of several generations of thinkers. Whereas Aristotle records the difficulties he encounters, the Later Mohists only give us the final result. The impression of elegance and terseness attached to the Later Mohists' system however is deceptive. Not only did the Later Mohists record the difficulties they had encountered, but they also, not infrequently, warn the beginner in dialectics against possible logical pitfalls. My task will be to find out whether any of these problems can be placed in the context of a doctrine of categories. The experience on which Aristotle's early discovery of the categorial scheme is based is the conflict between logical and linguistic structures. Aristotle had observed this conflict through the 'spectacles' of the Greek language. In what follows, I shall demonstrate that the Later Mohists experienced, though in a different linguistic setting, a situation similar to Aristotle's. It turns out indeed that homonymy is the gravest difficulty the Later Mohists had to face. In their summa on dialectics, they devoted considerable space to the problems of homonymy. They provide us, for example, with a whole list of ambiguous terms.[66] A very useful test to decide whether anything resembling a categorial division had existed in ancient China is to see whether the phenomenon termed 'focal meaning' (see above) had come to be recognized. Consider the following proposition.

> Different kinds (*lei*[ab]) are not comparable. Explained by: measuring.
>   Which is longer, a piece of wood or a night? Which do you have more of, knowledge or grain? Which is the most valuable, aristocratic rank, one's own parents, right conduct, a price? Which is higher, a deer or a crane?
> *(Mohist Canon,* B 6; Graham 1978: 357)

In the first example, *chang*,[ac] 'long', can signify either a quantity (a long piece of wood) or a time (a long night).[67] In the second example, *duo*,[ad] 'much', has a qualitative and a quantitative meaning; the third example gives four different senses of *gui*,[ae] 'dear': high social rank (quality), beloved parents (relation), noble conduct (action), expensive goods (quantity). In the fourth case, *gao*,[af] 'high', is ambiguous as to whether a size or a relation is stated. Theorem B 6 thus shows that categorial distinctions are not unknown in ancient China. There too, these distinctions came to light as a result of a strong preoccupation with definition. The most important result for our inquiry is that when the Later Mohists draw distinctions, these appear to coincide exactly with categorial distinctions also made by Aristotle. Moreover, the tie that holds together the four senses of *gui*, 'dear', can be equated with the Aristotelian 'focal meaning'.

I have shown earlier that for those writing and thinking in classical Greek, the morphological markings of a word are a very important clue to its categorial value, although they have to be alert to the 'foes of the categories'.

---

66   Graham 1978: 323–36 (theorems A 76 to A 87).
67   This ambiguity is also exploited by one of the twenty-one paradoxes of chapter 33 of the *Zhuangzi*. Paradox 12 states 'A tortoise is/lives longer than a snake.'

If categories are also marked in classical Chinese, we shall have to look there not for morphological clues, but rather for syntactical markings, since classical Chinese is an uninflected language. Indeed, in Chinese a grammatically unmarked word cannot by itself (unlike 'slave' in Greek, for example) induce the philosopher into error, because such a word alone cannot purport to belong to a type other than that to which it actually belongs. It follows from there that in classical Chinese a whole syntactic structure is required to produce a distorting effect. Consider, to this purpose, a text taken from the Later Mohists' treatise on *Names and objects*.

> Name and object do not necessarily go together. If this stone is white, when you break up this stone, all of it is the same as the white thing; but although this stone is big, it is not the same as the big thing.
>
> (NO 1; Graham 1978: 470–71)

Every part of a white stone is white, but not every part of a big stone is also big. This means, for the Later Mohists, that 'big' and 'white' cannot belong to the same category. The Later Mohists' problem arises out of the fact that *bai*,[ag] 'white', and *da*,[ah] 'big', here behave syntactically in exactly the same way. There is, however, a logical difference between 'white' and 'big': the latter belongs to the category of quantity, whereas the former is a quality. Another text of this same treatise argues in a similar way.

> If this horse's eyes are blind, we say that this horse is blind; though this horse's eyes are big, we do not say that this horse is big. If these oxen's hairs are yellow, we say that these oxen are yellow; though these oxen's hairs are many, we do not say that these oxen are many.
>
> (NO 18; Graham 1978: 492)

The examples chosen by the Later Mohists are mainly elementary paradigm cases. Nobody, I believe, would be misled by terms such as 'white', 'big' or 'blind'. Nevertheless, we must not leave out of account the fact that the Later Mohists' summa is more a handbook of dialectic than a complete and detailed exposition of the Mohist philosophy.[68] Consequently, the examples chosen are easy and obvious cases, designed to bring out the principle of the fallacy rather than listing individual cases.[69] Just like Aristotle in the opening paragraphs of the *Categories*, the Later Mohists use uncontroversial and intuitively clear examples.[70] The most astonishing aspect, however, if we compare Aristotle to the Later Mohists, is the facility the latter have in

---

68   Since the Mohists are utterly convinced of the immutable truth of the philosophy of Master Mo (Mozi), the rational reconstruction of this doctrine and the coining of the rules of dialectic are, for them, one and the same undertaking.

69   'We are again reminded that the ultimate purpose of disputation is practical, to equip us to approach the problems of government with clear heads', writes Graham when commenting on NO 6 (Graham 1978: 476).

recognizing categorial distinctions. Once the Later Mohists acknowledge the fact that a word has several meanings (like *gui*, 'dear', see above), they are also able to subdivide these meanings along categorial lines, without using Aristotle's rather complicated logical criteria.

Until now, I have been looking at the Later Mohists' achievements from a rather 'Aristotelian' perspective. I shall round off this study with a few considerations on how the Later Mohists have understood themselves, and on what they think they were doing when we say that they have been distinguishing between Aristotelian categories. Let me return to the beginning of *Names and objects*, where a categorial difference between a 'big' and a 'white' stone had been set up. The Later Mohists represent this difference in the following way.

> In all cases of naming otherwise than by reference to number or measure, when you break up the object all of it is the thing in question.
>
> (NO 1; Graham 1978: 470–71)

This explanation shows that categorial differences are seen against the background of a general theory of naming. Where Aristotle distinguishes between, presumably, ontological categories, the Later Mohists speak of different kinds of naming. But 'naming by reference to number or measure' (see NO 1) is, roughly, the equivalent of the Aristotelian category of quantity; 'naming by shape and characteristics' (see NO 2) recalls the category of quality; 'naming on the basis of residence and migration' (see again NO 2) can be equated with the Aristotelian category of 'where?' The list of the Later Mohists stops here, but there is evidence that they were able to identify most of the other Aristotelian categories.[71]

With these considerations, I have prepared the reader for a reassessment of Graham's conclusions. Graham has seen, rightly I think, that the Aristotelian categories have an ontological flavour, whereas the Later Mohists' 'categories' are clearly criteria for naming correctly: 'The definitions of Chinese philosophy are therefore conceived as presenting, not what is essential to being X, but what is indispensable to being called "X". In either case, however, there is the same exclusion of the accidental.'[72] The Aristotelian *ti esti*, 'what is it?' thus is the equivalent of *he wei X*,[ai] 'what is X called?' in Chinese. This difference, however, is the result of a different cultural attitude to language and naming. The Greek philosophers in general deny to language any capacity for faithfully mirroring the true nature of reality. They try

---

70   For an application of these principles to a concrete case, see, for example, the way in which the Later Mohists establish the categorial difference there is, according to them, between 'love (people)' and 'ride (horses)', developed in NO 14 and NO 17 (Graham 1978: 485–92).

71   See also the proposition B 3 (Graham 1978: 352–55), which draws categorial distinctions between *dou* 'fight' and *er* 'two', as well as between *miao* 'blind' and *bai* 'white'.

72   Graham 1986e: 378.

therefore to construct (or discover) a more firm reality beyond and independent of language, like Plato's ideas or Democritus' atoms. The first Chinese philosophers' confidence in language, on the other hand, has not been shattered in the same way. They believe that a set of rules for the proper use of language is sufficient to clear up all the confusion language might generate. In this way, the Chinese logicians are disadvantaged by the fact that classical Chinese is a logically better organized language than Greek and Indo-European languages in general. The more misleading the language, the higher, finally, the philosophical awareness of the speakers using it.[73] The problem of categories arises, in ancient China as well as in Greece, in the context of a theory of definition. Aristotle asks for what a thing essentially is; the first Chinese philosophers ask for what is indispensable to being called X. Despite this apparently fundamental difference, both approaches start from a common point, namely, from the experience of category confusions, provoked by misleading semantic or syntactical structures. I have shown that, as a consequence of the fundamental structural differences between Greek and Chinese, the mechanisms that are at the basis of these confusions did act in diverging ways. The hypothesis of the influence of language on the structure of categorial distinctions however has revealed itself as false. Different languages have different means of distorting logical categories, but the distorted categories are, so far as we have seen in this study, the same, despite the fact that, for Aristotle, the categories are epistemological or ontological entities as opposed to the categories of naming of the Later Mohists. In my opinion, categories, as they appear in Aristotle's and in the Later Mohists' writings, are symptoms of interference between linguistic and logical structures, which means that the problem of categories only arises within such zones. The structure of language only influences the way in which categorial structures may be discovered, and the extent to which these structures are unveiled. If Aristotle's list of categories is longer and more elaborate than the Later Mohists', this only proves that Aristotle had to fight against a language whose structure is more hostile to categorial distinctions than classical Chinese.

---

73   Lau 1952–1953.

Chapter 5

Words for Atoms – Atoms for Words

Comparative Considerations on the Origins of Atomism in Ancient Greece and on the Absence of Atomism in Ancient China

Introduction

Atomism is a theory which states that matter is composed of small, indivisible and inalterable parts, invisible to the eye. The combination or the separation of atoms explains all material changes in the world. This appears to be so simple and yet so fundamental a theory that its very absence in another culture almost inevitably pushes us to seriously question the quality of the philosophical achievements of that culture. 'The fundamental idea of atoms,' Needham writes,[1] 'could be expected to arise in all civilizations independently, since everywhere men were engaged in cutting up lengths of wood, and the question would inevitably arise as to what would happen if successive cuttings were to go until the uncuttable was reached.' Heidel saw the origins of the corpuscular theory 'in the dateless age before the birth of history'.[2] Bachelard thought that the scientific theory of atomism was basically an explication of intuitions', like Lucretius' famous picture of the sun illuminating fine particles in a dusty room.[3] Piaget even postulated atomism as a fundamental cognitive stage in the child's mental development.[4]

Needham himself did try to provide an answer to the puzzle: 'Atomism is one of the most familiar features of European and Indian theorizing, yet although at various times some Chinese thinkers watered its seeds, the idea never took root among them, presumably because it was out of harmony with those organic presuppositions on which Chinese thought was based' or 'It must now be made clear, as a further preliminary, how Chinese physical thinking was dominated throughout by the concept of waves rather than of atoms.'[5] However, this type of explanation is clearly unsatisfactory, because

---

1   Needham 1962: 3. Compare Needham 1962: 1 ('Just as Chinese mathematics was algebraic rather than geometrical, and Chinese philosophy organic rather than mechanical, so we shall find that Chinese physical thought [...] was dominated by the notion of waves rather than particles.')
2   Heidel 1911: 171.
3   Bachelard 1933. The picture is first mentioned by Aristotle, *De anima* 1.2; 404a1f.
4   Piaget and Inhelder 1978: 99f.
5   Needham 1962: 3.

the problem is shifted to an ethnological level where it is then left unanswered or even declared unanswerable.[6]

Another, related, line of argument starts from the assumption – explicit or not – that atomism simply *could* not arise in China, because change and natural phenomena were embedded there in a fundamentally different paradigm. Granet writes: 'Au lieu de constater des successions de phénomènes, les Chinois enregistrent des alternances d'aspects.'[7] Needham, finally, gives another interesting hint: 'Now it is a striking, and perhaps significant, fact that the languages of all those civilizations which developed atomic theories were alphabetic.'[8] But the fundamental idea that is behind the alphabet is also widespread in China, as Needham himself has noticed. We find it operating in the solid and broken lines of the hexagrams of the *Book of Changes*.

The absence of atomism in China is also sometimes explained by the general lack of interest in scientific problems. This explanation is hardly to the point, because even Greek atomism was not, strictly speaking, a scientific theory, as we shall see. The origin of the theory of atomism in ancient Greece is closely linked to the overall development of Presocratic philosophy, and is paradigmatic for the unfolding of ancient Greek philosophy as a whole.[9]

Atomism probably did not arise from trying to cut up wooden sticks to the infinite. Atomism, at least as it is understood in the context of ancient Greek philosophy, is primarily an *epistemological* theory,[10] not a scientific theory of the structure of matter. The strong points of atomism are above all its ability to explain not only the phenomenon of change and our perception of it, but also the quite common experience of conflicting appearances, that is, where different persons have mutually incompatible perceptions of one and the same object, like the same honey tasting sweet to one person, and bitter to another, ill, person. According to Theophrastus, Democritus had explained this phenomenon by the different physical, atomistic, constitutions of the healthy and the sick man: the same well-rounded honey atoms produce different sensations on the sick and on the healthy body, explaining thereby why the corresponding perceptions are also different.

The theory of atomism of Leucippus and Democritus is the logical outcome of this first phase of philosophical speculations on the phenomenon of change. The predecessors of Leucippus, Democritus and later Epicurus are Empedocles and Anaxagoras, and indirectly also Parmenides, Melissus and Zeno. The

---

6   Lloyd 1990: 5 ('[…] we should be clear that in general to appeal to a distinct mentality is merely to *redescribe* the phenomena that are found puzzling or in need of explanation.')

7   Granet 1934: 329.

8   Needham 1962: 13.

9   Bayley 1928: 9 ('[atomism] was no brilliant and isolated invention, but the natural issue of a long series of speculations of the early physical philosophers.' Everything 'pointed to atomism as the ultimate conclusion'). See also Canto-Sperber et al. 1997: 72.

10   See Kirk, Raven and Schofield 1983: 404 ('[…] Democritus was particularly occupied with the epistemological basis of atomism,' referring to Aristotle, *De generatione and corruptione* A,8; 325a2f., translated *ibid.*, pp. 407–408).

problem of atomism can be isolated from the general outcome of the issue whether China had science or not. Ancient atomism is not yet science. Atomism may or may not lead to science: the Indians and the Arabs did have atomism, but that did not lead them straightforwardly to science. The issues of scientific thinking and of atomism have to be kept apart.[11]

Is it worth investigating why such a simple and elementary theory did not arise in pre-Han China? But what can really count as an 'explanation' in this domain? Can we still follow Needham, for example, who thinks that there was another *kind* of explanation that predominated in China, namely the wave-model rather than the corpuscular model? This type of discourse makes us fall back into the mentality paradigm, 'where the only evidence of the mentality postulated is the very data that that postulate is supposed to help us to understand.'[12]

If the comparative approach is to yield more than a mere *description* of what is felt strange or different in another culture, and eventually lead us on to the way of an *explanation* of these differences, we will have to admit that the principles explaining the presence, the absence, or the particular configuration of a facet of the 'other philosophy' must also at the same time explain why this facet is present, absent, or different in our 'home philosophy'. For our case, this means that to explain the absence of atomism in ancient China is at the same time also to find out why and how atomism arose in ancient Greece. While explaining why the Chinese did not develop atomism, we explain at the same time why the Greeks did. But neither solution – atomism or its absence – is a norm, in relation to which the other would be the defect. Historically speaking, the absence or the presence of atomism in a culture must be considered as a contingent event, not a necessary outcome. There is not one distinctive principle (like the 'wave-model') that is to be held responsible for its absence, but we will have to look for a whole series of events and facts that are somehow linked and whose concatenation gives us – or does not give – the atomic theory. This, alas, requires much more preparatory work, philological, historical and interpretative.[13]

The Conceptual Prerequisites of Atomism in Ancient China

The point I want to emphasize is that there is no epistemological obstacle that could have prevented the first Chinese philosophers from creating a theory of atomism. I would even like to go a step further and show that there could have been atomism in ancient China, in the sense that all the necessary conceptual

---

11   Scharfstein 1998: 203. Although Scharfstein devotes a whole chapter (ch. 6) of his comparative history of philosophy to atomism, he does not – curiously, one might add – raise the problem of the absence of atomism in ancient China.
12   Lloyd 1990: 142.
13   See Lloyd 1996: 213–14.

prerequisites for such a theory had existed or were developed at that time.[14] To this purpose, I shall discuss a certain number of relevant Chinese texts. Interestingly enough, some of these texts have even been taken to prove that there was atomism in China.

Epistemological problems are not at all unknown in ancient China, and the absence of atomism cannot therefore be accounted for by a supposed general lack of interest in epistemological and scientific matters. We also have to resist the temptation to explain away this difference – the lack of atomism in ancient China – simply by arguing that the Chinese have in fact never raised the epistemological problem of change, or had even been incapable of doing so. The writings of the Later Mohists (third century BC) contain many passages where the problem of change is explicitly discussed. Furthermore, there is a treatise of the sophist Gongsun Long (third century BC) which bears the significant title *Tongbianlun*[a] 'Thinking Through Change'.[15] Moreover, the problem of change pervades the whole Chinese intellectual tradition in a variety of ways through one of its major works, the *Yijing*, the *Book of Change(s)*.

The conception of a large mass being composed of small and imperceptible units is indeed widespread in the philosophical literature of the Warring States period, as the following two texts may show:

> A mountain is accumulated (*ji*[b]) earth; the sea is an accumulation of thin streams of water.
>
> (*Xunzi*, ch. 8, p. 95, *Zhuzi jicheng* edition)

This text shows a philosophically unbiased reflection on the relations between the great and the small. The following text is a more refined version of the same problem:

> The *Book of Changes* says: A deviation as slight as an autumn spikelet causes an error of a thousand miles.
>
> (*Shiji*, ch. 130, p. 3298, *Zhonghua shuju* edition)[16]

There is another text worth quoting in this context, namely the famous ten theses of the sophist Hui Shi (fourth century BC), listed in chapter 33 of the *Zhuangzi*. The first and the second theses are particularly revealing:

> *Zhi da wu wai, wei zhi da yi.*
> *Zhi xiao wu nei, wei zhi xiao yi.*[c]
> The greatest has nothing outside it, call it the Great One.
> The smallest has nothing inside it, call it the Small One.

---

14   Hall and Ames have tried to show that the Chinese culture had developed options that were 'either rejected or left undeveloped within our own culture' (Hall and Ames 1995: 181). The case of atomism would be an example working the opposite way.
15   Translated in the last essay '"To Be" in Greece and China' in this volume.
16   Also to be found in chapter 23 of the *Liji*; the quotation from the *Yijing* is not in the transmitted text, nor in the published manuscripts from Mawangdui.

Wu hou bu ke ji ye, qi da qian li.[d]
That which has no thickness (bulk, dimension) cannot be accumulated (heaped up), yet its size is a thousand miles.

(Zhuangzi, ch. 33, p. 223, *Zhuzi jicheng* edition)

These propositions are sometimes, wrongly I believe, interpreted as implying an atomistic picture of the universe or alluding to it. 'This seems to be one of those not infrequent places where the ancient Chinese thinkers paused at the door of atomism without ever going in,' comments Needham.[17]

The first of Hui Shi's theses uses the significant expressions *zhi xiao* and *xiao yi*, 'the smallest' and 'the Small One'. The text does not say, however, that the Great One is composed of Small Ones. The terms *wuwai* and *wunei* ('that which has nothing outside it' and 'that which has nothing inside it') are used in the *Guanzi* and the *Lüshichunqiu* in purely cosmological contexts, such as the description of the action of the *qi*[e] 'cosmic matter' or 'cosmic breath'.[18] The structure of the *qi*, however, is never understood as being atomistic; the *qi* is rather conceived as a condensing and rarefying substance, much in the style of the elemental changes of the air in Anaximenes[19] or in Diogenes of Apollonia.[20] *Qi* has indeed many more affinities with the pseudo-Aristotelian concept of prime matter than with atomism, as Hatton has shown.[21]

It has to be noted that the second of Hui Shi's paradoxes connects in terminology (*ji*[f] 'heap up') as well as in content with the first two texts. The point Hui Shi wants to make in his second paradox is clearly this: great changes may be brought about by minute factors. This idea is also expressed in the above-mentioned quotation from the *Book of Changes*, to which Hui Shi's second thesis even seems to be a verbal echo, if not a commentary, because he also uses the phrase 'a thousand miles'.[22] I would even like to claim that since Hui Shi's second thesis bears so close a resemblance to a text from the *Book of Changes*, nobody, in ancient China at least, could have read it in a sense different from the one intended there.

---

17 Needham 1956: 194.
18 For the concepts *wuwai* and *wunei*, see *Guanzi* (ch. 36 and ch. 11) and *Lüshichunqiu* (ch. 15.3).
19 Cf. Anaximenes fragment 13 A 6 DK = 148 KRS, pp. 151–52.
20 For a similar idea in a Chinese context, see Ho Peng Yoke 1985: 3–5. Interestingly enough, early translators of Chinese texts had sometimes rendered *qi* as 'atom', as Graham notes (Graham 1985: 57) See also Moritz 1973: 123–24.
21 Hatton 1982. Shallow and superficial is Feng Jingyuan 1985, who, for example, relies for his analysis of the Western notion of matter on *Xifang zhexue yuanzhu xuandu* [= A selection of original writings of Western philosophers], Beijing, 1981–1982, 2 vols. This selection of texts mistranslates several crucial passages (the most blatant example surely is: vol. 1, p. 42, section 6, Empedocles, no. 5, that is fragment B 8 of Empedocles, noted D 8 there) in such a way that even key arguments of Presocratic philosophy, such as the famous *ex nihilo nihil*, do not appear to have been fully understood.
22 See also chapter 64 of the *Daodejing*.

Although Hui Shi's famous sayings cannot be equated with atomism, they nevertheless exhibit, like other texts from this same period, a strong awareness of the problem of the infinitely small.[23]

The reason why Hui Shi's second thesis is sometimes viewed in an atomistic context is perhaps to be found in the tentative translation of *wu hou*[g] (literally 'that which is without bulk') by 'atom', popularized at the beginning of the twentieth century by Forke and von Zenker.[24] Let us investigate if this way of translating *wuhou* is really justified.

The expression *wuhou* is frequently cited as a topic for discussion among the dialecticians (*bianzhe*[h]) in ancient China.[25] The only surviving document in which *wuhou* occurs in a technical and logical sense is the *Mohist Canon* (*Mojing*). The expression there occurs in a geometrical context, however. The Later Mohists define the notion of *hou*[i] in the following way:

> *Hou* (having bulk/thickness/dimension) is having something than which it is bigger.
> (*Mohist Canon*, A 55; Graham 1978: 305–306)

Hou is an important concept because it enters into the definition of *duan*,[j] 'starting-point' or 'end point', that is, geometrical points that have a limiting function.[26]

> The *duan* (starting-point) is the unit without dimension which precedes all others.
> (*Mohist Canon*, A 61; Graham 1978: 310)

There is no doubt that we are here in the presence of a kind of geometrical atomism, or rather of atomism in a geometrical context.[27] The interesting feature of *wuhou*, as it occurs in the *Mohist Canon*, is that it perfectly illustrates the idea of 'theoretical divisibility'. The concept of theoretical divisibility, as Furley has pointed out, is not to be equated with the idea of physical divisibility. Theoretical divisibility is the conceptual basis for atomism in the physical sense: 'the physical divisibility of an object entails its theoretical divisibility; but the converse is not true.'[28] The point of this remark is that reflections on the problems of the infinitely small and on infinite divisibility are presupposed by a theory of physical atomism, but that more is required to develop a theory of atomism.

---

23   See, e.g., *Zhuangzi*, ch. 17 and also ch. 25.
24   Von Zenker 1926: 257; Forke 1901–1902: 23.
25   For *wuhou* as a topic of the dialecticians, see *Xunzi*, ch. 2, p. 18, *Zhuzi jicheng* edition; *Hanfeizi*, ch. 41, p. 302, *Zhuzi jicheng* edition; *Lüshichunqiu*, ch. 17.2. See also *Zhuangzi*, ch. 3, p. 19, *Zhuzi jicheng* edition.
26   On the limiting functions of geometrical points, see Aristotle, *Metaphysics* 1060b12–16; *Physics* 220a9–11.
27   This is the view of Needham (Needham 1959: 92; see also Needham 1954: 155). Elsewhere, Needham says that 'atomism in the physico-chemical sense never played any role of importance in traditional scientific thinking' (Needham 1968: 96).
28   Furley 1967: 4.

It is well worthwhile mentioning that the Later Mohists also have coined the concept of *wujiu*[k] 'that which has no duration'.[29] We can safely assume that the concept of *wujiu* is not to be understood in the sense of a time-atom,[30] but rather as a boundary for periods of time, just as the starting-point (*duan*), which is 'without bulk' (*wuhou*), also has a limiting function for measured rules, as we have already noted. This interpretation of *wujiu* as a boundary is also the more plausible one on the ground that the Later Mohists have developed a theory of potential infinity to solve the paradoxes of infinite divisibility. Conceiving the moment, or the instant, as a time-atom leads to paradoxes, in China as well as in ancient Greece. Zeno's arrow has, in ancient China, a surprisingly close counterpart:

> When the arrow is at its fastest there is a time when it neither travels nor is at rest.
> (*Zhuangzi*, ch. 33, p. 223, *Zhuzi jicheng* edition;
> translation Graham 1989: 81)

The paradox hinges, like Zeno's, on the fact that motion and rest at one moment are impossible. If a period of time is conceived as being composed of moments (*to nun* in Greek), Zeno's paradox, just as its Chinese counterpart, cannot be avoided.

All this shows that the purely theoretical problem of infinite divisibility and units without magnitude had not escaped the minds of the first Chinese philosophers. However, no trace of atomism is to be found in ancient China.

It can be shown that even the idea of physical divisibility is well known in ancient China. Take the following text:

> A stick one foot long, if you take a half every day, will not be exhausted for a myriad generations.
> (*Zhuangzi*, ch. 33, p. 224, *Zhuzi jicheng* edition)

A more elaborate version of this paradox is to be found in the *Mohist Canon*.[31] The solution to this problem given by the Later Mohists comes very close to the Aristotelian answer. Like Aristotle, the Later Mohists admit only potential infinity. But here too, there is not the slightest tendency towards a theory of atomism.

Needham enumerates three more Chinese candidates for the notion of atom: *wei*[l] 'minute', *kuai*[m] a small piece' and *ji*[n] 'germ'. The term *wei* does indeed share one feature with the Western atom, namely its imperceptibility. This is not imperceptibility in a physical sense, however, but in a sense of not

---

29 For the concept of *wujiu* 'without duration' in the *Mohist Canon*, see Graham 1978: 298 (theorem A 50).

30 On the problem of time-atoms, see Sorabji 1979. See also Plato's *Parmenides* 156C–157A and *Mojing* A 44, A 50 (of names fitting to the objects they name) in Graham 1978: 295–99.

31 See proposition B 60 (Graham 1978: 432–33).

noticing the faint signs that foreshadow an imminent change.[32] The other two terms, *kuai* and *ji*, never really appear in an atomistic context, as Needham himself acknowledges.[33]

The idea of the infinitely small can even appear quite naturally in texts where no cosmological speculations are intended.[34]

> Therefore the sage, when he speaks about great things, nobody in the world is able to sustain them; when he speaks about small things, nobody in the world is able to break them further down.
>
> (*Zhongyong*, ch. 12)

The foregoing analysis has plainly shown, I hope, that the ancient Chinese philosophers did not lack the conceptual prerequisites for atomism. Neither were they incapable of raising the problem of change, to which, as we know, the Greek theory of atomism was meant to be one or the only answer. This situation must render the explanation of the absence of atomism in ancient China all the more challenging.[35]

The Conceptual Embedding of the Atomist Theory

If atomism is seen only as a problem of cutting up wooden sticks indefinitely, one misses a very important point. Atomism, as a primary epistemological theory, is not an isolated element, but appears to be embedded into a whole philosophical *problématique*. Once posed, the problem of change gives rise indeed to a vortex of what I shall call 'concomitant theories of atomism'. Here is a tentative list of these theories:

(a) *Sense perception is deceitful.* The human senses are bad witnesses. This theory is a sister-theory of atomism, for two reasons: first, we cannot see atoms, and are hence incapable of apprehending the true nature of things (Democritus B 9 DK = 549 KRS, p. 410). Moreover, our senses suggest,

---

32   *Lüshichunqiu* ch. 16.6; note the compound *qiuhao* 'fine autumn hairs' as an expression for the almost imperceptible (see above). But *wei* is not a candidate for atomism, because the elements that are termed *wei* are perceptible, but only for the sage, not for the fool. So the basic sense of *wei* is 'hardly perceptible'.
33   Needham 1962: 5.
34   Andrew Plaks has called my attention to this passage from the *Zhongyong*.
35   This conclusion is similar to the one reached by Sivin for cosmology and mathematical astronomy: the elements for building science in the Western way were there, but had not been drawn together (Sivin 1969). Harbsmeier (1998) shows most forcefully that the Chinese language is fully equipped to express the standard logical features and concepts current in Western thought. But he also notes: 'The question of whether rationality developed among the Chinese is entirely separate from the question whether the ways of speaking of the Chinese do or do not involve what we can recognize as logical trains of thought.' (Harbsmeier 1998: 261)

just as does language, that things are born out of nothing, or are annihilated (Melissus B 8 DK = 537 KRS, pp. 398–400). A third reason may be added: only atomism explains in a coherent way how conflicting appearances, such as for example the fact that the same honey tastes bitter to one person and sweet to another, are possible. We do not see atoms; hence, we do not see what is real; hence, conflicting appearances are not really logically contradictory. They may be explained by the hidden atomistic structure of the world.

(b) There is a strict *opposition between being and becoming*. Of changing objects, one cannot say that they really *are*. Unchanging atoms are the only real objects in the world. Greek ontology is not so much concerned with what is *there* as with what there *is*. Democritus would have conceded that there are colours, but not that these colours really *are*. Atoms possess a higher degree of reality than colours. Plato's great ontological innovation resides in the fact that he admits of 'degrees of reality', by introducing intermediate stages between Parmenides' nothing and absolute being.[36]

(c) There is, further, another equally strict *opposition between reality and appearance*. The atoms are not directly perceived. What is perceived therefore cannot be real, but only apparent.

(d) Next, it is worth drawing attention to a very famous epistemological principle that pervades ancient Greek philosophy, namely that *it is impossible to have knowledge of the changing*. Aristotle finds the right expression in the *Metaphysics: ou gar einai tôn reontôn epistêmên* (1078b16–17).[37] This principle is already very common in Plato.[38] Thus 'beauty in itself' *is* more, has a higher and more fundamental degree of being than individual instances of beauty, which may always appear ugly from some other point of view, such as the beautiful virgin when compared to a goddess (*Hippias major* 287E and 298A).

(e) *Language in general is deceitful*, and cannot bring us near to the true nature of things. Language suggests that things grow out of nothing and vanish into nothing. We shall quote hereafter three significant texts in which this principle is expressed, namely fragment 17 of Anaxagoras, fragment 8 of Empedocles and excerpts from fragment 8 of Parmenides (see below).

(f) *There is void*. The concept of the void is a logically necessary corollary of atomism. 'To distinguish one part of what *is* from another – in other words to account for plurality – Leucippus and Democritus introduced the concept of the void.'[39]

This short and necessarily sketchy presentation shows that Greek atomism is a member of a whole family of theories that somehow hang together. Notice,

---

36   Cf. *Republic* 479D. See also Bröcker 1959.
37   See also *Theaetetus* 179C1ff.; *Cratylus* 439E1ff.
38   For an overview, see Reed 1972.
39   Furley 1987: 118.

however, that the purely cosmological features of atomism are not ranked here within the concomitant theories. There is a simple explanation for this: the atomistic solution to the problems of change is an epistemological solution, not a cosmological one. To solve the antinomies of change, we only need to know *that* change is an exchange of place of previously existing elements, not *how* these movements of exchange actually take place. But cosmology precisely attempts to show how these movements of exchange take place or have taken place in the past. This then also means that Democritus' and Epicurus' cosmologies do not logically follow from their atomistic foundations.

The intimate connection that exists between atomism and the six above-mentioned concomitant theories will become all the more obvious later, especially in the light of the following observation: not only is there no atomism in ancient China, but also there is no trace of the six concomitant theories, as I want to show now.

(*a*) The theme of the epistemological critique of sense-perception is, as Graham has noted, treated only once in the whole corpus of ancient Chinese pre-Buddhist philosophical literature, namely in theorem B 47 of the *Mohist Canon*.[40] The epistemological context there, however, is quite different from the Greeks' concern with the unreliability of the senses. Moreover, the problem of 'conflicting appearances', that is, of two persons having different perceptions of one and the same object, is handled in a quite different way in ancient China. Take the following text from the *Lüshichunqiu*.

> The human eye perceives through reflection;[41] perceiving an object lying in the dark is in no way different from not perceiving at all. Men are similar as far as the conditions of reflection and darkness are concerned, but different as to what each one of them is able to make contact with or not. A soldier standing in the dark does not reflect the light; this is why he is not perceived. That which lies in the dark, the eye has no means of coming into contact with it. Not coming into contact with an object and nevertheless claiming to perceive it, this is self-contradictory.
>
> It is exactly the same with knowledge. The means whereby knowledge is obtained or not, are the same; but that which each one is able to make contact with or not, is different. The wise can grasp events that are still far away; the fool can only grasp what lies already right before him.
>
> (*Lüshichunqiu*, ch. 16.3; Chinese text)°

The burden of this text is to explain the difference between the wise and the fool. The task is complicated for us through the typically Chinese presupposition that the wise and the fool have initially the same physical and psychological condition. The sage, therefore, has no mysterious

---

40   Graham 1978: 417.
41   The reflection of the light falling on the object.

powers that would put him above other men. A common tenet of classical Chinese philosophy says precisely that everybody can become a Yao or a Shun.[42] The sage 'sees' the same objects as the fool: everything that is to be perceived is 'out there'. But the fool does not get in touch with it, whereas the wise man does. For the fool, the object of knowledge is like the soldier hiding in the dark. However, there are some people who can see in the dark; they are the analogues for the wise man who can foretell the outcome of obscure situations. The sage is able to perceive and inter- pret the small, nearly imperceptible signs that indicate future events, whereas the fool is incapable of noticing them:

> The wise man sees what is to come before it happens.
> (*Shangjunshu*, ch. 1, p. 1, *Zhuzi jicheng* edition)

This principle of the theoretical equality of all knowing persons also establishes the basic model for a theory of knowledge: as the object of knowledge is the same, and since there are no basic – or at least no irre- coverable – differences between the various knowing subjects, any defect in the process of knowing, and every difference in the quality of what is known, must be explained through the notion of artificial and accidental obstacles to knowing, that is, elements intervening between the knowing subject and the object of knowledge, like good or bad conditions of light, or simply other objects screening off the knowing subject from his object, but never intrinsic defects of the knowing subject.[43] The basic tenet seems to be, in ancient China, that if there are conflicting appearances, the perceiving subjects do not occupy the same moral status. The fool does not see a different picture; he sees only part of it, and only the less impor- tant parts. The sage sees the coming of the catastrophe; the fool does not, but they are facing one and the same object of knowledge.

(*b*)–(*c*)   The opposition between being and becoming and the opposition between appearance and reality correlated to it are both neatly tied up to the semantic values of the verb 'to be' in ancient Greek, as Kahn has shown.[44] Since the treatment of the verb 'to be' in classical Chinese is

---

42   These two figures are models of wisdom and moral conduct in ancient China.

43   The mirror of mind can be polished, as the *Zhuangzi* puts it: 'If a mirror is bright, it wards off stains; if the stains remain, it's that the mirror isn't bright. If you keep company long enough with a man of worth, you cannot go wrong.' (*Zhuangzi*, ch. 5, p. 32, *Zhuzi jicheng* edition) On the metaphor of the mirror, see the essay 'Light and the Mirror in Greece and China' in this volume.

44   The interdependence of these two aspects (appearance and reality; being and becoming) is spelt out very clearly by Kahn, who argues that the verb 'to be' combines the two features of reality and stability; see Kahn 1981. See also Kahn 1973a: 394, where he writes: 'The philosophers did not have to construct the antithesis of Being and Becoming: it was given to them fully preformed, in the stative-mutative system already described. They had scarcely more to do with constructing the antithesis Being and Seeming (or Reality and Appearance): it was given to them *almost* preformed [...]'.

totally different from its Greek counterpart,[45] we should not expect either to find such a combination of these two features of reality and stability in philosophical argumentation. Chinese philosophers do not look for hidden truth beyond or behind phenomena.[46] They rather try to find out the regularities in changing phenomena, or the rhythm of change.

(c)–(e)   The opposition which exists between appearance and reality is sometimes expressed by opposing an 'idle name' *xuming*[p] to 'reality' *qishi*[q] (cf. *Lüshichunqiu* ch. 18.1.) but no philosophical text in ancient China ever holds that language systematically deceives or distorts human understanding. The cryptic first chapter of the *Daodejing* only says that we cannot express the philosophical truth in our language, not that language is in itself deceitful. The manuscripts of Mawangdui, especially the four chapters of the Yellow Emperor *Huangdi sijing*, contain very illuminating passages on just this problem: going back to the origin of the world, we learn that things were named only *after* their coming into being out of the tenuous (*xu*[r]), and that only at this time did each thing receive its proper name.[47] This implies that language is fundamentally improper for describing events that have occurred prior to its own emergence. Language is used in these texts – and also in the *Daodejing* – precisely in such a way as to render this insight self-evidential.

Language may be brought into disorder by wicked social and political practice, as a famous passage in the *Lunyu* (13.3) suggests. Confucius' intention, however, is not to correct the Chinese language; immoral ministers and rulers have to correct their behaviour and must stop using the names of virtuous deeds to qualify their criminal actions, such as calling an aggressive war a punitive expedition.[48] Correcting language, rather, amounts to correcting human behaviour, so that it may conform to the standards of value embedded in language itself.

(d)   The problem of the knowledge of the changing is quite important in classical Chinese philosophy. We shall see later the quite original and at the same time very natural solution given to this problem by the Later Mohists and other philosophers in ancient China.

(f)   The absence of a concept of void (in the Greek sense of the term, of physical void) in classical Chinese philosophy is more delicate to ascertain. There is also the notion of *xu*,[s] which can be translated by 'void'. But the real meaning of *xu* is not 'void'. *Xu* rather designates the absence of any real, shaped, things. *Xu* is a reservoir of possible forms, not emptiness in a physical sense. Graham, for example, systematically renders *xu* by 'the tenuous', as for example in the opening lines of the cosmogony in the *Huainanzi*:

---

45   See Graham 1986d.
46   Sivin 1995a: 3.
47   Yu Mingguang 1993: 4; Chang and Feng 1998: 101. Translated in "'Contradiction is Impossible'", the first essay of the present collection.
48   The importance of naming in Chinese politics is well analysed in Defoort 1997.

> When Heaven and Earth were not yet shaped, it was amorphous, vague, a
> blank, a blur; call it therefore 'The Primal Beginning'. The Way began in the
> tenuous *xu* and transparent, the tenuous and transparent generated Space and
> Time, Space and Time generated the *qi*[t] [...] '
>
> > *(Huainanzi,* ch. 3, p. 35, *Zhuzi jicheng* edition;
> > translation Graham 1986a: 30)

This passage clearly says that the *qi,* the basic stuff of the universe, comes
after the tenuous, the *xu; qi* is never said to move in the tenuous, like
atoms move in the void.

The notion of *qi* is used in cosmological and medical contexts; it has to
be understood as a constant quantity of 'matter' that condenses and
rarefies, goes through different energetic states, but fills the whole
universe.[49] All we can say at this stage is that the concept of *xu* 'void' has
only a cosmological function, comparable to the chaos of ancient Greece,
not an epistemological one as in the theory of atomism. It might be added
that the void is correlated, or even equated, with non-being in Greek
thought. Since there is no concept of being similar to the Greek *einai* in
classical Chinese, we cannot expect either that the Chinese notion of void
bears the same overtones as *to kenon* or *to mê on* in Greek.

The basic meaning of *wu*[u] is 'absence of (shaped) things', not 'non-being'
or 'void', as a famous passage of the *Daodejing* shows:

> *Tianxia wanwu sheng yu you, you sheng yu wu.*[v]
> The creatures in the world are born from something, and something from nothing.
> > *(Daodejing* 40, p. 25, *Zhuzi jicheng* edition, Wang Bi text)[50]

The metaphysical problem posed by this sentence is quickly resolved if,
as Graham has pointed out, we come to notice that the Chinese *wu* does
not mean 'nothing', but only the absence of concrete things.[51] A parallel
passage from the *Huainanzi* further clarifies the core meaning of *wu:*

> It has no form but what has form is born from it, no sound but the five notes
> resound from it, no taste but the five tastes are formed from it, no colour but
> the five colours come about from it. Therefore what has (*you*[w]) is born from
> what does not have (*wu*[x]), the solid comes out of the tenuous.
> > *(Huainanzi,* ch. 1, p. 11ff., *Zhuzi jicheng* edition)

Wu is not therefore to be equated with the Western 'nothing' or even 'non-
being' (*nihil*), but designates an absence of concrete, or shaped, things.

---

49   *Qi* hence has strong affinities with the pseudo-Aristotelian notion of prime matter. On
     this problem, see Hatton 1982; Hatton 1988.
50   The text recently found at Guodian is different: *Tianxia zhi wu sheng yu you sheng yu wu*
     'The things of the world arise from being, and they arise from non-being'; see Henricks
     2000: 77–78, and notes.
51   See Graham 1986d: 343–51. See also Zürcher 1995.

Elsewhere in the *Daodejing* (chapter 2), it is said that *you* and *wu* give birth to each other, just like high and low determine each other. In chapter 11 of this same book appears a famous series of similes to illustrate the usefulness of 'what is not there'. The empty space delimited by the spokes in a wheel, the empty space left by the door and the windows in a house, the empty space left inside a vessel is what gives to these objects their usefulness.

There is, though, another possible candidate for void in Chinese, namely *kong*.[y] Its basic meaning is 'hollow'. It designates the empty space within a solid object.

> *Kong zhong zhi wu ze bei ye; jing zhong zhi wu da yu ye.*[z]
> That in the open air, there are no seas and ponds; that in a well, there are no big fish […]
>
> (*Lüshichunqiu*, ch. 13.7)

> If the house has not [enough] emptiness (*shi wu kong xu*[aa]), the wife and her mother-in-law will quarrel with each other.
>
> (*Zhuangzi*, ch. 26, p. 180, *Zhuzi jicheng* edition)

Kong is probably the term that comes closest to the Greek *void* (*to kenon*). The word for 'void' in modern Chinese is *xukong*.[ab] But *kong* is always used in its concrete sense, never in a more abstract and cosmological one.

The fact that atomism appears in ancient Greece in the company of the six above-mentioned concomitant theories means that our present investigation cannot be restricted to the explanation of the absence of atomism in ancient China, but must also take into consideration the absence of these concomitant theories.

Atomism and Ways of Speaking

The most fundamental element, and perhaps the very starting-point of atomism (and of the problem of change) in ancient Greece is the insight that language is deceitful. Not only does language give us a wrong picture of the phenomenon of change, but language is in general unreliable and therefore unable to provide the kind of firm knowledge the first Greek philosophers are looking for. The whole debate must therefore be shifted to a different, epistemological, level. Language is discarded and replaced by what can be called a philosophical theory, whose new concepts aptly replace the old and faulty ways of speaking ('atoms for words').

Let us start by exploring the motives that pushed the first Greek philosophers to pose the problem of change. It seems that some expressions of the Greek language directly suggest that things becoming do come out of nothing, and that things perishing disappear into nothing. But this is logically impossible. Language, therefore, must be wrong.[52] These words are mere 'names'. Three famous texts may be adduced:

> Another thing I will tell you: of all mortal things none has birth, nor any end in accursed death, but only mingling and interchange of what is mingled – birth is the name (*onomazetai*) given to these by men.
>
> (Empedocles 31 B 8 DK = 350 KRS;
> p. 291 for the translation)

> The Greeks are wrong to recognise coming into being and perishing (*to de ginesthai kai apollusthai ouk orthôs nomizousin hoi Hellênes*); for nothing comes into being nor perishes, but is rather compounded or dissolved from things that are. So they would be right to call (*orthôs kaloien*) coming into being composition and perishing dissolution.
>
> (Anaxagoras 59 B 17 DK = 469 KRS;
> p. 358 for the translation)

> Therefore it has been named all the names which mortals have laid down believing them to be true – coming to be and perishing, being and not being, changing place and altering in bright colour.
>
> (Parmenides 28 B 8, 38–41 DK = 299, 38–41 KRS;
> p. 252 for the translation)

All three texts agree on the following: the words currently used for describing the phenomenon of change in Greek suggest that the things undergoing change grow out of nothing or vanish into nothing. It would be quite rewarding to investigate the origins of these 'illogical' semantic representations of becoming and perishing and ask the question why native speakers of the Greek language have organized their ways of speaking in precisely this way. The real problem, however, does not arise out of these semantic representations alone, but grows out of the antinomy that is felt between them and an important philosophical postulate, namely that nothing can be born out of nothing: *ex nihilo nihil*.

This principle is considered to be the cornerstone of Greek philosophy. It is, as Aristotle notes in the *Physics* (187a27–35) and in the *Metaphysics* (K 6; 1062b25), the *koinê doxa*, the common opinion, of the first Greek philosophers. It amounts not only to the assumption that nothing comes into being out of nothing, but also that nothing comes to be out of what is not *it*.[53]

This rational philosophical postulate – a particular instance of the principle of sufficient reason – will not be questioned here, and I will even assume, on good grounds, its transcultural validity throughout this study. The postulate is indeed never contradicted in classical Chinese philosophy. Moreover, there are several texts that bear direct evidence of the first Chinese philosophers' readiness to recognize this postulate as logically compelling. A famous

---

52   On this point, see also Kahn 1973c: 155–57 ('Eleatic view of names').
53   Furley 1987: 117.

chapter in the *Liezi*, namely 'The questions of Tang',[54] states the following, quite Parmenidean reasoning, in its very opening lines:

> T'ang [Tang] of Yin asked Chi [Ji] of Hsia [Xia]:
> 'Have there been things from the very first?'
> 'Unless there were things from the very first, how would there be things now?'
>
> *(Liezi,* ch. 5, p. 51, *Zhuzi jicheng* edition;
> translation Graham 1989: 79)

This piece of reasoning strongly connects with one of the arguments Parmenides had developed to prove that Being is eternal, for nothing could have moved it to come into existence later or earlier.

A treatise of the sophist Gongsun Long, the already mentioned *Thinking Through Change*, builds its paradox of change on the tacit assumption of the validity of the rational postulate that nothing comes out of what is not *it*.[55] There is hence no reason to admit that the 'common opinion' of the Presocratics did not also operate in ancient China.

The philosophical intention of atomism, like its earlier Empedoclean and Anaxagorean versions, is clearly directed towards the solution of the antinomy which is felt between the rational postulate which declares that nothing comes to be out of nothing and between the illogical connotations attached to some of the Greek words for change. If my claim that the theory of atomism arises out of a conflict between the exaction of logic (*ex nihilo nihil*) and the facts of language (the semantic connotations of some of the Greek words for change) is found to be acceptable, and if we can assume the transcultural validity of logical principles, it follows that our main task will be to compare the ways in which the words for change are used and understood in both cultures.

The Words for Change (Greece)

The semantic field of change is radically different from other semantic fields, such as the field of colour-terms, or the field of types of snow and sand, the standard examples of linguistic relativity in the textbooks. Patterns of change are much less culture-bound. Although there are many individual instances of change in nature and although every language has to impose, by virtue of the principle of linguistic economy, a basic typology on forms of change, the diversity of expressions for change is not as large as might be expected, and the cluster of these expressions is correspondingly far more uniformly distributed among the languages which are of interest to us in the present context. With colour-terms, the semantic range of each term depends on the total

---

54   The beginning of this chapter 5 of the *Liezi* stems, as Graham (1986c: 271) has convincingly argued, from the unabridged *Zhuangzi*.

55   For a translation of this text, see the last essay '"To Be" in Greece and China' in this collection.

number of colour-words available in the corresponding language. The semantic field of expressions for change, however, is limited by the possible logical types of change. This logical structure of the semantic field of change is not at all transparent to a native speaker. In the period of the Presocratics, there is much guessing as to what kinds of change are to be ranked as basic. We have to wait until Aristotle to find a stabilized version of types of change, classified according to logical criteria.

It is interesting, in this context, to start from Aristotle's list of types of change in the *Categories* (chapter 14; 15a13 and following). There had been several earlier attempts at classifying types of change in Plato's dialogues, and also in the definitions and divisions of the Platonic Academy and in Aristotle's *Topics*.[56] Aristotle's list in the *Categories* presents itself as the culmination of all these earlier classifications, and lists six basic types of change:

> *genesis* and *phthora*
> *auxêsis* and *meiôsis*
> *alloiôsis*
> *kata topon metabolê*

Although chapter 14 of Aristotle's *Categories* does not use the categorial grid to classify these various forms of change,[57] it is convenient to redistribute these six types of change among the four categories of substance, quantity, quality and space.

Aristotelian category	Greek expressions	translation
category of substance	*genesis* and *phthora*	becoming and perishing
category of quantity	*auxêsis* and *meiôsis*	increase and decrease
category of quality	*alloiôsis*	alteration
category of space	*kata topon metabolê*	(ex)change of place

The fact that these types of change fall under different categorial headings only goes to show that they are logically independent. A thing undergoing one type of change does not at the same time and in the same respect undergo any other type of change.[58]

---

56 For earlier attempts at classifying types of change in ancient Greece, see *Theaetetus* 181B–D; *Parmenides* 138B–C; 162B–164B; *Timaeus* 40B; 52Aff.; *Sophist* 248E; *Laws* 893Bff. An important document in this context is the Academic *Diaireseis* ('Divisions') § 12 (p. 44 Mutschmann = fragment 72 Gaiser). Further classifications of change appear in Aristotle's *Topics* 120b1; 121a32; 122a21–30; 122b32; 111b5ff.

57 For Aristotle's categorial divisions of change, see *Physics* III,1; 200b32–34; *Metaphysics* Z,7; 1032a12–15. For a comparative study on categories, see the essay 'Greek and Chinese Categories' in this volume.

58 Ackrill 1979: 112; Waterlow 1982: 105–106.

The remarkable fact about this list is that while the first three forms of change (substance, quantity, quality) all come into conflict with the rational postulate *ex nihilo nihil*, the last type, namely exchange of place, fully meets the rational requirements of that postulate. All forms of change offend the rational postulate, except the fourth one, which depicts change in terms of change or exchange of place, hinting at redistribution in space of previously existing objects. For the Atomists, change is indeed no more than the variations generated by the order, the position and the shape of assembling and separating atoms in the void. The only real type of change admitted by the Atomists therefore is change of place, since separation and mixture clearly are of this type, and order as well as orientation can also be reduced to it.

Without even bringing into play comparative material, we could conclude already that the Greek language has exerted a decisive influence on the Presocratics, insofar as it is directly responsible for the rise of the atomistic theory, for this theory had been devised to correct the logically wrong picture of change embedded in the Greek language. This claim may sound surprising. It has to meet, among others, the objection that the phenomenon of change is in itself paradoxical, and that language is but a repercussion of these paradoxical features. But even if we, Western trained scholars, are unable to view change as other than paradoxical, we cannot rule out *a priori* the possibility that there might be other languages describing change in a way that is plainly in agreement with the rational postulate that nothing comes out of what is not. After all, we only need to imagine a language in which change is naturally expressed as a rearrangement of pre-existing elements. In the remaining part of this study, I want to show that classical Chinese is just such a language.

Intermezzo: the Origins of Philosophical Language

What is required, to test our hypothesis of the linguistic origin of atomism, is a so-called 'exotic' language that is at the same time the vehicle of a high-graded philosophical tradition in which reflections upon the problem of change had been conducted. Moreover, the language we analyse must belong to a stratum of language that comes prior to the philosophical activity itself.[59] Once again, these rather strict experimental conditions can be met, if we agree to turn to the early cultural traditions of China and Greece.

If this line of argument is correct, the following hypothesis must hold: if the linguistic structures of the Chinese language do represent change as a re-arrangement of pre-existing elements, the theory of atomism as well as its concomitant theories cannot arise in that culture, precisely because such a theory is then unnecessary. The language itself then already gives the

---

59   On this problem, see the Introduction.

solution, ready-made. The answer to the problem lies already in the language ('words for atoms'), and is not projected out from it in a philosophical theory ('atoms for words').

The Words for Change in a Comparative Perspective

The best way to pursue our investigation is perhaps to revert to Aristotle's list of categories of change, and try to find their Chinese equivalents:

Category	Greek	Chinese	Translation
substance	*genesis* *phthora*	*hua*[ac] or *wei*[ad] *sheng*[ae] *si*[af] *cun*[ag] *wang*[ah]	change (into) to be born – to die subsist – perish
quantity	*auxêsis* *meiôsis*	*sun*[ai] *yi*[aj]	increase – decrease
quality	*alloiôsis*	*bian*[ak]	alteration
space	*kata topon metabolê*	*yi*[al]	(ex)change of place

This list, as anyone familiar with classical Chinese will have noted, gives indeed the most basic Chinese terms for 'change'. There are, of course, many other Chinese expressions that can be translated by 'change', such as *gai*,[am] *yi*,[an] *dong*,[ao] *ge*,[ap] *geng*,[aq] *xi*.[ar] These expressions do not appear to be philosophically important.

The list given above is also corroborated by a group of theorems (A 45 to A 49) from the *Mohist Canon*.[60] There is, though, an important asymmetry in the first row, because the main term for describing in Chinese what the Greeks had called substantial change is not, as one might expect, *sheng* and *wang*, but *hua*. But the term *hua* does not have, strictly speaking, a single Greek equivalent. Furthermore, it does not have a clear antonym either. The now familiar expression *bianhua*[as] for designating 'change' in Chinese is simply a nominal compound grouping together the two most important forms of change. The compound does not yet occur in the *Lunyu* and the *Mencius*. We find it sparingly in texts such as the *Lüshichunqiu*, the *Xunzi* and in the later, syncretistic, chapters of the *Zhuangzi*.[61]

The standard pair of antonyms for substantial change in Chinese, *sisheng*[at] and *cunwang*,[au] does not function in the same way as the Greek *genesis* and *phthora*. The last pair is probably even unknown as such in the West. The core

60   See below.
61   Swanson 1984: 69.

meaning of *cun*[av] is 'to keep on existing as before', or 'to survive'.[62] The term rather points to an object *resisting* change, for example a state keeping its integrity under evil circumstances.

The bare list of expressions for 'change' does not tell us anything. We also have to know the semantic representations a native speaker of Chinese used to attach to each of these terms. We would like to know, for example, if *hua* also suggests, like its Greek counterparts, a generation out of nothing or a vanishing into nothing. Before analysing the definitions of these terms of change given by the Later Mohists, let us have a look first at the ways in which they are used in less technical contexts. We shall begin our investigation with a text from the *Sunzibingfa*.

> There are not more than five musical notes, but the *bian*[aw] of these five notes never exhausts the possibilities of what can be heard; there are not more than five basic colours, but the *bian* of these five colours never exhausts the possibilities of what can be seen; there are not more than five tastes, but the *bian* of these five tastes never exhausts the possibilities of what can be tasted.[63]
>
> (*Sunzibingfa*, ch. 5, pp. 69–70, *Zhuzi jicheng* edition)

I have left the term *bian* here untranslated to attract the attention to its essential meaning, which is something close to 'interplay' or 'combined effect'. This basic meaning also emerges from other, quite common uses of *bian* in classical Chinese, such as the phrase *bian hu si*,[ax] to express the fact that someone's face changes its colours under an emotive shock. *Bian* also occurs very often with antonyms, such as *li hai zhi bian*[ay] 'the alternations of advantage and prejudice'. One basic sense of *bian* hence is 'interplay of elements', as appears also from the expression *tian bu bian qi chang*[az] 'Heaven does not change its constant order' (*Guanzi*, ch. 64), meaning that the seasons do not change their fixed order.

Here are some more uses of *bian*: *bian yan*[ba] means 'to break an oath' (*Lüshichunqiu*, ch. 20.3); *you tun tan yi bian qi yin*[bb] 'he also ate charcoal to modify his voice' (*Lüshichunqiu*, ch. 20.1). *Bian fu*[bc] means 'to change one's clothes', as opposed to *yi yi*[bd] which means 'exchange clothes', and hence 'to disguise' (*Lüshichunqiu*, ch. 12.3 and 18.6).

Jin shui yi bian er yi duo yi.[be]
Now, the water level has already changed and has grown much higher.

(*Lüshichunqiu*, ch. 15.8)

---

62   Trauzettel 1970. The modern Chinese term for 'existence' is *cunzai*. See also the essay '"To Be" in Greece and China' in this volume.

63   In a parallel passage in the first chapter of the *Huainanzi* (ch.1, p. 11, *Zhuzi jicheng* edition), the term *hua* is used instead of *bian* in the case of the five tastes. This might be due to a different way of considering the mixing and the formation of the five tastes. In the *Lüshichunqiu* (ch. 14.2), the term *bian* is used to qualify the preparation of tasty food.

This sentence means that the river has left its usual course (marked out by wooden sticks in the story) and taken a new one as a result of a sharp rising of the floods. Hence another fundamental aspect of *bian* is that the object that undergoes this type of change does not change its basic aspect or identity. The change is only qualitative. The object does not become what is not *it*.

> *Pi ruo Zhongshan zhi yu. Chui yi lu tan san ri san ye er si zhi bu bian.*[bf]
> Compare it to the jade from the Zhong Mountains. Even if you heat it in a charcoal brazier for three days and three nights, the brilliance of its colour will remain unaltered.
>
> (*Huainanzi*, ch. 2, p. 22, *Zhuzi jicheng* edition)

For our purpose, these results are rather interesting, because the Chinese *bian* appears to be free from any such illogical or paradoxical representations as those that had bewitched the Presocratics' minds. The atomistic solution is even hinted at, though only in a subliminal way, with the understanding of *bian* as an interplay or a rearrangement of pre-existing elements. *Bian* is furthermore considered to be quantifiable: an object may *bian* five or ten times in a row.

> *Pi zhi ruo liang yi. Bing wan bian. Yao yi wan bian.*[bg]
> Compare him to a good physician. If the illness changes ten thousand times, he also changes the medicine ten thousand times.
>
> (*Lüshichunqiu*, ch. 15.8)

In a few passages, however, *bian* has an even more marked sense. Take the following passage from the *Huainanzi*:

> *Fuzi jian he zhi san bian ye.*[bh]
> The Master sees the three varying aspects of the grain.
>
> (*Huainanzi*, ch. 10, p. 157, *Zhuzi jicheng* edition)

The three *bian* of the corn are the grain (*su*[bi]), the sprouts (*miao*[bj]) and the ear of the grain (*sui*[bk]). The passage quoted above echoes a saying from the *Lunyu*.

> *Zixia yue: Junzi you san bian. Wang zhi yan ran, ji zhi ye wen, ting qi yan ye li.*[bl]
> Zixia said, A gentleman has three varying aspects: seen from afar, he looks severe, when approached he is found to be mild, when heard speaking he turns out to be incisive.
>
> (*Lunyu*, ch. 19.9; translation Waley 1945: 226)

We could nearly have translated: 'The gentleman appears under three different forms', for the saying describes the changing appearance of the superior man. It is indeed rather remarkable that a term denoting some form of change directly relates to what we call a 'form of appearance'. Note, however, that the unity between the object and its forms of appearance is not disrupted. What appears, rather, are the very qualities of the object and not its treacherous appearances.

We shall turn next to the pair of terms *sun* and *yi*[bm] 'diminish', 'increase', the proposed counterparts of the Greek *auxêsis* and *meiôsis*. The meaning of these terms is quite clear. The question which interests us is to see whether the phenomenon of increase and decrease gives rise, as in ancient Greek philosophy, to paradoxes, in the sense that a decreasing or increasing object could be thought of as ceasing to be what it is, or becoming what is not it. Aristotle, in *De Generatione and Corruptione* (A,5), gives a good survey of the way in which this problem presented itself to the first Greek philosophers. For the present purpose, one of the questions Aristotle raises needs, for reasons that will become more apparent later, special attention. Aristotle asks why it is the thing to which something accedes that is said to grow, and not the thing which accedes, or both (*De Generatione and Corruptione* A,5; 321a29f.). If the strawberries in my garden grow larger after a timely spring rain, we say that the strawberries grow larger, not the water that is added to them, nor the strawberries plus the water. Similarly, we say that the capital grows, not that the interest grows. In a quite fascinating study, Jacquinod has tried to determine the fundamental semantic value of the Greek term *auxô* 'augment'.[64] The gist of his argument is to show that the Proto-Indo-European root **aug-* does not mean 'to increase', but rather designates a process of growth ('bringing forth') starting possibly from zero. The central semantic value of *auxô* hence would be 'to cause to grow', where it is left open, as in the English verb 'to develop', whether the process starts from zero or from already existing material. It is easy now to see the origins of the philosophical problem: if the increase starts at point zero, we come into conflict with the rational postulate *ex nihilo nihil*, as the beginning of Parmenides' fragment 8, where the expression *pê pothen auxêthen* 'How and whence did it grow?' (B 8,7 DK 296,7 KRS, p. 249) occurs, plainly shows.

But let us go over now to the Chinese counterparts, *sun* and *yi* 'diminish', 'increase'. Here, too, the Chinese prove to be quite original: *sun* rather means 'to take away from' than 'decrease', and *yi* rather means 'to add to' than 'increase'.[65] We see at once that none of the Greek paradoxes of change can arise if we speak of the object that has grown as an object 'to which something has been added', or of the object that has been diminished as an object 'of which something has been taken away'. Here is an example:

Ru shui yi shen, ru huo yi ri, yi yun er yi yi.[bn]
[...] if water becomes deeper, if fire becomes hotter, they [the people] cannot but go into the other direction.

(*Mencius*, I,B,10)

---

64 Jacquinod 1988.
65 See also *Daodejing* 42; *Lüshichunqiu* ch. 15.8.

A literal translation of *shui yi shen* would amount to saying that 'water has been augmented by deepness', and a literal translation of *huo yi ri* would be 'fire has been augmented by hotness'.

One could argue, in this case, that the Chinese simply were not aware of the problem, or that they turned round the problem, by using other types of expressions. The Later Mohists, however, *had* noticed the danger of paradoxes. But they did not take the Greek way.

The next expression for change, *yi*,[bo] is not problematic either. The basic meaning of *yi* is quite easy to guess from a sample of representative texts.

Gu zhi wei shi ye, yi qi suo you yi qi suo wu zhe.[bp]
In Antiquity, the market was for the exchange of what one had for what one lacked.
> (*Mencius*, II,B,10; translation Lau 1983: 92)

Yi xiao yi da.[bq]
Replace a large thing by a small one [i.e. an ox by a sheep].
> (*Mencius*, I,A,7)

Huizi yi yi, bian guan.[br]
Master Hui disguised himself and altered his headdress.
> (*Lüshichunqiu*, ch. 18.6)

The expression *yi yi* does not simply mean 'to change clothes', but rather 'to exchange clothes', that is, 'to disguise'. And this makes sense in the context of the story that is told, namely Hui Shi's disaster in Wei that obliged him to flee in disguise. Note, however, that *yi* is not used with *guan* 'cap', probably because the cap is a sign of manhood. So, at least, Hui Shi did not flee in womanish clothes!

Mai yu, yi ye.[bs]
Buying and selling is exchanging.
> (*Mohist Canon*, A 85; Graham 1978: 332–33)

Song ren yi zi er shi zhi.[bt]
The people from Song exchanged their children to eat them.[66]
> (*Lüshichunqiu*, ch. 20.6)

Gu zhe yi zi er jiao zhi.[bu]
In ancient times, people exchanged their children to bring them up.[67]
> (*Mencius*, IV,A,18)

Yizi si yi yi tianxia.[bv]
Master Yi thought about (ex)changing the world [...].
> (*Mencius*, III,A,5)

---

66   They were forced to do so by famine, but obviously did not want to eat their own children.
67   The goal was not to bring up sons to be against their fathers because of corporal punishments.

Master Yi is a Mohist. Mencius cannot here use the term *hua*,[bw] because this would imply that the Mohist is after a *better* world; he cannot use *bian*[bx] either, because it would suggest that Mohism proposes an *alternative* (but similar) world order, which is unacceptable for Mencius. The use of *yi*[by] here, then, suggests that Master Yi would like to put *another* world in place of the present. The whole dialogue indeed shows that Mencius considers Master Yi's views as utopistic and unrealistic, going against the natural order of the world.

It is, at first sight, quite remarkable to notice that one of the most funda-mental expressions for 'change' in classical Chinese, namely *yi*,[bz] has the basic meaning of 'exchange'. Classical Chinese hence comes fairly close to the ways of speaking invented by the Greek Atomists, because for them, the separation and mixing of atoms really is a constant exchange of place. More-over, the basic image of change that is behind *yi* seems to be cyclical change. The cyclical view of change is fairly obvious in many texts from the classical period, above all from the *Book of Changes* and its earliest commentaries. But I would like to keep the cosmological features out of this debate. Atomism, as it has been developed in ancient Greece, includes cosmological aspects. But it is obvious that an explanation of change in terms of a redistribution of pre-existing and unchanging elements is not at the same time committed to a theory about *how* this redistribution is to be conceived.

The term *sheng*[ca] 'to be born' is always used with a subject, or is construed passively with a subject implied. Hence the problem of something coming out of nothing cannot arise under these conditions. One of the rare passages where the origin of what is born is not clearly stated occurs in the *Zhuangzi*, chapter 25.

> *Wan wu you hu sheng er mo jian qi gen, you hu chu er mo jian qi men.*[cb]
> There is something out of which the myriad things are born, but nobody knows its root; there is something they have come out of, but nobody knows its door.
>
> (*Zhuangzi*, ch. 25, p. 172, *Zhuzi jicheng* edition)

Later again in the same chapter we read the following:

> *Shaozhi yue: si fang zhi nei, liu he zhi li, wan wu zhi suo sheng wu qi.*[cc]
> Know-little asked: 'Within the four directions, inside the six-way-oriented, from what does it arise, that from which the myriad things are born?'
>
> (*Zhuangzi*, ch. 25, p. 174, *Zhuzi jicheng* edition; translation Graham 1981: 152)

There is also the expression *sheng yu*[cd] 'born from' or 'arise out of'.[68] This latter sense, however, is nearly always abstract. The expression *sheng* does not suggest, therefore, a birth out of nothing, like the Greek *genesis*. There is another term that might raise problems, namely *wang*[ce] 'destroy'. *Wang* is

---

68   Fu (1973: 376–78) argues that the meaning of *sheng* is really 'comes before', and not 'produce' or 'bring forth'.

often translated 'vanish' or 'perish', but its basic meaning is 'to lose'. If a state perishes, there is no vanishing into nothing; the owner changes, or the territory is divided up in another way.

Let us go over now to the most problematic expression, namely *hua*.[cf] This term does not occur very often in early texts. It is totally absent from the *Book of Songs*, from the *Lunyu* of Confucius, and occurs only five times in the *Mencius*. In this latter text, *hua* invariably means 'to improve (morally)', except in the following passage:

Qie bi hua zhe, wu shi tu qin fu, yu ren xin du wu xiao hu.[cg]
Furthermore, does it not give one some solace to be able to prevent the earth from coming into contact with the dead who is about to decompose?
(Mencius, II,B,7; translation Lau 1983: 90)

It is possible that the term *hua* is used in this text in a more rhetorical way, as a euphemism, or even as a taboo, in place of the cruel notion of death. Later in the *Zhuangzi*, the term *hua* has come to mean simply 'death', as for example in chapters 2 and 6:

Qi xing hua, qi xin yu zhi ran.[ch]
When the body dissolves, the same happens to the heart.
(Zhuangzi, ch. 2, p. 8, Zhuzi jicheng edition)

Soon Master Lai fell ill, and lay panting on the verge of death. His wife and children stood in a circle bewailing him. Master Li went to ask after him. 'Shoo! Out of the way!' he said. 'Don't startle him while he *transforms* (*hua*).'

He lolled against Lai's door and talked with him. 'Wonderful, the process which fashions and transforms us! What is it going to turn you into, in what direction will it use you to go? Will it make you into a rat's liver? Or a fly's leg?'
(Zhuangzi, ch. 6, p. 43, Zhuzi jicheng edition;
translation Graham 1981: 88)

These texts are, however, already philosophically 'contaminated', because they build a philosophical interpretation of the phenomenon of death upon the core meaning of *hua* 'to transform'. Note, however, that the principle of 'mass-conservation' appears to be respected throughout the text. The text also clearly says that it is this dying person, identified by a personal pronoun ('you' *ru*[ci]), which becomes either a rat's liver or a fly's leg. Although the paradox of an object becoming what is not it is not redissolved, the problem of something vanishing into nothing, or coming out of nothing, does not arise: one object is 'replaced' by another one, keeping the ontological accounts in balance. In another, similar context, the book *Zhuangzi* uses, however, the term *bian*[cj] (see ch. 18, p. 110, *Zhuzi jicheng* edition; death of Zhuangzi's wife). But this usage might well have an intended philosophical undertone: life and death are conceived as *alterations* of a single world-stuff and come after one another just like the four seasons.

The idea of transformation or transmutation is often also expressed by a simple *wei*,[ck] or else by the expression *hua wei*,[cl] or *hua er wei*,[cm] literally 'by change becomes [...]'. The syntactical constructions used with *hua*, or *hua wei*, always imply that it is one definite object, say A, that transforms into B, or becomes B:

Shen yin hua wei kong sang.[cn]
Her body was therefore transformed into a hollow mulberry-tree.

(*Lüshichunqiu*, ch. 14.2)

Yu hua er wei niao.[co]
The fish changed into a bird.

(*Zhuangzi*, ch. 1, p. 1, *Zhuzi jicheng* edition)

In some syntactical constructions, there may also be other verbs before *wei*:

Fu shui xiang dong ze ning er wei bing.[cp]
When water approaches the cold, it freezes and (so that it) becomes ice.

(*Huainanzi*, ch. 2, p. 21, *Zhuzi jicheng* edition)

Zhuang Zhou meng wei hudie.[cq]
Zhuang Zhou became a butterfly in his dream.

(*Zhuangzi*, ch. 2, p. 18, *Zhuzi jicheng* edition)

The core meaning of *hua* clearly is natural change: one thing transforms itself into another thing:

Luan zhi hua wei ji.[cr]
The fact that the egg transforms into a chicken.

(*Huainanzi*, ch. 20, p. 351, *Zhuzi jicheng* edition)

Shi mu jiang hua erwei mu, bu neng zhi mu;
shi sheng ren hua er wei nongfu, bu neng zhi nongfu.[cs]
If you make wood out of the carpenter, he cannot keep in order the wood anymore; if you make a peasant out of a sage, he cannot keep in order the peasants anymore.

(*Lüshichunqiu*, ch. 18.6)

Qi ri hua wei hu.[ct]
After seven days, he became a tiger.

(*Huainanzi*, ch. 2, p. 20, *Zhuzi jicheng* edition)

Gu Lizi yue: Fei gou bu de tu. Gou hua er wei tu, ze bu de tu.[cu]
Therefore Master Li said: 'Without hounds, you cannot get hares; if you change the hounds into hares, you cannot get hares anymore.'

(*Lüshichunqiu*, ch. 17.4)

Hua designates the most deep and radical form of change.

Chang qian er bu fan qi chu ze hua yi.[cv]
If one is moved away for a long time without being able to return to one's initial position, then one changes.

> (*Xunzi*, ch. 3, p. 30, *Zhuzi jicheng* edition)

This passage from the *Xunzi* even seems to imply that the borders between different forms of change – between *bian* and *hua* – are perhaps fixed by the degree or the intensity of the observed change.

As far as appears from these texts, some of the Greek paradoxes surrounding the concept of transformation could and should have arisen in China too. The term *hua* clearly also bears the overtones of something changing into what it is not, or what is not it. If these paradoxes did not arise, we could conclude, at first sight, that the first Chinese philosophers were not as metaphysically minded as their Greek counterparts, and that these problems were, for them, out of focus. But this does not hold. Fortunately enough, we do have useful comparative material, preserved in the *Mohist Canon*. The Later Mohists provide us indeed with a list of definitions for all the major concepts of change. The very strategy of these definitions – as I read them – is to avoid falling into the paradoxes of change, not by correcting the use of language or by introducing a new, philosophical, terminology, but simply by showing that the real and profound normal meanings of the words for change in Chinese are exempt from paradoxes.

Theorems A 45 to A 49 are indeed devoted to the definition of expressions for change.[69] Theorem A 45 defines *hua*,[cw] A 46 *sun*,[cx] A 47 *yi*[cy] (definition now lost). The term *yi*[cz] appears in theorem A 45 and A 48 and seems to be taken as primitive and undefinable. Three more terms for 'change' are listed in theorems A 47, A 48 and A 49, namely *xuan*[da] 'circle round', *yun*[db] 'rotate' and *dong*[dc] 'stir'. These minor or derived kinds of change will not be analysed here, except for a brief consideration of *yun* 'rotate'. But the term *wei*,[dd] which is listed in theorem A 85, has to be taken into account, because one of the senses of *wei* (level-tone) precisely is 'to transform'.

The term *bian*[de] occurs only three times in the *Mojing* (B 7, B 29 and B 30) and is apparently not considered to be sufficiently technical or problematic to retain the attention of the Mohist logicians. The list of the terms for change is closed by two theorems (A 50, A 51) dealing with expressions for the unchanging and the necessary (*zhi*[df] and *bi*[dg]).

The Later Mohists' definition of *sun*[dh] is already quite revealing:

Sun, bian qu ye.
Bian ye zhe, jian li (correct to: *ti*) *ye. Qi ti huo qu <hou> cun, wei qi cun zhe sun.*[di]
Sun (reduction/loss) is the removal of some without the rest. (theorem)
'Some but not the rest': it is a unit in a total. Of its units, if one is removed and the other remains, we say that the one which remains is reduced. (explanation)

> (*Mohist Canon*, A 46; Graham 1978: 296)

---

69   Graham 1978: 295–98.

The lost definition of *yi*[dj] 'increase' had probably been parallel to *sun* 'decrease'. The process of reduction, according to the Later Mohists, must not be conceived as a partial annihilation of an object. This way of describing the phenomenon of decrease would indeed lead to paradoxes, as early Greek philosophy amply demonstrates. The expression 'decrease' (*sun*) applies, as the Later Mohists suggest, to the object from which something has been taken away. We call the already diminished object 'diminished', not the diminishing object or the process itself. Moreover, the diminishing object is considered as a whole losing one of its parts, which means that the loss is already ontologically inscribed in the structure of the object, like a breaking point.

The Later Mohists, however, do not give a stipulative or a philosophical definition of the notion of decrease. All they do is to bring out the standard meaning of the term, as a comparison with the results of our analysis given above shows. They do not share the critical attitude to language of the Presocratics.

The notion of *yun* 'rotate' is defined in terms of *yi* 'exchange'; rotate is to change round: *yun, yi ye*[dk] (theorem A 48).[70] Rotation is simply defined as a continuous movement of exchanging places. In proposition B 23, the term *yi* 'exchange' is used to describe the inversion of the image in a concave mirror.[71]

The most interesting case is the definition of *hua* 'transform':

> *Hua, zheng yi ye.*
> *Ruo wa wei chun.*[dl]
> *Hua* (transformation) is the distinguishing marks (*zheng*) of one thing exchanged for the distinguishing marks of another. For example, a frog becoming a quail.[72]
>
> (*Mohist Canon*, A 45; Graham 1978: 295, slightly changed)

This definition builds upon another word for change, namely *yi*, whose basic meaning is, as we have seen above, 'exchange'. The definition of one concept by several more basic concepts (*more geometrico*) is the fundamental idea that lies behind the *Mohist Canon*.[73] It is therefore especially significant that the notion of *yi* 'exchange' is judged to be the most basic for analysing change. *Hua* is a more complex notion, but can be defined in terms of *yi* and *zheng*. The most surprising, however, is still to come. What are these *zheng*[dm] 'distinguishing marks' that are exchanged when the object 'transforms'?

---

70   Graham 1978: 296–97.

71   Graham 1978: 381–84.

72   This example is puzzling. But there had probably been a common belief in ancient China about such transformations. A whole series of similar examples of one animal transforming into another at a given time of the year can be gathered from the famous *Yueling* 'Monthly ordinances' of the *Lij* and the opening chapter of the first twelve books of the *Lüshichunqiu*.

73   See the essay 'Philosophy and Geometry in Early China' in this volume.

The semantic range of *zheng* is fairly broad and goes from 'evidence' to 'forebode'. The following texts relate the notion of *zheng* directly to the process of change:

Fan guo zhi cunwang you liu zheng.[dn]
There are six signs that tell whether a state is going to subsist or perish.
(*Yinwenzi*, ch. 2, *Zhuzi jicheng* edition)

Bing wei zhan er xian jian bai zheng, ci ke wei zhi bing yi.[do]
To see the signs (*zheng*) of defeat before the battle is fought, this may be called being expert at war.
(*Shiji*, ch. 7, p. 304, *Zhonghua shuju* edition)

Gu shengren jian hua yi guan qi zheng.[dp]
Therefore it is by watching the signs that the sage recognizes the transformations.
(*Huainanzi*, ch. 13, p. 220, *Zhuzi jicheng* edition)

Shengren zhi suoyi guo ren yi xian zhi. Xian zhi bi shen zheng biao.[dq]
It is by seeing in advance that the sage is superior to other men. To see in advance, it is inevitable that one examines the distinguishing signs and marks.
(*Lüshichunqiu*, ch. 20.8)

The most basic meaning of *zheng*[dr] seems to be 'distinguishing sign', 'the tests of what a thing is'.[74] Stress is laid on the knowledge of future events, of indications pointing to the future transformation of an object or a situation. In this case, the distinguishing signs are not overt, but hidden, and only a sage can appreciate them.

The clue for the understanding of these passages is that in a situation that is going to change, we have the simultaneous presence of contradictory *zheng*, comparable to old Yin and Yang lines in a hexagram. This is the most basic fact about change.[75] Moreover, these distinguishing marks, if rightly interpreted, give a clue to the future development of the situation.

This conception of change contains a very original philosophical solution to the process of transformation. The transformation from A to B extends over a certain period of time. During this process, there is a partial coexistence of 'distinguishing marks'. To describe an object as a frog, we need to see a certain amount of distinguishing 'frog-marks'. If they are present, the description 'frog' correctly applies. At some earlier stage, the marks of the tadpole had been more numerous. During the process of change, the tadpole-marks are replaced by the frog-marks, while the 'ontological' unity of the object is preserved: it is this tadpole in front of my eyes that is transforming into a frog. The most important assumption therefore is that the changing object preserves some kind of identity throughout the change: the egg *is* the chicken; the

---

74   Graham 1978: 295.
75   For this aspect, see Gernet 1994.

tadpole *is* the frog; the ice *is* water; Zhuang Zhou *is* the butterfly. This also explains why the process of *hua* is sometimes reversible, or even iterative, if the same object undergoes several, successive transformations.

There was no need, in ancient China, to develop an ontological theory. In the Chinese context, the problem is already solved, because the language gives in itself the right 'ontological' answer: *hua* only implies an exchange of 'distinguishing marks', not a vanishing into nothing, or a birth out of nothing.

This attitude greatly simplifies the problem of change, because it is 'reduced' to the problem of correctly describing change. The discussion of the problem of language and change that we find in the Later Mohists' writings hinges almost exclusively on the problem of setting down the conditions for describing change coherently. The Chinese words for change are in order as they are; only the conditions for their correct application have to be laid down. The Later Mohists do not propose to change the use of the terms for change. Nor did they develop an ontological theory, like atomism, to correct the normal, faulty, ways of speaking.

The description of changing objects raises only one crucial problem in the Mohists' perspective: how are we to describe the changing object at the time it changes from A to B? Take the example of the tadpole becoming a frog. At what stage of the transformation shall we change our ways of naming, and use 'frog' rather than 'tadpole'? Roughly speaking, the process of change can be divided into five stages:

1   the tadpole has only the distinguishing marks of the tadpole;
2   one quarter of the distinguishing marks are already those of the frog;
3   the distinguishing marks are even for the frog and the tadpole;
4   only one quarter of the tadpole's distinguishing marks remain;
5   we have only the distinguishing marks of the frog.[76]

At stage 2, there are better reasons for calling the object a tadpole, whereas at stage 4, we have better reasons to call it a frog. The problem arises with stage 3, when there are just as many distinguishing marks of the frog as there are of the tadpole. From there it follows that we have equally good grounds for naming the animal that transforms a frog than we have for naming it a tadpole. The Later Mohists agree with this way of presenting change. Their solution to the problem is to restrict this third phase to the shortest possible amount of time. At this crucial stage, the object may be both X and non-X.[77] It is precisely in this context that the Later Mohists make use of the concept *wujiu*[ds] 'the durationless', just to make sure that the moment at which the description of the changing object at phase 3 expresses a contradiction is virtually

76   Note that each one of these five stages may also be described the other way round. For stage 1, we could have said, 'there are not yet any distinguishing marks of the frog', and so on.
77   See theorem A 50 in the *Mohist Canon* (Graham 1978: 298).

durationless.[78] In this way, the Later Mohists also solve the problem of the knowledge of the changing. It is impossible, for them too, to have knowledge of the flux. But this does not rule out the possibility of knowing: we can know change if we are able to recognize and point out the still hidden signs (*zheng*[dt]) of an imminent change.[79]

This conception of change may also explain the fundamental role played by the *Yijing* in the whole of Chinese thought, because the transformation of one hexagram into another through old Yin and Yang lines is a prototypical illustration of this concept of change: the whole circuit of change stays within the frame delimited by the hexagram system. The problem of a hexagram vanishing into nothing to free the place for the following would be absurd in this context. There is a secret direction in the process of change. The diviner may get at it by manipulating his stalks; the sages – they never cast the stalks – know in advance where the process will lead them.[80]

We know change if we know the future object. And that is all one can know about change. The first Greek philosophers had declared that knowledge of the changing was impossible. The Chinese conception of change does not deny this fact. What is more important to the first Chinese philosophers is the outcome of change: we do not know the changing,[81] but we know what the changing object is going to be in the future, if we are wise enough to see the important distinguishing marks.

The notion of an 'orientated change' is prominent also in another famous Chinese concept, namely *shi*,[du] which can be translated as 'propensity',[82] 'hidden tendencies', 'configuration', 'constellation', 'circumstances'.[83] If we compare this concept with Aristotle's analysis of change – which is explicitly directed against atomism – we notice very soon that the Greek *dunamis* denotes pure potentiality, because the goal and the direction of change lie concentrated in the notion of form, which is that towards which change is directed. *Shi*,[dv] on the contrary, does not capture an endless number of possible developments, but rather points to hidden tendencies, to outcomes of a

---

78   There is a striking parallel to this argument in the *Metaphysics* of Aristotle. At K 6 (1062b26f.), Aristotle reports that 'some thinkers claimed, paradoxically, that a thing which became white was both not-white and white in the first place.' See Lloyd 1966: 113–14.

79   To know is to predict accurately. A similar conception is also defended in the *Chunqiu fanlu* ch. 8/10b SBBY edn; see Ames and Hall 1987: 50–56; Ames 1988: 268–69.

80   The *Book of Changes*, in a sense, never predicts anything. The cosmic processes of change are known anyway, at least to a sage. The oracle only tells the person seeking advice what his actual situation in this process is. The oracle re-orientates the lost, but does not predict.

81   The Later Mohists (*Mojing*, theorem A 5) point out that there is an important difference between knowing and seeing: seeing ceases with the disappearance of the object of sight; knowledge, however, stays after the object of knowledge has disappeared (Graham 1978: 266–69).

82   See Jullien 1992.

83   For an overview of the various shades of meaning of this concept and its historical evolution, see Ames 1983: 65–107.

situation that are significant for human action and that can also be provoked or exploited by the one who is capable of discerning these tendencies. The potential of change, in ancient China, is *knowable*, though only to the wise. There is no reservoir of endless possibilities. The wise know the special circumstances, the right moment, to act. *Shi*[dw] denotes the special circumstances, favourable occasions, particular situations that are or that can become relevant to human action. It is a concept that has originated not in the realm of natural science, but in the one of human action. This aspect is sometimes obscured by the fact that the philosophical texts, to illustrate their conception of *shi*, frequently adduce examples of natural events. But even so, what matter are the advantages that can be got out of these.[84] The limits of *shi*, nevertheless, are delimited by what one might call the 'physical laws':

> *Sui you guo shi zhi li bu neng zi ju qi shen fei wu li ye shi bu ke ye.*[dx]
> Even the strongest of a country cannot lift up his own body. It is not that his strength is defective; it is because this is not within the range of his possibilities (*shi*).
>
> (*Xunzi*, ch. 29, p. 348, *Zhuzi jicheng* edition)

This means that, even with the knowledge of the hidden resources proper to the sage, nothing supernatural or humanly impossible can be achieved on the basis of *shi*. According to the context, *shi*[dy] may be rendered as 'circumstances', 'occasion', 'crucial position'.[85] This is due not to an inherent ambiguity of the Chinese term, but to a different conceptualization of the notion of change in ancient China.

As the problems of economics, political and military science come first into focus, the conceptualization of the notion of change also starts, in ancient China, from this direction, and not from natural science as in ancient Greece. The philosophical problems posed by the notion of change in both cultures partially overlap – it is the same 'philosophical continent' – but the specific directions in which the concept spreads are dictated by philosophical environments that stress, in one case, human activity, in the other, natural events. Change, of course, also enters into cosmological speculations in ancient China. These, however, are subsequent developments, that keep the original anthropocentric colour of the primitive concept.

The most important element we should note, again, is that *shi* does not suggest either that an event grows out of nothing. On the contrary: *shi* always denotes 'hidden tendencies', that is, developments that are already present, like the energy in the drawn crossbow.[86]

The results of this comparative analysis of the words for change are very revealing: none of the Chinese words for change has concomitant representations similar to the Greek idea that a thing grows out of nothing or vanishes

---

84   See, for example, the chapter 'Dishi' of the *Sunzibingfa*.
85   Jullien (1992: 25) paraphrases 'potentiel né de la disposition'.
86   Cf. *Sunzibingfa*, ch. 5, p. 72, *Zhuzi jicheng* edition.

into nothing.[87] Most of the Chinese terms, on the contrary, describe change as a rearrangement of pre-existing elements, and none of them suggests that a thing vanishes into nothing or comes out of nothing. Even the most radical type of change (substantial change, *hua*) holds fast to the basic 'ontological' unity of the transforming object. None of the concomitant representations violates the logical postulate *ex nihilo nihil*. The philosophical solution found by the Greek Atomists, Empedocles and Anaxagoras lies *in nuce* in the Chinese language ('words for atoms').

Finale: the Boundaries of Philosophical Language

There is yet a more radical conclusion to be drawn: the limits between philosophical and ordinary ways of speaking are themselves culture-bound. What is philosophical in one culture may be already lexicalized in another, and what is lexicalized in one culture may turn up as a philosophical theory in another. Just as philosophical terminology may over time become the sedimentary rocks of ordinary ways of speaking (as Aristotle's 'actual' and 'potential'), so too it may happen that, as with atomism, philosophical theses developed in one tradition existed already at the level of ordinary ways of speaking in another.

---

87 Here, the Chinese language does not stand alone, for Warlpiri, an Australian language, apparently also lacks words that would describe a coming out of nothing or a making out of nothing and uses, instead, only words that suggest transformations of previously existing things. See Hale 1986.

Chapter 6

Light and the Mirror in Greece and China

Elements of Comparative Metaphorology

Introduction

The starting-point of my investigation is the discovery of the following, highly paradoxical situation: although metaphors are theoretically banned from philosophical discourse in ancient Greece, Plato, the Presocratics, and even Aristotle rely very heavily on metaphorical expressions, whereas in ancient China, where the metaphorical way of arguing is not condemned, but rather encouraged, metaphors are only sparingly used and we hardly find any reflections or theories focusing on them. There are, in ancient China, many anecdotes, parables, allegories, metaphors and analogies, but the specific technique of using systematically one, better known domain, to conceptually recategorize another, at first sight totally different, but more obscure domain, is not recognized as a specific philosophical problem. In the Greek philosophical tradition, on the other hand, there is a great discrepancy between the theoretical attitude to metaphor and the way in which metaphors are actually used, because the philosophers do not comply with rules established by themselves.

Metaphors, in the Western tradition, had long been perceived as a peripheral, cognitively reducible, phenomenon. According to the Aristotelian interpretation, the way in which a philosopher expresses his theories is independent of the contents of thought he wants to convey. The ideal the philosopher aims at is an unambiguous, abstract, formal and rigorous expression of his theories. If it turns out that the philosopher nevertheless falls short of this ideal, he either did so deliberately in order to adapt his wording to a particular audience, or he had simply failed sufficiently to purify his message. In both cases, however, it is customarily agreed that, if his text still contains figurative language, this is due to the fact that the philosopher has reached, at that time, only a *provisional* stage of expression. He offers, for the time being, only provisional formulations of rational modes of expression not yet available to him, but nevertheless already adumbrated in the metaphors he uses.

This means that, if the Greek philosopher Empedocles tells us that the sea is the sweat of the earth,[1] or if Confucius compares cultural refinement to the

---

1   Empedocles, fragment A 25 DK = 371 KRS, quoted in the essay 'The Origin of Logic in China'.

coat of a tiger,[2] they only do so because the proper philosophical terminology is lacking at the moment of writing, supposing thereby that such a perfect, abstract and philosophical language exists, independently from the figurative ways of representing it, and that the figurative way of signifying cannot add anything to the original content of their thought.

This view, accordingly called the *substitution theory of metaphor*, also implies that it is possible to substitute, at a more advanced cognitive stage, rational expressions with literal meaning for these provisional metaphors.[3] It postulates that the figurative way of expressing philosophical theories is always merely provisional and always inferior to rational and abstract ways of expressing these same contentsof thought.[4] It also implies that rhetorical figures are merely a matter of choice, and that Plato, for example, could have chosen different metaphors – or perhaps no metaphor at all – to express his theory of forms.

The presupposition that lies behind the substitution theory of metaphor is therefore that there is a clear-cut distinction between content and form, and that one and the same content may be expressed through various forms and that one and the same content may also be recognized as identical when appearing in different forms. Plato's conception of *good* rhetoric in the *Phaedrus* rests upon the presupposition that science and knowledge must exist *before* they can be expressed in a rhetorical discourse and hence that figures of speech have no ontological role to play. For Plato, the art of speaking could not have more than an ancillary function. Philosophy, being concerned with truth, does not need anything beyond the plain exposure of truth to be convincing.

Modern, cognitive theories of metaphor have gradually led to a re-evaluation of metaphorical language, by recognizing the irreducible cognitive – and hence onto-logical – value of metaphors and by negating the content–form distinction and its epistemological implications.[5] Philosophers, linguists and cognitive scientists have also maintained that many metaphors are absolute and unavoidable, which means that it is sometimes impossible to find an equivalent formulation in a corre-sponding, rational language, capable of conveying the same contents of meaning.

---

2   *Lunyu* 12.8. The term 'human nature' (*xing*) is seemingly not yet available to Confucius, because, as the *Lunyu* tell us, 'the Master did not speak about nature [...]' (5.13). The term *xing*, however, *does* occur in the *Lunyu*, but not, however, in the technical sense the term has acquired later with Mencius and Xunzi.

3   For a standard definition of metaphor, see Johnson 1981: 6 ('A metaphor is an elliptic simile useful for stylistic, rhetorical, and didactic purposes, but which can be translated into a literal paraphrase without any loss of cognitive content.')

4   A modern representative of this view is Searle (1981). Searle distinguishes between a speaker's utterance meaning and a literal sentence meaning.

5   The cognitive view of metaphor goes back to the American literary critic Richards (Rich-ards 1936). Interestingly enough, Richards is also the author of a book on Mencius (Rich-ards 1932). It is highly probable, then, that his new theories about metaphors grew out of his contact with Chinese philosophy. Black's *interaction view of metaphor* is cognate to the cognitive theory of metaphor. For Black, metaphor is an irreducible cognitive phenomenon that arises out of the interaction of one conceptual structure on another (Black 1981). For a modern re-interpretation of Aristotle's theory of metaphor in a cogni-tive sense, see Kirby 1997.

The major part of contemporary discussions on metaphor start therefore from the insight that metaphors not only serve to express already prefigured (but not yet formulated) contents of thought, but also that metaphor is a cognitive force by itself, able to guide or misguide thought or even fundamentally organize, or reorganize, its structure.

However, if the philosopher cannot do without metaphors and if his metaphorical production is guided by his native tongue, we seem to be driven to the conclusion that some of the more basic differences between civilizations might ultimately be reduced to the presence or absence of a limited set of root-metaphors. Lakoff's and Johnson's claim that human thinking, perceiving and acting is structured by metaphors, and the fact that metaphors differ from one language to another, indeed strongly implies relativism. The challenging claim of their book is precisely that the whole conceptual system of a language is fundamentally metaphorical in nature, and that all thinking and acting ultimately proceeds from a system of – largely unconscious – beliefs grounded in a set of interrelated metaphors.[6]

Rorty's influential work on the metaphor of the mirror should also be mentioned in this context.[7] Rorty's main thesis is that Western metaphysics has been dominated, up to now, by optical metaphors, such as light or the mirror. The human mind has been pictured, throughout the history of Western philosophy, as a huge mirror, faithfully trying to reflect reality or mischievously distorting it. Our philosophical convictions are therefore influenced by this root-metaphor of the mirror.

At first sight, it seems tempting to try to reduce the main differences between the Chinese culture and other cultural areas to basic differences in the underlying metaphorical system. The truth is, however, that ancient China shares many metaphors with our own tradition. The cognitive metaphors used by the first Greek and the first Chinese philosophers are not as different as the general cultural contrasts between these two civilizations might lead us to expect. One of Lakoff's and Johnson's favourite metaphors ('argument is war'), for example, is even quite common in ancient China, not to speak of the metaphors of light and of the mirror, which can be found in both traditions and which we shall examine later in this study. The military expressions *fu*[a] 'submit', and *sheng*[b] 'win', are widely used to designate victory and defeat in a debate in classical Chinese. These similarities, however, should not obscure the fact that the Chinese perception of war and conflict is entirely different from the Western.[8]

---

6   Lakoff and Johnson (1980) seem to argue in favour of linguistic relativism, since they believe that metaphors structure our experience and that metaphors are different from one language to another. The work of Kittay on metaphor also seems to imply linguistic relativism. She writes: '[…] metaphors are always relative to a set of beliefs and to linguistic usage which may change through time and place – they are relative to a given linguistic community.' (Kittay 1987: 20)

7   Rorty 1980.

8   Kamenarovic 2001; Jullien 1995; Lloyd 1996.

Although the tendency to argue about philosophical problems in terms of manufactured artefacts and of natural properties of things is present in Greece as well as in China, there is a marked difference in the way these metaphorical expressions are used.[9] The most striking aspect is the uniformity in the use of metaphors in China. There is a limited range of stock metaphors, like the wood that has to be carved, or the jade that has to be polished. These metaphors are then used by nearly every school which discusses the specific philosophical problem – human nature, for example – with which these metaphors are conventionally associated.

This is not to say that the cross-cultural exploration of metaphors should be neglected.[10] My point is, simply, that there is no predictable overlap between differences in the metaphorical make-up and other cultural differences.

The paradox mentioned at the beginning of this essay should already have given rise to the suspicion that the Western way of doing metaphorology might be vitiated, right from the start, by our, Western, ways of looking at metaphors and by our Western habits of analysing the relations between language and reality. We have already noted in the Introduction that the Western tradition usually *opposes* thinking to language, as if both were necessarily antagonistic factors. This attitude also operates in the ways in which metaphors are treated in the Western, especially Greek, context, no matter if we adhere to the substitution theory of metaphor or to the modern cognitive views. As a consequence of this, we will have to be extremely careful not to re-project our Western attitude on the Chinese material, but, on the contrary, try to discover the specific Chinese locus of metaphor.

Comparative Metaphorology – the Philosophical Problem

Metaphors belong to a continuum of figures of thought that comprises analogies, parables, similes, examples, allegories and comparisons. Their basic function might be described as 'structure-mapping', because one, generally less well known domain, is reformulated or recategorized in terms of another, better known one. A metaphor is often an unusual, surprising and at first sight nonsensical formulation (for example, 'the heavenly clockwork'), which puts our conceptual apparatus 'under pressure' and may eventually lead to a re-arrangement of our cognitive framework.[11]

Metaphors are also a general linguistic phenomenon and seem to act primarily as semantic innovators. We use metaphors when the proper name for a thing or an event is lacking. Quintilian already noted that metaphors are

9   For a collection of examples in ancient China, see Keightley 1989.
10   A good example would be the metaphor of the way as opposed to the metaphor of the crossroads. The metaphor of the crossroads is rarely used in the classical Chinese tradition (*Lüshichunqiu*, ch. 22.3), but is extremely common in Greek philosophical writing (theme of the *bivium*).
11   See Turner 1988: 3. For a general overview of the field, see Johnson 1981; Ortony 1994.

necessary because of the original poverty of language.[12] The link that ties together the philosophical and the normal linguistic notion of metaphor is, I think, the pretension to inaugurate a novel way of viewing things. This might indeed be the reason why the first Greek philosophers were instinctively driven to use metaphors. The problem, however, is whether this means of expression is a legitimate one.

Central to the Western debate about metaphor is the question whether the firmly rooted distinction between the literal and the metaphorical,[13] first worked out by Aristotle, is at all a justifiable one. Aristotle, as Lloyd notes,[14] has used this distinction in a polemical way, because he condemns many theories of his predecessors on the ground that they use figurative, that is, metaphorical language, in giving definitions. Metaphors are already banned from the philosophical discourse in the *Topics* (139b34f.) where Aristotle says that every metaphorical expression is obscure.

Aristotle's condemnation of metaphor and figurative language, when put into a comparative perspective, cannot be explained solely by the desire to obtain pure and abstract knowledge. There are no *a priori* reasons that would discredit the cognitive pretensions of a metaphorical expression as such. Figurative language, I guess, is problematic only because there is no way to ascertain whether everybody attaches the same meaning to a proposed metaphor. Dead or conventional metaphors may be (and are) used without danger in argumentation, precisely because nobody doubts the meaning of these expressions. Metaphors can become valid tools for argumentation only if it is possible also to reach an agreement on a metaphorical basis; this in turn presupposes that different persons must understand metaphors in exactly the same way. Hence the following principle: the more conventional a metaphor, the greater its chances of acceptance in an argumentative context. Creative and original metaphors, then, are not very likely to gain immediate and universal acceptance, not because they are metaphors, but simply because there is no way of making sure that everybody understands a new metaphor in the same sense.[15]

These remarks give us a clue to the understanding of the first-mentioned paradoxical situation: it appears indeed that the use Chinese philosophers

---

12   The creative nature of metaphors had also been noted by Dumarsais, who had argued that metaphors were necessary because of the original poverty of the vocabulary. See also Black 1981: 69 '[...] metaphor is a species of catachresis, which I shall define as the use of a word in some new sense in order to remedy a gap in the vocabulary; catachresis is the putting of new senses into old words.' and Fontanier [1821–1830] 1977: 157: 'On a aussi remarqué que les langues les plus pauvres sont les plus figurées, c'est-à-dire, les plus tropologiques; que les peuples les moins civilisés, et surtout les sauvages, ne s'expriment que par Tropes.'

13   This distinction is at the heart of the substitution theory of metaphor.

14   Lloyd 1990: 21; cf. Aristotle, *Posterior Analytics* 97b37f.

15   Kittay 1987: 19 '[...] it is important to notice that an expression is not metaphorical in an absolute sense. It is metaphorical only relative to a given conceptual organisation in which certain categorisations capture similarities and differences taken to be salient for that language community.'

make of metaphors is often conventional and highly codified;[16] Greek philosophers, on the other hand, prove to be extremely creative and individualistic, to the extent that none of them would ever resort to a metaphor or to a comparison that had already been used by another philosopher!

The conventional element in the Chinese way of arguing is fairly conspicuous. This constellation fits in well also with the observation that the Chinese language in general is much poorer in philosophical terminology than classical Greek. Plato and the Presocratics, on the contrary, have greatly enriched the Greek language, especially through new metaphors.

Metaphors and Rhetoric in China and in Greece

Metaphors are embedded in the much larger domain of rhetoric and are supposed to act, just like other rhetorical tools, on the transmission of the message and its impact on the audience rather than upon its content. If one detaches the art of speaking from its philosophical settings, one could indeed rest with the impression that rhetoric is, like linguistics, a fully fledged, cross-culturally invariant discipline and that there are a given number of rhetorical devices and figures every culture is bound to discover sooner or later.[17]

The rhetorical figure of *antonomasia*, for example, well known from Western handbooks, is also quite common in classical Chinese. In the following text, the name of the Yellow Emperor is used to signify 'the cleverest emperor'.[18]

> Hence, those whom the law condemns, the ruler accepts, and those whom the magistrates seek to punish, the higher officials patronize. Thus law and personal inclination, high official and lowly magistrate, are all set at odds, and there is no fixed standard. Under such circumstances even *ten Yellow Emperors* could not bring the state to order.
>
> *(Hanfeizi*, ch. 49, p. 344, *Zhuzi jicheng* edition;
> translation Watson 1964: 105, slightly modified)

The rhetorical structure of the following text is also quite obvious. It exhibits the rhetorical figure of *antistrophe*, the repetition of the same word or phrase at the end of successive clauses.

> Somebody had lost his axe. He suspected his neighbour's son. When he watched him walking, he saw him stealing the axe;[19] when he saw his face – axe-stealing!

---

16   The material collected by Keightley (Keightley 1989) shows that only simple and straightforward images are used, even in Daoist contexts.

17   See, for example, Unger 1994; Zhang Zhenhua 1991; Heidbüchel 1993. All these works start from a Western list of rhetorical tropes. Less rigorous and systematic is Lu Xing 1998.

18   *Antonomasia*: 'use of an epithet or patronymic, instead of a proper name, or the reverse'.

his way of talking – axe-stealing! His behaviour and his undertakings, none of it were not axe-stealing.

Then the man searched in his cave and found his axe. When he saw again his neighbour's son the next day, his behaviour and undertakings were not axe-stealing anymore. It was not because his neighbour's son had changed, but because he himself had changed. Changing is not becoming different; it is to be obstructed by something.

(*Lüshichunqiu*, ch. 13.3)

The expression *qie fu ye*[c] 'axe-stealing' is repeated at the end of no fewer than four consecutive sentences, and gives a vivid impression of what is really on the mind of the man who had lost his axe and who suspected his neighbour's son of having stolen it.

Examples such as these could easily be multiplied, and the task of contrastive rhetoric therefore looks like being promising and useful. The fact that a limited number of figures of speech appear to be overtly language-dependent, because they use phonetic or syntactic elements peculiar to some languages cannot, of course, ruin the general and universal pretensions of rhetoric,[20] and the existence of typically Chinese rhetorical figures cannot ruin these pretensions either. Harbsmeier has shown that there are also differences on the level of the cultural anthropology of the writing process.[21] He has noticed that the figure of *aposiopesis* 'falling silent in mid-sentence' seems to be absent from pre-Buddhist Chinese prose. 'The pre-Buddhist Chinese have no need for summary through indirect speech, simply because summarizing and reducing a message to the essentials is part of the *overall cultural mode of writing* in the first place. If writing does not purport to be mimetic of the actual flow of speech then there is less need to mark off the non-mimetic character of the summary.'[22]

One could thus be satisfied with Chinese rhetoric in this contrastive sense and exclude philosophical problems from consideration. But the problem with rhetoric is that it is not just an art of speaking and persuading. Far from being philosophically innocuous, rhetoric carries within itself epistemological presuppositions that can render cross-cultural applications very delicate.

---

19   This is a case of *zeugma*, two different words linked to a verb which is appropriate to only one of them. It is an example, too, of a case where rhetoric overrides grammar. I am indebted to Christoph Harbsmeier for these remarks.

20   See, for example, Villard 1984: 208: 'To show the difference between Japanese and French metaphors would be the same as pointing out the syntactical differences there are between Japanese and French [...]' (my translation). Although it is true to say that rhetoric is limited by the rules of grammar, Max Black's definition seems over-confident when applied to classical Chinese texts. He writes: 'So the writer or speaker is employing conventional means to produce a non-standard effect, while using only the standard syntactic and semantic resources of his speech community. Yet the meaning of an interesting metaphor is typically new or 'creative', not inferable from the standard lexicon.' (Black 1986: 23)

21   Harbsmeier 2001: 147–51.

22   Harbsmeier 1995: 55.

Its hermeneutic embedding into Western intellectual history further complicates the issue of Chinese rhetoric. The art of speaking has been and still is important in the West precisely because of the everlasting tension between rhetoric and philosophy. The status of rhetoric in the West has constantly changed, and the current 'rhetoric revival' is but the most recent in a long series, after the 'Second Sophistic movement' in Greco-Roman Antiquity, Renaissance rhetoric, French rhetoric of the seventeenth century, Burke, Perelman, and so on. The status of rhetoric invariably goes down when this tension loosens and when rhetoric is considered to be no more than a catalogue of figures of speech ('tropology') or a clever method of distorting philosophical truth through artful manipulations of language. Ricoeur and Genette use the expression 'restricted rhetoric' for the kind of rhetoric from which argumentative techniques are excluded.[23]

Is it possible at all to recover an authentic Chinese concept of rhetoric when our Western perceptions of rhetoric are not at all settled? Is it a sensible attitude at all to look for Chinese rhetoric? Rhetoric might indeed be a typical Western problem, for which there is no exact equivalent in China.

We will have to pay attention to several important differences. Western rhetoric is traditionally located within a continuum of disciplines that include grammar and dialectic. No signs of such a tripartite division (the *trivium* of the Middle Ages) are visible in ancient China, where neither logic nor grammar emerge as independent branches of knowledge in the classical period. *Bian,*[d] roughly the Chinese equivalent of dialectic, includes rhetorical as well as logical, semantic and even psychological considerations, and thus comes much closer to Aristotle's rhetorical project than any modern form of rhetoric that is restricted to a theory of tropes.[24] Although the art of speaking – at least the art of pleading at court – seems to have been taught in ancient China, no handbooks from this period survive.[25] The document that comes closest to a treatise of philosophical rhetoric is the *Mohist Canon* (*Mojing*), where we find a system of rules and devices which demonstrate the basic tenets of the Mohist school and at the same time defend these tenets against attacks from outside. But this is certainly a very special use of rhetoric.

Rhetoric, however, is more than a technique. Figures of speech and tropes (sometimes also called 'figures of thought') are not the whole of rhetoric. Persuasion always starts from arguments; but argumentation can only proceed within an already established epistemological framework. Perelman was one of the first to point out that there is a systematic relationship between

---

23 Ricoeur 1975: 13–18; Genette 1972.
24 It is worth noting that the Arabic world had received a 'longer' version of Aristotle's *Organon*, including the rhetorical writings, the *Rhetoric* and the *Poetics*. See Brunschwig 1991.
25 The *Zhanguoce* is perhaps a collection of model speeches; but the text does not include theoretical considerations. Deng Xi (see *Lüshichunqiu*, ch. 18.4) is said to have taught people how to plead at court.

the content and the form of an argument.[26] The ways of arguing, far from being neutral, influence the very issue of the debate.[27] The problem of metaphor must therefore also be examined in its argumentative context.

Philosophical Uses of Metaphor in China and in Greece

The fundamental difference which exists in the way Greek and Chinese philosophers use metaphors in their discourse is best shown by working through several examples.

> *Fu shui zhi xing qing, tu zhe gu zhi. Gu bu de qing.*
> *Ren zhi xing shou, wu zhe gu zhi. Gu bu de shou.*[e]
> It is the nature of water to be limpid; mud makes it turbid. So it fails to be limpid.
> It is the nature of man to live long; outer things trouble (disturb) him. So he fails to live long.
>
> (*Lüshichunqiu*, ch. 1.2)

From a Western perspective, the second occurrence of 'trouble, disturb' is metaphorical, because it looks as if we were moving from a physical sense to a more spiritual one.[28]

Upon closer inspection, however, it turns out that this metaphorical discourse does not operate in the same way as its possible Western counterparts. First, there is this curious habit of enumerating, point after point, all the relevant metaphorical correspondences. In a Western context, 'trouble longevity' would have been enough to induce the metaphorical mapping. We would have been aware then that there was no good term in Chinese for saying 'disturb' in a spiritual sense, and hence accept its provisional replacement by a more concrete and physical substitute.

Nature of water	Nature of man
limpidity	longevity
mud	outer things
disturb (trouble)	disturb (trouble)
muddy water	shortened life

26   Perelman and Olbrechts-Tyteca 1970. Perelman was a student of the Belgian philologist and philosopher Dupréel. Dupréel is at the birth of the modern rehabilitation of the Sophists, and thus, indirectly though, also of the contemporary rhetoric revival. See Dupréel 1980.
27   See Perelman 1977: 138.
28   'Trouble' comes from the French 'troubler', which means, 'cause to be turbid' and 'disturb'. The metaphor is also the same in Greek, where we have *tarassô* and *ataraxia*.

The table shows that 'trouble, disturb' is not the only metaphorical term, but that every term from the left-hand column is potentially metaphorical as well. The term 'mud' is indeed often used in Daoist texts to speak of the 'political affairs' of the world. The Chinese use of metaphor thus seems to fit also the basic Western use of metaphor: take one discourse and transpose it on to a totally different domain.

But there is a problem here, because the Chinese metaphor does not try to establish a parallelism between two domains, but rather wants to show that there is a *convergence* between them: the nature of water behaves in exactly the same way as the nature of man. There is not an accidental linguistic coincidence between these two domains, but an essential link through their nature. One and the same nature is responsible for the properties of water and for man's longevity. There is no passage from a physical to a spiritual sense here, as a Western reading of this text would suggest, but a basic unity within one and the same domain.[29] We are still not very far away from Aristotle's conception of metaphor, for whom resemblance was also the major stimulus of metaphors: to be good at metaphors means to be good at perceiving similarities.[30]

The kind of resemblance invoked in our text from the *Lüshichunqiu* is not chosen at random. It is a *natural* resemblance. As such, however, especially in a Chinese context, it also has explanatory functions. What is natural, in Chinese, is often expressed by the formula *ziran*[f] 'what is so by itself'. To explain a phenomenon thus often means explaining what is natural in it. And the basic postulate is that there must then be a resemblance between all other phenomena that are also natural.

The art of metaphorical invention, in ancient China, often means to find out just what is natural in a process and thus also separate from it what is merely artificial.

> Gaozi said, 'Human nature is like whirling water. Give it an outlet in the east and it will flow east; give it an outlet in the west and it will flow west. Human nature does not show any preference for either good or bad just as water does not show any preference for either east or west.'
>
> 'It certainly is the case', said Mencius, 'that water does not show any preference for either east or west, but does it show the same indifference to high and low? Human nature is good just as water seeks low ground. There is no man who is not good; there is no water that does not flow downwards. Now in the case of water, by splashing it one can make it shoot up higher than one's forehead, and by forcing it one can make it stay on a hill. How can that be the nature of water? It is the circumstances being what they are. That man can be made bad shows that his nature is no different from that of water in this respect.'
>
> (*Mencius*, VI,A,2; translation Lau 1983: 160)

---

29   This, probably, is also the reason that has lead Pauline Yu (1987) to ban the very expression of 'metaphor' from her analysis of the nature of Chinese poetry.
30   *Rhetoric* 1459a: *to gar eu metapherein to to homoion theôrein estin.*

Mencius' way of arguing here is not cognitively neutral. His argumentation creates its own framework by the systematic exploitation of the contrast between good, natural, *self-explaining* qualities and bad, artificial, *reducible* qualities. Mencius presupposes that there is an essential link between the nature of man and the nature of water. The natural properties of water match the good qualities of human nature, whereas the artificial properties of water match the 'perversions' of human nature. The very way Mencius presents his arguments already includes a philosophical doctrine, namely that natural qualities are good and prevail over artificial and acquired ones and that there is a uniform concept of nature underlying both the basic constitution of water and the basic constitution of man. The water-metaphor is a typically Chinese root-metaphor, unknown in the West in that form. Sarah Allan has tried to show that the importance of the water-metaphor in early China is related to the belief that the nature of cosmos and the nature of man are basically one. The problem for the first Chinese philosophers, therefore, was to find an adequate metaphor to express this insight. Water itself perfectly illustrates this natural way of the cosmos. Any metaphor, therefore, which well describes water, must also be useful in describing the basic law of the cosmos. Hence also the cognitive value of the metaphor of water in ancient Chinese thought.[31]

Natural qualities are not only self-explaining, but also *cognitively* prior to artificial qualities, because artificial qualities can then be explained as deviant. The formal rhetorical device and the material content are interdependent. Here is another example:

> Gaozi said, 'Human nature is like the *qi* willow. Dutifulness is like cups and bowls. To make morality out of human nature is like making cups and bowls out of the willow.'
>
> 'Can you', said Mencius, 'make cups and bowls by following the nature of the willow? Or must you *mutilate* the willow before you can make it into cups and bowls? If you have to *mutilate* the willow to make it into cups and bowls, must you, then, also *mutilate* a man to make him moral? Surely, it will be these words of yours men in the world will follow in bringing disaster upon morality.'
>
> (*Mencius*, VI,A,1; translation Lau 1983: 160)

The metaphorical element is brought in here by the expression 'mutilate', *qiang zei*,[g] used to describe both the violence done to the wooden material and the violence done to the 'human' material. It is even precisely this pivotal expression of 'mutilate', common to both domains, that induces the crucial metaphorical 'transference of meaning' from one semantic field (craftsmanship) to another (human nature).[32]

Gaozi holds that dutifulness, *yi*,[h] is external to human nature; Mencius, on the other hand, takes it to be internal, arising spontaneously from the inborn tendencies of the human heart. The significant element about this dialogue, however, is the fact that Mencius does not try to find a rival metaphor to

---

31   See Allan 1997.

Gaozi's, centred, for example, on the *inborn* nature of dutifulness. Neither does Mencius make efforts to dredge out the 'literal' meaning of Gaozi's thesis; he does not attempt to reformulate it into a more neutral and more rational language. What Mencius does, instead, is to show that Gaozi's metaphor fails to map one of the corresponding elements of the case at issue: mutilation is not a natural element. Gaozi then proposes several other analogies to clarify his position,[33] but is rebuked each time by Mencius, who shows that the 'transference of meaning' (Kittay) proposed by Gaozi does not hold. Mencius is ready to find better metaphors than Gaozi, or to 'correct' Gaozi's metaphors; he never suggests that Gaozi's metaphorical way of arguing is, on the whole, the wrong approach.

Positions as distinct as those of Mencius and Gaozi hence may be expressed as a 'dialogue in metaphors', because both, in spite of their disagreement, still want to show their theories as being grounded upon the nature of things, and assume that their way of saying things is perfectly adapted to this task. This means that both Gaozi and Mencius agree upon the validity of the wood-metaphor; their discussion really should show who is using the metaphor at its best.[34]

These dialogues between Mencius and Gaozi, as well as many other, similar texts, show that the argumentative *value* of metaphorical expressions is never questioned in ancient Chinese philosophical texts. Mencius never objects to Gaozi's use of figurative language. Even the Later Mohists, the most rational-minded philosophers in ancient China, resort in a systematic manner to illustrations and comparisons, as we shall see later. Also, the specific technique of combating a proposed metaphor with a (better) counter-metaphor seems to be unknown in the West, where counter-metaphors can only be used to destroy the very use of metaphors in argumentation and hence show the refusal of the interlocutor to engage into a metaphorical debate.[35]

In the context of Greek philosophy, the use of metaphors is even theoretically prohibited. One of Aristotle's attacks against the theory of forms starts with an objection against its metaphorical clothing:

---

32   The expression 'transference of meaning' is borrowed from Kittay 1987: 258 '[…] the transference of meaning, which Aristotle took to be the critical feature of metaphor, can be seen as a process in which the structure of one semantic field induces a structure on another content domain.' And again Kittay 1987: 36 'More precisely, in metaphor what is transferred are the relations which pertain within one semantic field to a second, distinct content domain.' The 'transference of meaning', in Chinese metaphors and analogies, is generally linked to the presence of a 'pivotal' expression, (or *focus*, in Max Black's terminology), like *qiang zei* 'mutilate' in the text of Mencius, which can take a share in both semantic fields.

33   See *Mencius*, VI,A,2–4; these arguments are based on the natural properties of water.

34   I owe this remark to Sarah Allan.

35   In ancient China, this technique is occasionally used to refute an argument, but never to invalidate the very process of analogical or metaphorical argumentation. See Leslie 1964.

To say that the Forms are paradigms, and that other things participate in them, is to use empty phrases and poetic metaphors.

(*Metaphysics* A 9; 991a19–22)

In spite of this, metaphors are widely used in early Greek philosophical discourse, not only commonly recognized metaphors, but also and above all new and creative metaphors. Here is a Greek example now, taken from book 6 of Plato's *Republic*.

'You are aware,' I said, 'that when the eyes are no longer turned upon objects upon whose colours the light of day falls but that of the dim luminaries of night, their edge is blunted and they appear almost blind, as if pure vision did not dwell in them.'

'Yes, indeed,' he said.

'But when, I take it, they are directed upon objects illumined by the sun, they see clearly, and vision appears to reside in these same eyes.'

'Certainly.'

'Apply this comparison to the soul also in this way. When it is firmly fixed on the domain where truth and reality shine resplendent it apprehends and knows them and appears to possess reason; but when it inclines to that region which is mingled with darkness, the world of becoming and passing away, it opines only and its edge is blunted, and it shifts its opinions hither and thither, and again seems as if it lacked reason.'

'Yes, it does.'

'This reality, then, that gives their truth to the objects of knowledge and the power of knowing to the knower, you must say is the idea of good, and you must conceive it as being the cause of knowledge, and of truth in so far as known. Yet fair as they both are, knowledge and truth, in supposing it to be something fairer still than these you will think rightly of it. But as for knowledge and truth, even as in our illustration it is right to deem light and vision sunlike, but never to think that they are the sun, so here it is right to consider these two their counterparts, as being like the good or boniform, but to think that either of them is the good is not right. Still higher honour belongs to the possession and habit of the good.'

(*Republic* 508D–509A; translation Shorey 1980)

The equivalence between light and knowledge appears to be at the very heart of the *Lichtmetaphysik*.[36] The basic tenet of this hypothesis is that being, knowledge and truth are inevitably expressed in the diverse languages by the means of the metaphor of light. Plato uses this type of discourse many times, as the passage quoted above amply shows. In the *Sophist*, non-being is called 'the dark place' and being, 'the luminous region' (254A). We can spell out the equivalencies there are between light and knowledge with the help of a table of correspondences:

---

36   See Bremer 1973; Bremer 1974 (with bibliography) and Bremer 1976. See also Blumenberg 1957; Luther 1965 and Luther 1966.

Vision	Knowledge
eye	soul
light	truth
darkness	confusion, falseness
visible objects	knowable objects
artificially illuminated objects	changing objects
naturally illuminated objects	unchanging objects
bad sight	opinion
clear sight	knowledge

Even if we can represent the Platonic metaphor of light in the same way as the Chinese metaphors in a table of correspondences (see above), we must pay attention to several very important differences. First, there is no convergence here between the two domains, of sight and knowledge. There is a transition from less perfect to more perfect ways of knowing, from perceiving with our eyes to perceiving with our minds.

From the point of view of the construction of the philosophical discourse, Plato does not make efforts to lay bare, systematically, all these correspondences. His rhetorical technique rather tries to take, at random, one term out of the left-hand column and 'marry' it with a predicate from the right hand column. He coins expressions such as: *katalampei alêtheia* 'truth throws light upon something' (*Republic* 508D5), *doxazei te kai ambluôttai* 'opines with the sight blurred' (508D8).

This metaphorical proliferation, however, is surely intentional in Plato's work. The more he uses metaphors, the more their cognitive inability must become apparent. Moreover, this strategy also prepares the reader for the general conclusion, namely that truth is not to be found in language. The very use of metaphors shows at the same time also their philosophically inferior status. The mind must go beyond metaphors towards another type of reality, a kind of reality metaphors cannot hold within them, but only hint at. So even if Plato thinks that metaphors cannot express philosophical truth, it takes him many metaphors to say just that!

Metaphors and Philosophy in China and in Greece

One of the reasons why metaphors, and the analogies and comparisons derived from or embedded in them, have a better argumentative value in ancient China, is because their content is already codified in the linguistic competence, and does not need to be guessed or reconstructed, unlike Greek metaphors, by the hearer.[37] The problem is whether the proposed metaphor matches and explains all the points at issue; the actual principle of metaphorical argumentation, however, is never questioned.

Even if metaphorical expressions are not a fundamental philosophical – or even literary – problem before the *Wenxin diaolong* of Liu Xie (chapter 36, *Bixing*[i]), this does not mean that the phenomenon as such had not been noticed and discussed in early China. I would claim that the distinction between what we call metaphorical and literal could have been made in ancient China. We find there indeed the notions of 'phrasing' (*ci;*[j] *yan*[k]) and of 'communicative intent' (*yi*[l]) of a saying. In a famous – very 'rhetorical' – passage, Zhuangzi declares:

> The net is the means to get the fish where you want it; catch the fish and you forget the net. The snare is the means to get the rabbit where you want it; catch the rabbit and you forget the snare. Words (*yan*) are the means to get the idea (*yi*) where you want it; catch on to the idea and you forget about the words.
>
> *(Zhuangzi*, ch. 26, p. 181, *Zhuzi jicheng* edition; translation Graham 1981: 190, slightly modified. See also *Lüshichunqiu*, ch. 18.3)

In the *Lunyu*, this conception is expressed even more directly:

> The Master said: Speech – get [the idea] across, that is all!
>
> *(Lunyu* 15.41)

The same idea appears also in the *Lüshichunqiu:*

> Wordings (propositions, formulations) are the outer marks of 'communicative intents' (*yi*). To mirror the outer marks and discard the communicative intents is mistaken. Therefore, the men of old put the words aside once they had achieved the communicative intents.
>
> *(Lüshichunqiu*, ch. 18.4)

These texts show, at least, that the separation between the content and the expression of thought, one of the prerequisites for the distinction between the literal and the metaphorical, had been made in ancient China, and hence that there is nothing like an 'epistemological obstacle' (in Bachelard's sense) which could have prevented the first Chinese philosophers from building a theory of metaphor upon this distinction. The reason for this difference in attitude to metaphor must therefore be sought at another level.

---

37   A good example of a widespread and conventional metaphor in ancient Chinese philosophy is the metaphor used for expressing the abstract notion of causality through the image of the gate. 'There is only one gate to it' means that there is only one way of bringing about an effect; 'there are one hundred gates' on the contrary means that an event may have many different causes. See, for example, *Mozi*, ch. 8; *Mozi*, ch. 48; *Shangjunshu*, ch. 5; *Xunzi*, ch. 17, and *Lunyu* 6.17. See also the essay 'The Origin of Logic in China' in this volume.

Even if no thinker in ancient China has made an attempt to separate figurative meaning from literal meaning, this does not mean, as we have already noted, that the distinction as such could not have been made. There is indeed, in ancient China, the distinction between the intention, *yi*,[m] and the 'wording' of a saying, which is analogous to the one between literal and figurative meaning, but does not have the same function: it is recognized that it is possible to communicate one's *yi*, 'intention', also without resorting to language; the notion of literal meaning, in its Western sense, *cannot* be referred to outside of a linguistic code. Moreover, a communicative intent may be unconscious to the one that has it and does not even need to be formulated, but an interlocutor may guess it.[38] The most faithful rendering of *yi* is, in my opinion, 'communicative intent', because this translation draws away the notion from the domain of mentalism and psychologism.

Contrast again the notorious mistrust of Western philosophers in metaphors to the following, very optimistic, text from the *Shuoyuan*, a collection of sayings compiled by Liu Xiang in the first century BC:

> A client said to the King of Liang:
> 'Hui Shi [a famous sophist] always uses skilful comparisons when he argues about a subject. If you forbid him illustrative comparisons he won't be able to speak.'
> The King agreed. At the audience next day he said to Hui Shi: 'When you speak about something I wish you would simply speak directly [*zhi yan*[n]], without illustrative comparisons.'
> 'Let's suppose we have a man who does not know what a *dan*[o] [crossbow] is', Hui Shi said. 'If he says "What are the characteristics of a dan like?" and you answer "Like a dan", will it be conveyed to him?'
> 'It will not.'
> 'If you proceed to answer instead "A *dan* in its characteristics is like a bow, but with a string made of bamboo", will he know?'
> 'It will be known.'
> 'It is inherent in explanation [*shuo*[p]] that by using something he does know to convey what he does not know one causes the other man to know. To give up illustrative comparisons as you are telling me to do is inadmissible.'
> 'Well said', said the King.
> > (*Shuoyuan*, ch. 11, p. 4A7–4B1, *Sibu congkan* edition;
> > translation Graham 1978: 444–45)

The sophist Hui Shi is well reputed for his comparisons and analogies. Nearly all of his transmitted sayings are based on analogies, metaphors and comparisons.[39] The dialogue from the *Shuoyuan* is crucial for an adequate understanding of the role of metaphors and analogies in ancient China. The text quoted above discloses several important features. Stress is laid on the *cognitive*

---

38   See, for example, *Lüshichunqiu* ch. 18.3.
39   Hui Shi is known, throughout the pre-Han philosophical literature, for his skilful analogies; see Reding 1985: 301–47, where a French translation of all this material can be found.

aspect of the allegorical element, as the use of the term *shuo* 'explain' shows. The text even declares that, without comparison, there is no explaining at all. Similes, parables and metaphors proceed from what the hearer knows to make him understand things he does not (yet) know. Finally, the text justifies the use of comparisons by itself using a comparison – the metaphor is at the same time the message.

The expression *zhi yan* 'speak directly' is the most interesting in the present context, because it is the closest equivalent we can get in China to the Western concept of 'literal meaning'. *Zhi yan*, however, is a quite normal expression in classical Chinese and means, 'to speak overtly'.[40] But it may also be itself a metaphor, because it means – literally – 'speak in shortcuts'. Hui Shi simply wants to say that, in some cases, the most efficient, and hence the shortest way to convey meaning is through similes and metaphors.

Viewed from a Western point of view, these theories should rather have *favoured* a rich metaphorical language in ancient China. But, as we have already noticed, just the opposite of the expected result has taken place.

In early Greek philosophy, on the other hand, we see an 'inflation' of metaphors. The metaphorical prodigality of Western philosophy is an aftermath of the Presocratics' negative attitude to language in general.

If the burden of expressing the true aspects of reality is not laid on language, but on extra-linguistic means, the philosopher gets thereby also the right to use words in more indirect, plethoric, metaphorical ways. Plato sometimes even uses his metaphors in a contradictory manner. When he says, for example, in the seventh book of the *Republic* (516B) that the philosopher will be able to see and contemplate the sun itself, he uses not only a counter-intuitive image – looking straight at the sun hurts – but contradicts what he had said himself a few lines before (515C–D; *cl. Phaedo* 99D–E) of the prisoners in the cave, namely that their eyes will be hurt if they look at the sun.

There is nothing wrong in using metaphors even in these contradictory ways. But the very use Plato makes of his metaphors already shows what he thinks of them: they are not able to hold philosophical truth. Metaphors – as language in general – can only have a propaedeutic, or protreptic function. Plato's attitude to language – and to philosophy – is reflected in his attitude towards metaphors.

Light and the Mirror – Three Examples of Metaphoric Discourse

In the remaining part of this essay, I shall concentrate upon a special group of metaphors, namely upon metaphors related to the problem of knowledge.

---

40   *Lüshichunqiu* ch. 23.1; 23.5. The anti-rhetorical attitude of the compilers of this text is notorious. But see also *Xunzi*, ch. 5, *wei ke zhi zhi*, 'It is impossible to reach one's goal directly' (p. 53f., *Zhuzi jicheng* edition). The expression *zhi zhi* is contrasted with *qu de* 'get it in an oblique way' (*ibid.*, p. 54).

Cognitive metaphors are indeed the figures where the problem of the relationship between the content of thought ('what is said') and the medium of
thought ('how it is said') is the most acute. I shall try to outline the cognitive
topology of the metaphor of light and its cognates in a comparative perspective. The idea I would like to put forth, and to test, is simply this: although I
agree that metaphors are a general linguistic and cognitive phenomenon, I
suspect that their basic aspects and the way in which they are used in philosophical discourse may vary – in quite unexpected ways – according to the
linguistic structure and to the linguistic community in which these metaphorical expressions are embedded, and hence that the theories developed to cover
the phenomenon of metaphor are also dependent upon this community. More
precisely, what I want to suggest is that different attitudes to metaphor depend
upon different attitudes to language in the first place.

To answer this question, we shall turn to China and Greece, right at the
beginning of their philosophical traditions. We are fortunate enough to have at
our disposal the raw material we need, namely metaphorical thinking and
expressions centred around similar themes and used for the same purpose,
namely to try to explain the process of knowledge. Among these metaphors,
we shall focus on metaphors using the image of light and the mirror, insofar as
they are used to understand knowledge. It is important, for the project undertaken here, that we concentrate upon one and the same metaphorical domain.
Differences in attitude towards metaphorical expressions can only be tested
against a common background.

The most general trait of metaphor, namely explaining the unknown or the
more obscure in terms of what is better known, is amply illustrated in the way
expressions for seeing and sight have been used to paraphrase the phenomenon of knowledge. This appears immediately from the fact that most of the
standard expressions for knowing and understanding are derived from expressions whose homeland is the domain of sight. This remark is true for the
Greek as well as for the Chinese language. That many Chinese characters for
knowing are directly related to the semantic domain of seeing need not be
demonstrated at great length.

Ming[q] 'clear'; *an*[r] 'obscure, stupid'; *hun*[s] 'blind, confused'; *guang*[t] 'bright',
are some of the most obvious examples. Less apparent is the fact that expressions like *zhi*[u] 'to know' may refer directly to visual appearances, as in the
following example.

> *Wen hou bu yue. Zhi yu yan se.*[v]
> Duke Wen was not pleased; one could *know* it from the colour of his face.
> > (*Lüshichunqiu*, ch. 24.3)[41]

---

41   There are similar expressions in early Greek; see for example Homer, *Iliad* XV, 422:
      hektôr d' hôs enoêsen anepsion ophthalmoisin ('Hector knew through his own eyes that
      his cousin [...]').

The importance of the metaphor of light for expressing the idea of knowing and understanding in ancient Greek philosophy has been pointed out many times.[42] The metaphor itself is not an invention of the philosophers. It is already present in Homer as well as in early Greek poetry. The Greek *oida* (literally 'I have seen') means 'I know'. This word goes back to the Indo-European **weid*, from which the Latin *vidi* ('I have seen, I know') and the Greek *idea* and *eidos* are derived. *Noein* and *gignôskein*, two further Greek words for 'to know' are also rooted in the domain of sight.[43] *Theôrein*, an expression which has come to mean, 'contemplate', and from which 'theory' is derived, goes back to the noun *theôros*, whose primitive meaning is 'spectator'. These examples could easily be multiplied.[44]

For the purpose of this essay, it will be enough to point out that many expressions for 'knowing' and 'understanding' have originated in the domain of sight, from where they have been transposed, already at an early, pre-philosophical stage,[45] into the domain of knowing, and that these expressions have nearly lost their primitive meaning. The linguistic raw material for expressing the idea of knowledge and understanding through the metaphor of light and vision is thus basically the same in both cultures. This does not mean that the metaphor of light is the only metaphor used in this domain. The metaphor of 'grasping' is occasionally used, but also in both traditions.[46] The Chinese expression *jie*ʷ 'to connect' also relates to knowledge, as we shall see later.

Although the root-metaphor of light finds immediate philosophical ramifications, it would be rash to pretend that this metaphor *predetermines* the kind of philosophical theory derived from it. The defenders of the German *Licht-metaphysik* hold that there is a distinctive set of philosophical doctrines which try to express the link between being, truth and knowledge through the metaphor of light. Although it is admitted that this form of metaphysics has a historical development of its own, they do not seem to take into account the possibility that a different attitude to metaphor might also change its argumentative applications, especially in philosophical surroundings where the notions of being and truth do not appear to have the same value as in ancient Greek philosophy. The material from Chinese philosophy presented here will somewhat correct their claims.

My comparative investigation into the metaphorology of light will proceed from three case studies selected from the early Chinese philosophical literature.

---

42   See, for example, Saffrey 1990 (with bibliographical references); Tarrant 1960; von Fritz 1966: 52. The semantic link that exists in Homeric Greek between the notion of truth (*alêtheiê*) and light has been meticulously explored by Levet (1976: 106–23).

43   See Luther 1966; Snell 1978: 22–26 and 41–43; Onians 1998: 15.

44   In the Indo-European linguistic tradition, there is also a link between speech and the metaphor of light. The evidence is collected in Bremer 1974: 192–97. The word (*logos*) is conceived as 'revealing' or 'making clear' (*dêlôma*).

45   See also Bremer 1976: 8, where he declares that his goal has been to follow up a way of thinking that leads to *Lichtmetaphysik*, but still comes before philosophy and metaphysics.

46   See Luther 1966: 29 and Luther 1965: 483.

The first example comes from the writings of the Later Mohists; the second from chapter 2 of the *Zhuangzi*. The third example will be devoted to a peculiar aspect of the metaphor of light, namely to the image of the mirror.

The Later Mohists' Treatment of Metaphor

The purpose of my first example is to show the Later Mohists' use of figurative expressions, especially in the domain of seeing and perceiving. I shall start with a small corpus of Mohist theorems on knowledge. The purpose of this section from the *Mojing* (theorems A 3 to A 6) is to provide an analysis of all the different aspects involved in the phenomenon of knowledge. Here is the text.[47]

A 3
Zhi, cai ye.
Zhi ye zhe, suo yi zhi er bi zhi. Ruo ming.[x]
Knowledge (the faculty) is the capability.
Knowledge (the faculty): it is necessarily through it that knowledge comes about.[48]
(Like the eyesight.)

A 4
Lü qiu ye.
Lü ye zhe, yi qi zhi you qiu ye er bu bi de zhi. Ruo ni.[y]
Thinking (knowledge as an activity) is the seeking.
'Thinking': by means of one's knowledge (the faculty), one seeks something, but does not necessarily find it. (Like peering.)[49]

A 5
Zhi jie ye.
Zhi ye zhe, yi qi zhi guo wu er neng mao zhi. Ruo jian.[z]
Knowledge (act of knowledge) is the connecting.
Knowledge (act of knowledge): by means of one's knowledge, having passed the thing one is [still] able to describe it. (Like seeing.)

A 6
Zhi ming ye.

---

47   I follow the edition of Graham 1978. The translation is sometimes slightly changed.

48   One of the immediately preceding theorems of the *Mojing* has explained the difference between a necessary condition and a sufficient and necessary condition (theorem A 1, p. 263f. in Graham's edition). The concept of a necessary condition is also illustrated there by an example taken from the visual domain: 'The becoming manifest, the appearing (*xian* written by the Mohists with the man-radical) of a visual object is a necessary condition to its being seen.'

49   *Ni* 'look askance'. See also *Zhuangzi*, ch. 23, p. 153, *Zhuzi jicheng* edition; (Graham 1981: 190) where a critique of knowledge as an instance that tries to fix things is offered through the metaphor of staring at things.

Zhi ye zhe, yi qi zhi lun wu er qi zhi zhi zhe zhu. Ruo ming.[aa]
Knowledge (result) is clearness.
Knowledge (result): by means of it, in discourse about the thing one's knowledge (act of knowledge) of it is apparent. (Like clearness of sight.)

(Graham 1978: 266–69)

In these theorems, the Later Mohists try to pin down different senses of knowing:

1   Theorem A 3 puts forward the aspect of the *capacity* or the *faculty* (*cai*) of knowing; the graph is *zhi*.[ab]
2   Theorem A 4 insists on the *activity* of knowing: trying to know does not necessarily yield a result. It is merely exercising one's faculty of knowing.
3   Theorem A 5 describes the *act* of knowing, the hitting on some content of knowledge; the original Mohist graph is presumably *zhi*.[ac] The Mohists do not attach to this graph the standard meaning 'wisdom', but the more technical one 'act of knowing', a meaning not recognized or standardized in the classical Chinese written language.[50]
4   Theorem A 6 describes the final product of knowledge, the *achievement* or the *result* of the process: after pursuing and finding the objects of knowledge, one becomes wise, one has knowledge; the original Mohist graph is presumably *zhi*.[ad]

We would say, then, that *lü*[ae] 'thinking' really is the 'peering' of thought; and that wisdom is the 'clearness of sight' of the mind, to use standard metaphorical expressions.

Theorems A 3, A 5 and A 6 apparently try to define one and the same concept, namely *zhi* 'knowledge'. It is highly probable, as Graham has pointed out, that all three senses of *zhi* recognized by the Later Mohists were originally also graphically differentiated.[51] One notices indeed that the Mohist graph for 'wisdom' (*zhi*[af]), now written with the sun-radical (*zhi*[ag]), used to be written by them with the heart-radical.[52] So possibly the Later Mohists were trying to make special graphical as well as semantic distinctions, or trying to fix their semantic distinctions also graphically, but they had to use the metaphor of light to make clear what they meant.

More important for our purposes are the examples and comparisons used by the Later Mohists. Each one of these four theorems is indeed illustrated by a different expression for 'seeing'. The occurrence of *ming*[ah] in theorem A 3 as well as in theorem A 6 points again perhaps to a graphical distinction peculiar

---

50   One example of this special Mohist usage also survives in the *Lüshichunqiu*, ch. 16.3; see below. For other instances, see Graham 1978: 268–69.
51   Graham 1978: 266.
52   Proved by the graphic corruption of the original *zhi* written with the heart-radical underneath the graphically similar *shu*. See Hu Shi 1922: 87.

to Mohist circles, because *ming* has two senses, namely 'clear' and 'eyesight'.[53]

The point the Later Mohists want to make is this: 'knowing' is exactly parallel to 'seeing', under four different heads: there is a *capacity* for knowing and seeing; there is an *activity* of knowing and seeing; there is an *act* of knowing and seeing; there is a *result* of knowing and seeing.[54] It is possible, therefore, to explain knowing in terms of seeing, because both seem to obey to the same epistemological criteria. The Later Mohists simply assume that these criteria are evident in the case of seeing, and propose to take them over to the less well known domain of knowing, thus proceeding, like Hui Shi in the previous example, from the known to the unknown, in order to make the other person know. In short:

Capacity	capacity to know	*zhi*	capacity to see	*ming*[55]
Activity	seek to know	*lü*	peering	*ni*
Act	effectively know	*zhi*	see, perceive	*jian*
Result	be wise	*zhi*	clearness of sight	*ming*

But the main goal of the Later Mohists is not primarily to point out the similarities between seeing and knowing, and try to make people know the properties of knowing through the properties of seeing; they rather use this commonly recognized similarity already as a kind of argumentative platform, only to point out, in theorem A 5, that there is an important difference between knowing and seeing: seeing ceases with the disappearance of the object of sight; knowledge, however, stays (*jiu*[ai]) after the object of knowledge has disappeared. Moreover, proposition B 46 of the *Mohist Canon* clearly points out the difference between knowing and perceiving: what is perceived through the 'five roads' *wu lu*[aj] does not last, just as perceiving ceases with the disappearance of the corresponding object of sight.[56] Knowledge, however, lasts (*jiu*) beyond the disappearance of the object, as theorem A 5 had pointed out. The Later Mohists also use, in this context, another visual metaphor, namely the metaphor of the wall. They imagine an object placed behind a wall and ask what we know about this object when we only know its name. If this object is a horse, we know beforehand, *a priori* (*xian zhi*[ak]) that it has hooves and that it has a mane, but we do not know whether it is black or white.

The main function of the metaphor of light is therefore not to point to some new and hitherto unnoticed or unknown aspect of knowledge; the primary goal is to keep both apart, and prevent the 'natural' metaphor from doing its

---

53　See again Graham 1978: 267.
54　See also Raphals 1992: 59.
55　*Ming* here means 'eyesight' (capacity to see).
56　Graham 1978: 415.

job automatically. The metaphorical use of the expressions for light is rather already *presupposed*; the important aspect is the subsequent restriction of the transference of meaning operated by the metaphor. This, really, is the astonishing feature of the Later Mohists' use of the metaphor of light, and this usage is, in my opinion at least, unparalleled in the West. The Later Mohists are not, like Plato, inaugurating metaphors; they are not looking for new and original metaphorical formulations to explore an obscure domain.[57] They rather build on the metaphor of light and its standard applications to the phenomenon of knowledge, and take these as their starting-point. This then also means that the Later Mohists presuppose, right from the start, that the metaphor of light is deeply rooted in the Chinese language and is generally acknowledged, and that it is part of the semantic competence of their audience. Our evidence is the fact that the Later Mohists, to make their point that true knowledge has to have unchanging and stable objects as its reference points, had to *restrict* the application of the metaphor of light.

Their metaphor does not lead us from a crude material sense to a novel and spiritual one. Nor is it introduced as a new or surprising element. While Western metaphors generally induce the awakening of a dormant connection in the cross-domain mapping engine, the Later Mohists rather try to restate more precisely an already assumed mapping. Their argumentative technique hence comes close to the one also adopted by Mencius in his discussions with Gaozi (see above).

Unlike the Later Mohists, Plato has coined many new expressions, like 'the eye of the soul' (*to tês psukhês omma*) in *Republic* 533D or 'the ray of the soul' (*tên tês psukhês augên*) in *Republic* 540A, or 'the true light' (*alêthinon phôs*) in *Phaedo* 109E. Plato is even sometimes inconsistent in his application of the metaphor of light, as we have already noted.[58]

Zhuangzi's Negative Metaphorology

The purpose of my second example is to reconstruct part of the metaphorical apparatus used in the second chapter of the *Zhuangzi* to discuss the problem of conflicting opinions. It will appear, from the metaphorical traces left in this chapter, that the metaphor of light is there used in a self-destructing manner, just as logic is used in this same chapter to deride logic. It goes without saying that a textual game of this complexity can only be played if its metaphorical rules are already familiar to the reader. This also presupposes, just as in the preceding example, that the reader is already familiar with the metaphor of

---

57   Tarrant 1960: 185: 'Plato's metaphors of light are used to denote the standpoint of the percipient subject. In another type of application they convey the quality of the object contemplated [...].'

58   It is therefore also easily understandable that metaphors once created by philosophers tend to sink into oblivion, as for example Parmenides' use of the metaphor of the sun and the eye to qualify the nature of his 'being'. See the brilliant study by Destrée (1998).

light and its use in representing the phenomenon of knowledge. My purpose, again, is to show that this metaphor must be deeply rooted in the linguistic competence and that Zhuangzi uses it, just like the Later Mohists, as a platform for his argumentation, and not, like Plato, as a medium for formulating new insights.

Zhuangzi's problem, as I reconstruct it, is this. How is it possible to use a standard metaphor in an oblique way, that is, to use it to show just the opposite of what it means normally? We have seen, in the previous example, that the Later Mohists have used the metaphor of light in its conventional acceptation, building upon the metaphorical competence of their audience. If Zhuangzi conforms to this use of the metaphor of light, that is, presupposes the standard identification 'knowledge equals brightness', but wants to destroy at the same time this standard conception of knowledge, the only way for him to do so is to use the metaphor in a self-destructing manner. This means that Zhuangzi has to show that light itself may also generate darkness and obscurity. Zhuangzi indeed succeeds in deconstructing the metaphor by using a conventional tool, like Mencius, namely, the opposition between natural and artificial properties. He wants to show that too much knowledge leads to ignorance, just as too much light (in one place) leads to darkness (in another place). It is quite remarkable to see that Zhuangzi here still exploits the standard value of the metaphor of light and its contrast between natural and artificial sources of light.

It can be shown, I believe, that the rhetorical effect Zhuangzi produces through the metaphor of light could hardly have been obtained if the standard interpretation of it was not already presupposed. The normal connotations of the metaphor of light point to the quality of the acquired knowledge: light has to be thrown on the object of knowledge; the more, the better. The knowing subject has to be enlightened; darkness and mist removed from his mind. The chances for knowing thus seem to be directly related to the intensity of the source of light.

Zhuangzi wants to show quite the opposite. But even here, his use of the negative version of this metaphor is not entirely creative, because it already exists as a popular saying:

> If a fire lights up one quarter of a room, most part of the room is dark.
>
> (*Lüshichunqiu*, ch. 26.1)

Note that this metaphor uses an artificial source of light, an element that will also be very important for Zhuangzi. The metaphorical use of the torch for representing knowledge is also attested, as the following text shows.

> Even if Duke Huan did not speak, [what he meant] was as clear as a torch lit in the darkness of night.
>
> (*Lüshichunqiu*, ch. 18.3)

We find the image also in later Daoist schools. Zhuang Zun, in his commentary on the *Daodejing*, still uses the same image of the torch: 'The wise man travelling in daylight depends on the sunlight available to all, while the fool insists on carrying his own torch.'[59]

When a torch is lit in a room, some parts of the room may become darker than they used to be before. I think that precisely this paradoxical theme is developed in large parts of chapter 2. It is already adumbrated in the first chapter of the *Zhuangzi* (with a parallel in the *Lüshichunqiu*, ch. 22.5):

> Yao resigned the Empire to Hsü Yu, saying: 'When the sun or the moon is up, if the torch fires are not put out, aren't we taking too much trouble to light the world? When the timely rain falls, if we go on flooding the channels, aren't we working too hard to water the fields? While you, sir, are in your place the Empire is in order, yet here I still am in the seat of honour. In my own eyes I do not deserve it; let me make you a present of the Empire.'
>
> (*Zhuangzi*, ch. 1, p. 3, *Zhuzi jicheng* edition; translation Graham 1981: 45)

This text contrasts natural with artificial light. Zhuangzi uses a metaphor that shows the superiority of the natural over artificial light, just as Mencius had tried to show that the natural properties of water are stronger than its 'man-made' and artificial properties. The same metaphor occurs elsewhere in the second chapter.

> Therefore formerly Yao asked Shun.
> 'I wish to smite Tsung, K'uai and Hsü-ao. Why is it that I am not at ease on the south-facing throne?'
> 'Why be uneasy', said Shun, 'if these three still survive among the weeds? Formerly ten suns rose side by side and the myriad things were illumined, and how much more by a man in whom the Power is brighter than the sun!'
>
> (*Zhuangzi*, ch. 2, p. 14, *Zhuzi jicheng* edition; translation Graham 1981: 58)

For Yao, to subdue these three remaining places would be the same as trying to be brighter than the greatest possible brightness, and hence add superfluous artificial brightness to the natural one.

Zhuangzi's strategy, in the second chapter, is to play off the metaphor of light against the metaphor of light. He looks at the metaphor just the other way round, and explores its negative values: what is normally enlightening at times may become dazzling; if there is competition between several, rival, sources of light, some areas will afterwards be darker than other areas, and light will thus, indirectly though, also be responsible for darkness and shade. It is interesting to note that Zhuangzi, as his goal is to show the negative sides of knowledge, also uses the negative, that is, the artificial side of the 'natural' metaphor of light.

---

59   Quoted from Nylan and Sivin 1987: 56.

Let us comment upon several key passages of this second chapter, where Zhuangzi tries to reflect upon the notion of contradiction, especially as far as it applies to debates between rival philosophical schools. Zhuangzi's deconstruction of the notion of *bian*[al] 'debate', 'dialectic' is worth noting. For Zhuangzi, everyone argues from his own viewpoint. Occupying different positions in space, time, or simply in society or in interest groups is a sufficient condition for also having different opinions. But each of these opinions is right, and is unconditionally right, although only within its proper sphere. It is meaningless, therefore, to think that one point of view is superior to or better than any other point of view or that there is some vantage point that could be superior to all other points of view. To convey this idea, I believe that Zhuangzi uses the image of one torch (that is, one philosophical position) trying to be brighter than another, or of trying to 'overshadow' another torch, or of trying to light up the large, dark room all by itself.[60] I shall try to show that all the metaphors of light used in chapter 2 proceed from precisely this image.

> The brilliant display (*zhang*[am]) of 'that's it' and 'that's not' is the reason why the Way is diminished (*kui*[an]).
>
> (*Zhuangzi*, ch. 2, p. 11, *Zhuzi jicheng* edition)

The expression *zhang* 'brilliant display' refers to the dazzling light of isolated torches, which try to illuminate all by themselves, but forgetting that they are limited in their brilliance not only by their 'sister-torches', but also by the limits inherent in artefacts.[61] Note that *kui* 'diminish' also connects indirectly to the metaphor of light, because it is used to describe the waning of the moon.

Perfect knowledge is possible, but only individually in a limited area. The more this area is illumined, the more the surrounding places become dark, not only for an observer from outside, but for the person illuminating.

> Chao Wen strumming on the zither, Music-master K'uang propped on his stick, Hui Shih leaning on the sterculia, had the three men's knowledge much farther to go? They were all men in whom it reached a culmination, and therefore was carried on too late a time. It was only in being preferred by them that what they knew about differed from an Other; because they preferred it they wished to illumine it, but they illumined it without the Other being illumined, and so the end of it all was the darkness [*mei*[ao]] of chop logic.
>
> (*Zhuangzi*, ch. 2, p. 12, *Zhuzi jicheng* edition; translation Graham 1981: 54–55)

This passage shows again how the illuminating function of knowledge ends up in obscurity if it tries to illuminate by violent and artificial means. Every

---

60   At the end of the forged chapter 4 of the *Gongsunlongzi*, we also find the theme of *liang ming* 'both shine' (said of ruler and minister contending with each other).
61   See also *Daodejing*, ch. 22 and ch. 24.

kind of knowledge is relative to time and place; only the sage knows how to assign its proper place to each piece of knowledge.

> By what is the Way *hidden*, that there should be a genuine or a false? By what is saying *darkened*, that sometimes 'That's it' and sometimes 'That's not'? Wherever we walk how can the Way be absent? Whatever the standpoint how can saying be unallowable? The Way is *hidden* by formation of the lesser, saying is *darkened* by its foliage and flowers. And so we have the 'That's it, that's not' of Confucians and Mohists. If you wish to affirm what they deny and deny what they affirm, by affirming what they deny and by denying what they affirm, the best means is *illumination*.
>
> (*Zhuangzi*, ch. 2, p. 9, *Zhuzi jicheng* edition;
> translation Graham 1981: 52, modified)

The strange formula *yi ming*[ap] then probably means 'let the natural light fall on it to light up only what naturally should be illuminated.' The difference between on the one hand the natural light of the sun or the moon and a torch on the other, is that the intensity of light decreases or increases as we approach the torch or move away from it, whereas natural light is uniformly distributed everywhere.

But there is perhaps a rhetorical figure, namely a pun, behind the formula *yi ming*. *Ming* is an expression used by the dialecticians, especially the Later Mohists, who define dialectic as the capacity to bring the difference between 'that's it' and 'that's not' to light (*ming shi fei*[aq]).[62] But the expression also means 'clearness of sight' and 'sagacity'. The philosophical debates between Mohists, Confucians and other schools simply disrupt the continuity of natural light and bring, with artificial light, also artificial darkness.

The metaphor of light and of overshadowing pervades this whole paragraph. The Way is hidden, darkened, 'overshadowed' *yin*,[ar] because there are now too many rival sources of light.[63] The dazzling light of bright torches prevents us now from seeing the less well illuminated spots and hence darkens the place.

The meaning of this metaphor is not, as a Western interpretation would suggest, a strife between the forces of darkness and ignorance against illumination and truth. It is rather a problem of perspective, because the primary meaning of *yin* is the shady side of a valley, which implies that the sunlight is there, but taken away by the other side of the valley. There is no absolute

---

62   Graham 1978: 473–75 (NO 6).
63   I disagree with Graham's interpretation of this passage. Graham writes: 'There is an unobtrusive metaphor which recurs throughout the chapter, that of throwing everything open to the light. It is assumed that when we judge between alternatives we turn the light on what we select as "It" and leave everything which is "Other" in darkness; it is in the wordless illumination which discredits all distinctions that the whole world is open to the light.' (Graham 1969–1970: 149) Darkness is not a matter of not turning the light upon what we select. Darkness, rather, comes about through an excess of illumination.

darkness confined to one side at the expense of the other. Darkness is a relative concept.[64]

Zhuangzi here wants to show that the metaphor of light, if it is used to signify truth, is a dangerous one. The brightness of one source of light is only possible at the expense of the darkening of another one. The image of brightness therefore unerringly calls for its opposite, namely darkness. If truth really is comparable to the brightest argument, then all losing or inferior arguments and positions are rejected into obscurity, while they happen to be only less bright than their rivals, or farther away from the person who listens to them.

But Zhuangzi's idea is that the brightness of an argument depends on how close the listener or spectator is to the source of light, that is, the particular, but still relative, position occupied by the person who argues. One torch may be brighter than another one, but only in a small, limited area.

The sage is capable of seeing the light, the natural light, and hence the portion of truth, there is in every particular position.[65] Every dialectical position and opinion has got some truth in it; the error is in trying to magnify the natural light of one's own position by artificial means and refusing to see the natural light that is also contained in rival positions.

> If there is disputation, this shows that something had not been seen.
>   (*Zhuangzi*, ch. 2, p. 14, *Zhuzi jicheng* edition)

Note also that the technical term for disputation *bian*[as] already holds within itself a visual metaphor, because the basic meaning of *bian* is 'to tell one thing from another', that is, to see the differences. The sage tries to see things 'in their natural light'.

> What is allowable is at the same time also unallowable; what is unallowable is at the same time allowable. To take a 'that's it' as one's criterion is also taking a 'that's not' as one's criterion; to take a 'that's not' as one's criterion is also taking a 'that's it' as one's criterion. This is why the sage never makes the beginning and lets things reflect (*zhao*[at]) in Heaven. This attitude is also taking a 'that's it' as one's criterion.
>   (*Zhuangzi*, ch. 2, p. 9, *Zhuzi jicheng* edition)

The expression 'lets things reflect (*zhao*) in Heaven' means that the sage tries to gain a vantage point. If he is able to judge things from the viewpoint of what in them is from Heaven, and does not move, pushed by his own interest, nearer to one thing than to another, he will be able to see the natural light

---

64   For another example of this kind, see *Lüshichunqiu* ch. 21.3, beginning, and also Hanfei's famous expression *you yin jian yang* 'from the shady observe the brilliant' (chapters 7 and 8). The ruler posts himself at the shady side, where he cannot be seen, but from where he can more easily observe his subjects exposed in the open daylight.

65   This is also the position of the later, so-called Syncretists, expressed at the beginning of chapter 33 of the *Zhuangzi*.

reflected by the things in a vast continuum, instead of the artificial, bright, disorderly light things mirror back when they are randomly, but violently lit up by shifting torches. The same image can also be found at the end of chapter 58 of the *Daodejing*: *shi yi shengren ... guang er bu yao.*[au] 'Therefore the sage [...] shines but does not dazzle.' In chapter 4 of the same text, we have the expression *he qi guang*[av] '[the Way] ... evens out its glare'.

Zhuangzi nevertheless would concede that this vantage point, however encompassing, is just as limited and relative as any other, particular, human view of the nature of things. But the sum of the dim reflections of the things is not brighter than the natural light of the sun itself and does not pretend to be brighter. It is perhaps possible, also, to interpret the obscure phrase *bao guang*[aw] (*Zhuangzi*, ch. 2, p. 14, *Zhuzi jicheng* edition) within the context of this same metaphor, and read it as 'cover up the light', which does indeed make sense in the context of the metaphor as I have reconstructed it. Here are a few more traces of the metaphor.

Ming jun zhi guo er hui.[ax]
The enlightened ruler, in governing the state, dims his light [...].
(Shen Buhai, fragment 4; Creel 1974: 353)

I have shown that the metaphor of light pervades large parts of the second chapter of the *Zhuangzi*. We have met the expressions *yin*,[ay] *ming*,[az] *jian*,[ba] *zhao*,[bb] *zhang*[bc] and *mei*.[bd] These expressions are, so to say, the metaphorical traces Zhuangzi's vision has left behind. But none of these expressions, it has to be noted, is in itself unusual, original or surprising in classical Chinese. Zhuangzi builds on the fact that the metaphor of light already belongs to the unconscious conceptual make-up of his audience, but he uses it to deconstruct the metaphor of light, by reversing its standard metaphorical meaning. The composition of the second chapter is at least partially due to this rhetorical technique.[66]

Zhuangzi is generally considered as a highly original thinker with an idiosyncratic imagery and style. But this example shows that Zhuangzi's writing also exploits the more common resources of the Chinese language and its metaphorology.

The Metaphor of the Mirror

The third example will be devoted to a peculiar aspect of the metaphor of light, namely to the image of the mirror. In ancient China, the metaphor of the mirror appears basically in two forms: the mirror itself, usually symbolizing

---

66 This example also warns us to be very careful with literary genres in such contexts. Raphals (1994) has indeed shown that the Western opposition between philosophy and poetry is not as strict in ancient China as it is in the West.

the mind, but also the mirror image, reflected in the mirror or sent to the mirror by various objects.[67] The first Chinese philosophers use both of these aspects in their efforts to provide a model for the mechanism of knowing and also for its defects.

The metaphor of the mirror is also used in ancient Greek philosophy, by Plato and Democritus. But the early Greek authors always use this metaphor for its *subjective* properties.[68] Plato uses mirror images to contrast true objects of knowledge with mere imitations and imperfect copies of it. He uses this metaphor to point out the ontological gap between the archetypal form and its sublunary copies. Human courage thus is but a faint copy of the eternal idea of courage. A mirror image is less valuable than its original for the simple reason that the image is ontologically dependent upon its prototype. Moreover, mirror images systematically distort the original, by inverting left and right, for example.[69]

In book 10 of the *Republic*, where Plato works at the exclusion of poetry from philosophical discourse, the notion of imitation is severely criticized. Three levels of reality are established: we have, first, the *idea* of a bed (independent of the human mind), then the *physical object* itself (created by a craftsman who takes the idea as his model) and finally the *image* of the bed (typically produced by the painter who in turn imitates the craftsman).[70] In this context, the metaphor of the mirror is brought into play to illustrate the notion of imitation in its two senses: the ontological dependence from the original and the deformation of the original. Imitation, for Plato, means necessarily distortion, because the painter, if he really wants to produce a good imitation, must not reproduce the true dimensions of the object he is representing, but rather must adapt these to the point of view of the spectator.[71]

We must not forget that the metaphor of the mirror has been used above all in modern Western philosophy and literature for the purpose of emphasizing the *subjective* aspects of knowledge.[72] The function of the metaphor of the mirror is to explain the possibility of subjective knowledge, that is, cases where one and the same object is perceived ('mirrored') in different

---

67   This aspect has been explored by Oshima (1983). But Oshima has not noticed that the metaphor of the mirror is part of a much larger metaphor-web; neither does his analysis mention the opposition between the natural and the artificial aspects of mirror images. See also the classical study by Demiéville (Demiéville 1947) where the difference between the pre-Buddhist and the Buddhist use of the metaphor of the mirror is pointed out.

68   See also Wunenburger 1997: 168f.

69   *Theaetetus* 193C; see also *Sophist* 239D and *Republic* 510A. I am aware of only one example of an objective use of the metaphor of the mirror in *Theaetetus* 206D.

70   The ontological dependency of imitations is often advocated in the *Republic;* see, for example, 532B and 510A, 402B; *Sophist* 239D.

71   *Sophist* 235D–236A.

72   A typical use of this metaphor is made by Leibniz (Monadology, para. 56), who compares each individual monad to a 'living mirror' which reflects within itself a complete picture of the world, but different from the picture reflected in the other mirrors. On the modern treatment of the metaphor of the mirror, see Konersmann 1991.

ways, or even distorted, by different knowing subjects, whose mind acts as a mirror.

It is worth noting, right from the start, that this contrast between objective and subjective knowledge seems to be totally absent from classical Chinese philosophy. The first Chinese philosophers do not share Plato's ontological preoccupation either. The two main Western uses of the metaphor of the mirror (subjective knowledge and ontologically inferior objects) being totally absent from classical Chinese philosophy, it is then not surprising to notice that the first Chinese philosophers never use the image of a *distorting* mirror.[73] Even if the mirror itself is an artefact, the metaphor never stresses the artificial and man-made aspects over the natural ones.[74] Take the following text from chapter 5 of the *Zhuangzi*.

> If a mirror is bright, it wards off stains; if the stains remain, it's that the mirror isn't bright. If you keep company long enough with a man of worth, you cannot go wrong.
>
> (*Zhuangzi*, ch. 5, p. 32, *Zhuzi jicheng* edition)

A well-polished mirror wards off stains; water-drops do not attach to it. The company of a sage 'polishes' the mirror of the student's mind, so that it becomes more and more receptive. Short as it is, this text nevertheless discloses one fundamental assumption of classical Chinese philosophy: the student's mind is, in principle, capable of reaching the same degree of perfection as the sage's mind. The difference between the student and the sage is explicable in terms of more or less well-polished mirrors, not in terms of fundamentally different or even qualitatively inferior, or mischievously distorting mirrors. The sage is thus not fundamentally different from the student, or other people.[75] The originally received mirror is flawless.

This principle of the theoretical equality of all knowing persons also underlies the basic model for a theory of knowledge: as the object of knowledge is the same, and since there are no basic – or at least no irrecoverable – differences between the various knowing subjects, any defect in the process of knowing, and every difference in the quality of what is known must be explained through the notion of artificial and accidental obstacles to knowing. These obstacles are elements intervening between the knowing subject and the object of knowledge, like good or bad conditions of light, or simply other objects screening off the knowing subject from his object, but never intrinsic defects of the knowing subject. This aspect is further confirmed by a text from the *Lüshichunqiu*.

---

73 See, for example, ch. 20.5 of the *Lüshichunqiu*, for a good example for the objectivity of mirror images in ancient Chinese thought.

74 In many cases, the natural aspect of mirror images prevails, inasmuch as the reflecting medium is the even surface of water!

75 This belief is also upheld by Mencius and by Xunzi in the moral domain: both declare that every man has the capacity to become a Yao or a Shun.

The human eye perceives through reflection. Perceiving an object lying in the dark is in no way different from not perceiving at all. Men are similar as far as the conditions of reflection and darkness are concerned, but different as to what each one of them is able to make contact with or not. A soldier standing in the dark does not reflect the light; this is why he is not perceived. That which lies in the dark, the eye has no means of coming into contact with it. Not coming into contact with an object and nevertheless claiming to perceive it, this is self-contradictory.

It is exactly the same with knowledge [*zhi*^{be}].[76] The means whereby knowledge is obtained or not, are the same; but that which each one is able to make contact with or not, is different. The wise can grasp events that are still far away; the fool can only grasp what lies already right before him.

(Lüshichunqiu, ch. 16.3)

The burden of this text is to explain the difference between the sage and the fool. The task is complicated through the typically Chinese presupposition that the sage and the fool have the same basic physical and psychological make-up. The sage, therefore, has no mysterious powers that would put him above other men. A common tenet of classical Chinese philosophy says precisely that everybody can become a Yao or a Shun. The difficulty, in the table of correspondences given below, is that the equivalent terms for *zhao*^{bf} 'reflect' and *ming*^{bg} 'blind' (in the sense of 'not reflecting') are not given for the domain of knowing. But this lacuna is easily filled, because we know from many other texts, that the sage is able to perceive and interpret the small, nearly imperceptible signs that indicate future events, whereas the fool is incapable of noticing them.

mu	eye	[*xin*]	mind
zhao	reflecting	?	
ming	not reflecting, blind	?	
jian	seeing	*zhi*	knowing
bu jian	not seeing	*bu zhi*	not knowing
jie	making contact	*jie*	making contact
bu jie	not making contact	*bu jie*	not making contact
[*ming*]	clearness of sight	*zhi*	intelligence
[*ming*]	blindness	*yu*	stupidity

The metaphor of the mirror is also used in ethical domains, to describe the perfect course of action a sage takes.

---

76   *Zhi* here means the act of knowledge, not wisdom; see above.

The utmost man uses the heart like a mirror; he does not escort things as they go or welcome them as they come, he responds and does not store. Therefore he is able to adjust himself to things without being harmed by them.

(Zhuangzi, ch. 7, p. 51, *Zhuzi jicheng* edition;
translation Graham 1981: 98, slightly changed)

'The sage does not use the heart to plan ahead, only to reflect the perfect image of the situation before he responds. Like a mirror, it reflects only the present, does not "store" the past experience which traps in obsolete attitudes', comments Graham.[77] Perfect knowledge and perfect action are one. Here, too, the image of the mirror is used for one of its natural properties, namely to reflect instantaneously, without adding anything of its own to the picture and without delaying its response.

Perturbations of the reflecting activity of the mirror are explained by natural causes, such as dust on a bronze mirror, or mud on the surface of water.

Confucius said: 'None of us finds his mirror in flowing water, we find it in still water.'

(Zhuangzi, ch. 5, p. 32, *Zhuzi jicheng* edition;
translation Graham 1981: 77)

And again:

When the sage is still, it is not that he is still because he says 'It is good to be still'; he is still because none among the myriad things is sufficient to disturb his heart. If water is still, its clarity reflects the hairs of beard and eyebrow, its evenness is plumb with the carpenter's level; the greatest of craftsmen take their standard from it. If mere water clarifies when it is still, how much more the stillness of the quintessential-and-daemonic, the heart of the sage! It is the reflector of heaven and earth, the mirror of the myriad things.

(Zhuangzi, ch. 13, p. 81, *Zhuzi jicheng* edition;
translation Graham 1981: 259)

Passion is an obstacle to a correct mirroring of the facts. Note, again, that passion does not distort the human mirror, it only stains it, just like an even surface of muddy water – often compared to the human mind when stirred up by the passions – is only accidentally and temporarily deprived of its original, perfect reflecting powers.[78] The mirror returns naturally to its original, perfect state. The epistemological contact between the human mind and the nature of things thus never breaks off in ancient Chinese thought. The mirror never gives of itself a wrong or distorted picture of reality. It may give an incomplete picture, due to incomplete mirroring of facts, or due to accidental damage to its mirroring surface.

---

77   Graham 1989: 192. The metaphor of the mirror also occurs in the second chapter of the second essay of the 'Four canons of the Yellow Emperor', the *Huangdi sijing*, discovered in Mawangdui in 1973; see Yu Mingguang 1993: 92; Chang and Feng 1998: 146–47: 'For people, he investigated them just as a mirror reflects them'.
78   See, for example, *Lüshichunqiu*, ch. 1.2; *Daodejing*, ch. 10.

Even Xunzi, a philosopher who insists heavily on learning and on the trans-formation of man's primitive nature, still uses the same basic metaphor of the mirror as Zhuangzi. Xunzi also invokes the natural reflecting properties of the mirror to explain the perceptual defects generated by temporary disturbances of the mirroring surface, the mind.

> Hence man's heart may be compared to a pan of water. If you lay it level and do not disturb it, the muddy settles below and the transparent above, so that it is adequate to see whiskers and eyebrows and discern the pattern of them. But if a faint breeze passes over, and the muddy is stirred up below and the transparent blurred above, you cannot perceive even the general outline correctly. It is the same with the heart. Therefore we guide it by pattern, nurture it by clarifying, and if no thing upsets it, it is adequate to fix the right alternative and the wrong and decide the doubtful and confusable. But if the smallest thing tugs at it, then the correct is distorted outside and the heart upset within, so that it is inadequate to decide between the broadest patterns.
>
> (*Xunzi*, ch. 21, p. 267, *Zhuzi jicheng* edition;
> translation Watson 1963: 131–32)

The metaphor of the mirror is here used exclusively in the sense of the natural properties and the natural defects of mirror images; Plato, on the contrary, uses mirror images to illustrate cases of systematic and irrecoverable distor-tion. So here again, the very use of the metaphor mirrors back the attitude towards knowledge, and hence also to cognitive metaphors.

Striking also is the fact that this metaphor of water and mirroring is well codified in ancient China. Its basic meaning does not change between its presumably early use by Confucius and its subsequent variants in the *Huainanzi*, the *Xunzi* and the *Zhuangzi*. In ancient Greece, it would have been utterly impossible to use a second time the metaphor of the river in the same sense as Heraclitus had already done, whereas it would presum-ably have been impossible, in ancient China, to use the metaphor of water and mirroring in a sense different from the one Confucius had inaugu-rated.[79]

There is no forced way that would lead us from the metaphor of light to only one well-defined metaphysical theory, or even to any metaphysical theory at all. Truth, being and knowledge are not necessarily tied to the meta-phor of light in the way the defenders of the *Lichtmetaphysik* would have liked it. If the role the metaphor of light plays in the Western tradition is more impor-tant, this is not due to the primary choice of one root-metaphor over another. As the philosophical use of metaphors already expresses a basic attitude towards the problem of knowledge, the ideal of knowledge that the philosopher seeks to obtain is mirrored back in the very choice of the developments he gives to his metaphors.

---

79   In the *Poetics*, Aristotle even declares that the faculty of inventing good metaphors is a natural gift, that is unique, and that cannot be learnt from others (1459a).

In ancient Greece, the metaphor of light depicts the eternal strife between light and darkness. Light tries to overcome darkness, just like rational thinking tries to overcome the dark areas of meaning by enlightening formulae. New light has to be thrown all the time, hence also the endless task of always inventing new metaphors and always giving new developments to root-metaphors.[80] Plato eventually enlarges the Greek philosophical vocabulary and confers through his metaphors new meanings to standard Greek expressions. The terms *idea* and *eidos*, for example, had not been used in a philosophical sense before Plato.

Ancient Chinese thinkers, on the other hand, use metaphors in a much more conventional way. Different thinkers seem to be well aware of the basic developments of the root-metaphors and largely agree as to their use in disputation. This is even true for Zhuangzi, when he reverses the standard use of the metaphor of light, because this move is only possible on the assumption that the standard meaning of the metaphor is well known.

Conclusion

In both cultures metaphors had been used for *cognitive* purposes. The question we have to answer, therefore, is how metaphors can convey knowledge. It is well known that the first Greek philosophers do not attach much credit to language and adopt, in general, a pessimistic attitude to its cognitive powers. Anaxagoras, Parmenides, Empedocles and Democritus note time and again that language is misleading.[81] This general mistrust in language is counterbalanced by an 'inflation' of metaphor: if language is fundamentally insufficient to grasp reality, the philosopher acquires, so to say, the right to use many, often tentative formulations in order to go beyond language. Unable to reach his aim with one, well adjusted shot, the Western philosopher tries to shoot, instead, as many times as he can, in the direction of his target, and then invites his spectators to guess where the target was from the scattered arrows lying around that had missed it.

This also gives us a clue towards a solution to our initial paradox: if language is considered to be an insufficient and untrustworthy means of communication, the philosopher will try to step over its boundaries and look for extra-linguistic standards – Plato's ideas, or Democritus' atoms – or try to overcome the limits of language through metaphorical inventions. The metaphors of the first Greek philosophers clearly point *beyond* language, but only because the normal ways of speaking are thought to be rationally insufficient. Metaphors, therefore, are not a legitimate means of expression in the mind of

---

80   A list of Greek philosophical neologisms related to the metaphor of light can be found in Luther 1966: 28.

81   Parmenides, fragment B 8 DK = 296 KRS; Anaxagoras, fragment B 17 DK = 469 KRS; Empedocles, fragment B 8 DK = 350 KRS.

the first Greek philosophers, but it is the only one available to them. The very way metaphors are used by the Greek philosophers is already witness to their basic attitude of mistrust in language. Metaphors, for them, are necessarily an indirect way of acquiring knowledge.

There is, thus, a curious dual aspect in early Greek metaphorology: the strategy of the multiplication of metaphorical expressions proves that the philosopher judges none of them sufficient alone to convey his true meaning; but the profusion of metaphors should nevertheless help to bring us nearer to true, non-linguistic and conceptual, knowledge by a kind of maximum metaphorical coverage. Even if this attitude leads in the end to an inflation of metaphor, the link of these metaphors to the 'gold reserve' of real meaning cannot be disrupted. Metaphors may not be a valid instrument of knowledge, but many metaphors are needed to show it. Hui Shi uses one metaphor to show that metaphors are indispensable to argumentation, whereas Plato uses many metaphors to show that we should not really use them!

The first Chinese philosophers adhere to what may, conversely, be called epistemological optimism.[82] They are confident in the language they use; even for Zhuangzi, as we have seen above, words are compared to nets catching fish: quite an optimistic picture indeed. The possibilities of the net coming up empty, or of its meshes being too wide, or of the breaking of the net are perhaps taken into account, but not the thought that the net might not after all be the best way of catching fish.

There is another, much more striking difference between the philosophical uses of metaphor in Greece and China: whereas the cross-domain mapping is ontologically insignificant in ancient Greece, the parallelisms Chinese metaphors point to are always highly significant. In ancient Greece, the role of metaphor is, precisely, to *dissociate* ontological levels by moving our attention from a crude material sense a novel spiritual one; in ancient China, on the other hand, the basic function of metaphors, namely to link one domain to another, is also exploited to show that there is an ontological connection between these different domains: different domains are shown to take a share in one and the same nature. This strategy validates and justifies the metaphor and gives it its argumentative power.

In other words, the first Chinese philosophers stress the *epiphoric* element of metaphor, that is, conventional metaphors that have long lost their disturbing impact. The epiphoric element (so-called 'dead metaphors') is opposed to the *diaphoric* element, that is, truly new and disturbing, challenging metaphors.[83]

We have also seen that the first Chinese philosophers are very sensitive to the contrast between natural and artificial aspects inherent in root-metaphors. But if metaphors are considered as valid cognitive tools, good metaphors are those that are able fully to match natural and spontaneous processes;

---

82   For this notion, see Metzger 1985–1987. See also Keightley 1990.
83   For the expressions 'diaphoric' and 'epiphoric', see MacCormac 1985.

metaphors depicting artificial and man-made circumstances therefore generally act as negative cases or even as counter-instances. Cognitive metaphors
of this type create their own framework by the systematic exploitation of the
contrast between good, natural, self-explaining qualities and bad, artificial,
reducible qualities. Philosophical options laying stress on the transformation of reality by man therefore reverse this strategy and tend to confer
greater value to illustrations from the human, man-made, domain.[84]

Part of the technical terminology devised by Western theoreticians to
analyse the phenomenon of knowledge is itself relative to Western conceptions of metaphor. The distinction between literal and figurative meaning is,
cross-culturally speaking, untenable, as modern discussions on metaphor
have come to teach us anyway. The notion of literal meaning in Western
philosophy seems to act as a barrier to the complete inflation of metaphors, as
a 'currency-refuge' to the arbitrary multiplication of figurative expressions.
Literal meaning should act – though only symbolically – as a criterion for
valid metaphor creation, for there must be some criterion for deciding
between good and bad metaphors: good metaphors lead to literal meaning.
Literal meaning is the target, while the metaphors are the arrows. Literal
meaning acts as a Platonic model (*tou onomatos eidos*, 'the model of the
name', *Cratylus* 390A5) to which the creator of a metaphor 'looks up'
(*Cratylus* 389B2; 389D6) before coining his new expression.

Perelman had already noticed that the distinction between literal and figurative meaning is not a hard fact, but a conceptual splitting that comes up within
metaphorical argumentation itself.[85] The very notion of literal meaning implies
a critical attitude towards the use of metaphors in argumentation. But if there is,
as in ancient China, already an agreement, not only on the principle of argumentation through metaphors itself, but on the suitable type of metaphors as well,
the notions of literal and figurative meaning become epistemologically
superfluous.[86]

We thus seem to be driven to the conclusion that Chinese is a wholly
'unmetaphorical' language.[87] At this point, however, we should pay attention
to an important peculiarity of the Chinese language. We really have to work
with two different codes, the spoken and the written language. Rosemont has
put forth very convincing arguments for what he calls the 'uniqueness' thesis
of the Chinese language.[88] The Chinese written language is not, as is widely
assumed for other, especially alphabetic, languages, a symbol system that is

---

84   A good example is *Lüshichunqiu* ch. 18.7. To illustrate the idea that man-made tools, like
     cauldrons, can be successfully used for many different purposes, Hui Shi counters Bai
     Gui's analogy of the 'regular use' of a cauldron with an analogy stressing the extraordi-
     nary – but no less important – use of the same cauldron.
85   Perelman and Olbrechts-Tyteca 1970: 549.
86   Derrida went even further and tried to show that metaphors are a philosophical problem
     only within classical Western metaphysics. The problem of metaphor, for him, is an
     invention of the philosophers. See Derrida 1971.
87   For a defence of this position, see Pauline Yu 1987.

derived from the spoken language, but a system which has its own rules of generating and communicating meaning.

The subject matter of the Chinese philosophy of language is the *written* code. The spoken Chinese language, with its numerous homophones, hardly permits any serious philosophical reflection on language, as the following example may show. Since the characters *ren*[bh] ('man') and *ren*[bi] ('benevolent') are homophones, sentences like the following are only interpretable in their written form:

> *Zi yue: Ren er bu ren, ru li he? Ren er bu ren, ru yue he?*[bj]
> The Master said, 'What can a man do with the rites who is not benevolent? What can a man do with music who is not benevolent?'
>
> (*Lunyu* 3.3; translation by Lau 1979: 67)

The character for 'benevolence' is composed of two elements, 'man' (*ren*[bk]) and 'two' (*er*[bl]), and 'benevolence' (*ren*[bm]) could then indeed be viewed as a metaphorical extension of *ren*[bn] 'man', signifying a man in the company of fellow men.

The interesting question to ask here is whether this unique code also bears in itself a special and unique attitude to metaphor and to the creation of new meanings. During the formative period of the Chinese writing system, the radicals had indeed been an important way to generate new characters. Take a series of cognate characters from Karlgren's *Grammata serica recensa*, for example the series 362 and 416:

tian[bo] = field
dian[bp] (man and field) = cultivate
tian[bq] (field and animal) = hunt

gen[br] = resist
gen[bs] (tree and resist) = root
gen[bt] (man and resist) = disobedient

We come to notice that radicals may be used to indicate the 'ontological' domain in which the core meaning (*tian* or *gen*) is to be articulated. At first sight, the process of adding a radical seems to be equivalent to what Kittay had termed a 'transference of meaning' except that the metaphorical creation is recognizable only at the graphic level.[89] The advantage the Chinese written

---

88   For a detailed exposition of the 'uniqueness thesis', see Rosemont 1974. The thesis is restated now in a more trenchant way as 'Appendix II Further Remarks on Language, Translation and Interpretation', in Ames and Rosemont Jr. 1998.

89   Note, however, that the systematic use of radicals appears only at a later stage in the formation of the Chinese written language (third to second century BC). Radicals, nevertheless, seem to have been used in a less standardized way even before these dates, as the newly unearthed texts teach us.

language has over alphabetical ones is therefore that it is able to establish conceptual distinctions that may not exist at the level of the spoken language.[90]

Furthermore, one is always struck by the number of different and seemingly unconnected meanings given for a single word in Chinese dictionaries.[91] Take the case of *zhi*,[bu] which can either mean 'to govern' (*zhi guo*[bv]) or 'to cure' (*zhi bing*[bw]). Neither of these expressions is metaphorical – or else both are – since we find the metaphor of illness applied in politics (for example *Lüshichunqiu*, ch. 15.8) and also the metaphor of the well-ordered state applied to the body in medical texts. It is impossible, thus, to define the literal and the figurative meaning of *zhi*, for there is no such distinction in Chinese. The meaning of *zhi* is – from a Western perspective – rather vague. But in Chinese, the need for spelling out its exact meaning in isolation – its literal sense – is never felt. The word gets its precision through the syntactical and semantic environment in which it is embedded. The process is one of narrowing down an initially rather broad and vague 'core' meaning to several more specialized ones. It would indeed be totally inadequate to view the Chinese characters as signs with very concrete meanings. Meaning, in Chinese, always emerges as a property of entire texts or sentences, and is never felt as the sum or the product of the meanings of the isolated words that make up these texts or sentences. Meaning is the result of a clever juxtaposition of characters. Puns are very often intentional. Parallelisms, which are considered as a rhetorical device in Western handbooks, are a basic way of generating meaning in Chinese texts.

Contrast the Chinese way of building sentences with the following Latin example. The sentence *Jacobus militem occidit* ('Jack kills the soldier') is made up of three words. These words can be rearranged in six different ways, yielding the following six sentences:

1 *Occidit Jacobus militem*
2 *Occidit militem Jacobus*
3 *Jacobus occidit militem*
4 *Jacobus militem occidit*
5 *Militem Jacobus occidit*
6 *Militem occidit Jacobus*

---

90 For an example, see the different terms for 'knowledge' coined by the Later Mohists. In the Western tradition, only Derrida seems to have used this very same device when he writes 'est' (*is*) barred like this: 'e̶s̶t̶' in his *Grammatology* (Derrida 1976).

91 Vandermeersch has a very interesting remark about this problem: 'Je dirais qu'en Chine l'écriture a été conçue originellement à la manière d'un algorithme, c'est-à-dire, en donnant à ce mot un sens très large, comme un instrument (constitué par un système de symboles graphiques) servant à soutenir un effort de structuration des représentations. Un peu à la façon dont l'algèbre a été créée pour symboliser des structures mathématiques, la première écriture chinoise a été créée pour symboliser des rapports entre certaines représentations religieuses, cultuelles, rituelles. Les formules très élémentaires qu'elle a servi à construire au stade initial se sont progressivement développées, puis déployées en suites de formules, comportant des références de plus en plus riches à la variété du monde; et l'écriture algorithmique primitive est ainsi devenue la langue écrite chinoise.' (Vandermeersch 1983: 256)

The emphasis is in each case different, and each of these six sentences seems to answer a different question: who killed, who was killed, did Jack kill or not, was the soldier killed or not, was it Jack or not, was the killed one a soldier? This constellation – six different sentences formed with the same invariant three words – immensely favours the idea that there is one fixed meaning embodied in different linguistic forms and thus opens up the path to the emergence of the notion of literal meaning. Each one of these six sentences has indeed the same 'propositional meaning' and the same truth-conditions. All the rest are stylistic and rhetorical variations.

In Chinese, on the other hand, the permutation of syntactic elements nearly always changes the meaning of the sentence. This feature, combined with the impossibility of attaching a fixed meaning to characters viewed in isolation, finally leads the first Chinese philosophers on to a very different path: meanings are not properties of words or sentences, they are messages – and so are metaphors.[92]

---

92   Ames and Rosemont Jr. (1998) also stress the communicative aspect of Chinese, as opposed to Western languages, as did Harbsmeier (Harbsmeier 1979: 114–15). The theory of metaphor that comes, in the West, closest to the Chinese view of metaphor is, curiously, Davidson 1978.

Chapter 7

'To Be' in Greece and China

Ontology, or the doctrine of being, is rightly considered as one of the main achievements of Western metaphysics, no matter how we finally judge the value of the tradition derived from it. But it has also been observed that, without the support of the Greek verb 'to be' (*einai*, *eimi*, *estin*), it would hardly have been possible to express the central tenets of ontology, let alone discover them.[1] Is it justified, then, to infer from the commonplace observation that ancient China has had neither a verb 'to be' comparable to the Greek *einai* nor a theory of being comparable to what Aristotle and Plato had constructed, that ontology simply *could* not arise in China? And if this is considered as a serious hypothesis, what are our opportunities for testing it?

At first sight it looks as if circumstances as clear as these would render unnecessary any comparative investigation: 'The dependence of Western ontology on the peculiarities of the Indo-European verb "to be" is evident to anyone who observes from the vantage point of languages outside the Indo-European family.'[2] The research work that is needed to put side by side the Greek and the Chinese linguistic material for expressing the notion of 'being' – whatever its equivalents in Chinese are – is, moreover, available. In the Chinese domain, we have Graham's *'Being' in Classical Chinese.*[3] The Greek counterpart of Graham's work is Kahn's monumental *The Verb 'Be' in Ancient Greek.*[4] Both works belong to the series *The Verb 'Be' and Its Synonyms: Philosophical and Grammatical Studies* inaugurated by the Dutch linguist John W. M. Verhaar some thirty years ago. This series is extinct now, and no final synthesis of the work done so far has ever been undertaken.

Kahn's goal is the analysis of the *pre-philosophical* uses[5] of the Greek verb *einai* 'to be' and the reconstruction of the linguistic raw material found by the first Greek philosophers.[6] After having tabulated all the different senses of 'being', mainly those of the Homeric corpus, Kahn proceeds to the more

---

1   Kahn 1973a: 2.
2   Graham 1989: 406; Jullien 2001: 29–31.
3   In: *The Verb 'Be' and Its Synonyms: Philosophical and Grammatical Studies; Part 6,* Dordrecht: Reidel, 1967, pp. 1–39. This works goes back to an earlier, more technical and sinological study, namely, '"Being" in Western Philosophy Compared With *shi/fei* and *you/wu* in Chinese Philosophy' (1960), reprinted in: *Studies in Chinese Philosophy and Philosophical Literature,* Singapore: The Institute of East Asian Philosophies, 1989, pp. 322–59 (= Graham 1986d).
4   Kahn 1973a.
5   On the importance of this feature, see also the Introduction.
6   Kahn 1973a: 9.

difficult task of finding out how the Greek language had eventually influenced the first Greek ontologists. Kahn's conclusion is that the Greek language has had a favourable influence upon philosophical thinking, because it had delivered to the first philosophers, 'ready-made', as he says himself, the basic principles of ontology: '[...] I want to suggest that it was, philosophically speaking, a happy accident and that the proper subject matter of ontology was in a sense delivered ready-made to the Greek philosophers in the system of uses of their verb.'[7] The subject matter of ontology, for Kahn, is the intimate connection that exists between predication, truth and reality. 'Whatever error the Greek philosophers may have committed in their doctrines of Being, it was not an error to suppose that predication, truth and existence (or reality) belong together in a single family of concepts, the topic for a single body of theory [...].'[8]

In admitting that the Greek language has had a favourable influence upon the first Greek philosophers, Kahn is compelled to start from fairly strong claims on the nature of philosophical thinking. 'But the connection between these three notions – truth, knowledge, and reality in the general sense entailed by the other two – is in no way a peculiar feature of Indo-European. The connections here are firmly grounded in the logical structure of the concepts of truth and knowledge, and similar connections must turn up in every language where human beings try to acquire information or try to test the reliability of what is told to them. [...] No language can do without these basic notions of truth, reality and fact.'[9]

Ancient Greek, therefore, is one of the most philosophical languages. Speaking Greek, for Kahn, is an advantage. 'It seems to me that this was a philosophical advantage, and that the language spontaneously brought together concepts which genuinely belong together.'[10]

Kahn thereby adopts a somewhat oblique position on the issue of linguistic relativism. He clearly admits that there is an influence of language upon philosophical thinking. He escapes from relativism, however, in claiming that the first Greek philosophers do not hit upon some parochial feature of the Greek language, but through the Greek language, discover *universally valid* structures of thinking. This conclusion is very elegant, because it saves the Greek language and the Greek ontology in one and the same move. Moreover, it also wards off the accusation of cultural imperialism, by attributing the discovery of ontology to happy linguistic circumstances rather than to the language itself. Kahn thereby seems to imply that the discovery of ontology within a culture with a different linguistic substratum would not have been impossible, but only more difficult.[11]

---

7 Kahn 1973b: 4. See also Kahn 1973a: 372; 403 ('a piece of good luck').
8 Kahn 1973a: 372.
9 Kahn 1979: 32; see also Kahn 1973a: 415.
10 Kahn 1979: 32 and p. 22.

It has to be said, in defence of Kahn, that his project was explicitly directed towards rehabilitating Greek metaphysics against its critics, mainly against those from the camp of analytical philosophy. The opinion that metaphysics rested nearly entirely upon a confusion between predication and existence, or between predication and identity, was still widespread in the late 1960s.

One can say that Graham's work also pays tribute, though not in the same sense, to the critique of metaphysics. In his study on the Chinese ways of expressing the Western concept of being, Graham shows in a quite subtle way that the major Western ontological texts, Anselm's ontological argument, for example, simply *cannot* be translated into Chinese, because that language totally lacks the idiosyncrasies of the Indo-European verb 'to be' upon which these arguments rest. The obvious conclusion that is to be drawn – Graham leaves it to the reader – is that the Chinese language has helped the Chinese philosophers to *avoid* metaphysics. One of the reasons stated by Graham – though only incidentally – why Chinese philosophy had sailed past Western-type metaphysics, is that the structure of the language already has affinities with the main antidote to metaphysics, namely symbolic logic: 'It may be noticed that in the functions here discussed classical Chinese syntax is close to symbolic logic: it has an existential quantifier, *you*[a] "there is", which forbids mistaking existence for a predicate […].'[12]

Kahn's and Graham's works, though on the same subject, now stand isolated, like monolithic blocks, side by side, leaving the philosopher, who wants to draw firm conclusions from them, in almost total perplexity. Indeed, if we are neither adversaries of, nor spokespeople for, metaphysics, what kind of conclusion could we possibly draw from Kahn's and Graham's studies? If the solution depends upon the value – if not the truth – of some kind of metaphysics, what is there to be done if we do not subscribe to that type of metaphysics? Are we allowed to accept Kahn's linguistic analyses even if we think that Greek metaphysics is but a heap of errors? We could equally well invert the situation: if we believe that Greek metaphysics is the wrong kind of philosophy, we must then also admit that the Greek language is philosophically worthless. If, on the contrary, we think that the discovery of metaphysics was a great discovery, we would then have to admit that the Chinese language is metaphysically worthless.

The weak point in Kahn's and in Graham's approaches lies in the fact that both have to issue judgements of value on the type of philosophy that is or is not contained in the languages they examine. Kahn, moreover, is also committed, without making this aspect explicit, to a whole theory on how

---

11   Kahn is not always clear about this issue, for he once wrote the following: 'Both histori-cally and linguistically, the philosophical project of ontology seems to depend upon – to have as a necessary condition – the possession of a verb *to be!*' (Kahn 1973b: 1) See also Kahn 1995: 157: 'I would suggest that ancient Greek is one of the most adequate of all languages, and that the possession of such a language was in fact a necessary condi-tion for the success of the Greeks in creating Western logic and philosophy [...].'
12   Graham 1989: 412. See also Graham 1965: 231.

thought is influenced by language. He starts from the assumption that the Greek language contains a 'tacit' metaphysics.[13] Faced with the objection that not every philosopher gets the same conclusions out of the same language, he meets it with the remark that language nevertheless 'exhibits various conceptual tendencies': '[...] different philosophers develop these tendencies in different ways. In this sense a large number of alternative ontologies are "latent" in the language; but the task of philosophers is not only to bring these tendencies out of hiding but to give them rational form by articulating them in systematic theories.'[14]

From Kahn's theory we should conclude that the first Greek philosophers are in the main good students of the Greek language, because each of them had properly grasped its lessons. This conclusion, however, as we shall see later, does not square at all with the historical and philosophical material that is at our disposal. Language, on the contrary, is rarely adopted as a teacher or a guide by the first Greek philosophers. What happens, rather, and I have already pointed to this feature many times in the foregoing essays, is that language is mostly criticized by the first Greek philosophers and even 'amended' by Plato and other philosophers.[15] The argument invariably is that language presents us a wrong picture of reality. We can quote many texts, where it is evident that the philosopher constructs his theory in opposition to some facet of the language he finds illogical.

> The Greeks are wrong to recognise coming into being and perishing; for nothing comes into being nor perishes, but is rather compounded or dissolved from things that are. So they would be right to call coming into being composition and perishing dissolution.
>   (Anaxagoras 59 B 17 DK = 469 KRS; p. 358 for the translation)

Philosophical theories are often meant to replace such 'faulty' ways of speaking. This is, as we shall see, particularly evident in the case of the Greek verb 'to be'. Before turning to this problem, let us first briefly state the basic linguistic and philosophical facts. The original datum is that classical Chinese uses a multiplicity of different expressions to render the senses covered by the unitary Greek verb 'to be' (*einai*).

---

13 Kahn 1973a: 2: '[...] each language has a built in conceptual structure [...] unconsciously presupposed by all thinkers who articulate their doctrines in that tongue.'
14 Kahn 1973a: 3.
15 This aspect is analysed in detail by von Fritz (1966). He shows, first, how Parmenides struggles against language without, however, going beyond it (von Fritz 1966: 10); then that Plato deliberately coins new words and inaugurates new meanings, especially to convey his doctrines on the notion of being (von Fritz 1966: 53–59).

Greek (uses of *einai*)	Chinese (supposed equivalents)
1 existence ('there are no gods')	*you, wu*[b]
2 to be as a copula, or predication ('Socrates is/is not a man')	*A B ye*[c] (A and B are nominal) *A fei B ye*[d]
3 the veridical use or the assertion that something is true ('it is as you say')	*ran*[e] *dang*[f] *shi, fei*[g]
4 localization ('Socrates is/is not in Athens')	*zai*[h] *you, wu*[i]
5 identity ('the Good is what is real')	*A ji B*[j]
6 roles and functions ('he is/is not a carpenter')	*wei*[k] (or falls outside the scope of the Greek 'to be')

Kahn postulates that the linguistic unity exhibited by the Greek verb 'to be' also points to a deeper conceptual unity. He starts by reducing these six senses to three: the existential use, the use as a copula and the so-called veridical use. Senses 5 and 6 may be understood as variants of 2, and sense 4 as a subset of 1. The veridical use ('it is as you say') is an original contribution of Kahn, for this sense had not been recognized as separate before.[16] Finally, Kahn tries to establish a kind of conceptual precedence between these three terms.

According to the traditional theory, the use of 'to be' as a copula had evolved out of the existential use. Meillet still believed that the Indo-European system of the nominal sentence had gradually weakened, so that it became necessary, at a certain time, to introduce a verb to tie the nominal elements together. The most adequate verb to assume this function was finally the verb 'to be'.[17] This theory, as Lanérès has observed, is not tenable, for nominal sentences continue to exist in Greek, along with copula sentences. Nominal sentences simply have different functions.[18]

Kahn's most original contribution – which he sometimes calls his Copernican revolution – is the insight that it is not the existential use that is primary, but the use of *einai* 'to be' as a copula. 'Once we carry out the modest Copernican Revolution which I propose, that is, once we reinstate the copula construction at the centre of the system, the other uses of the verb will easily fall into place. As the locative use is *included* in the copula construction, the corresponding lexical value "is present, is located (there)" obviously occupies a central

---

16 Von Fritz though mentions this sense ('Wahrsein') in passing (von Fritz 1966: 53).

17 '[…] il a fallu y introduire un verbe, aussi peu significatif que possible par lui-même. La racine *es qui signifiait "exister" s'est trouvée apte à ce rôle […]. Le verbe d'existence, perdant sa signification propre, a été réduit peu à peu au rôle de simple copule.' (Meillet and Vendryès 1963: par. 873)

18 Lanérès 1994.

position within the system and exerts some influence over many uses of *eimi* which are not merely statements of place.'[19]

Kahn, in fact, offers his own reconstruction of the evolution of the Greek verb 'to be'. In the beginning, that is for Proto-Greek speakers, he says, 'to be' only meant 'to be in some place'. This meaning was then transferred to new, abstract and metaphorical uses 'in which the intuitive spatial connotations were preserved.'[20]

The proto-philosophical system of the Greek verb 'to be', as Kahn reconstructs it, is then roughly the following. There are three fundamental uses: existence, use as a copula and the veridical use. To each one of these three fundamental uses corresponds a key notion of ontology: existence corresponds to reality, the veridical use to truth and the use as a copula to predication. The reason why Kahn thinks that ontology is delivered 'ready-made' to the first Greek philosophers is that the Greek language, using one and the same linguistic expression for these three fundamental notions, had somehow anticipated the insight that they are connected.[21]

This conclusion is, however, only a *post mortem* analysis of Greek philosophy, for no Greek philosopher has extracted precisely this tripartite scheme out of the Greek language, and it is not at all clear how the theories of the Greek philosophers are to be related to this scheme in detail.

Kahn's strategy, when he interprets ancient Greek ontologists, invariably amounts to crediting these thinkers with 'fused' rather than 'con-fused' senses of being.[22] He thereby undercuts all those arguments that attribute to Parmenides or Plato confused senses of being, but obscures, probably, the real origin of their philosophical thought, which I see as a struggle *against* language, not as a docile listening to its lessons.[23]

Another of Kahn's claims is also highly disputable. When he writes: 'But I shall contend that Parmenides, Plato and Aristotle were served rather than hindered by the fact that the language itself joins together the formal sign of predication with the notions of existence and truth',[24] he presents their efforts as a kind of translation of linguistic insights into philosophical reasoning. The philological and philosophical evidence, however, is on the other side. The Greek verb 'to be' has always been a source of problems for the Greek philosophers. There are, basically, three different attitudes: the first philosophers object that the Greek language is illogical; Plato corrects language by introducing new expressions, like *ousia*, that are supposed to solve the problem, or by inventing new senses of being; Aristotle tabulates the different senses of being and tries to accommodate to his theories as much as he can of the Greek

---

19   Kahn 1973a: 395.
20   Kahn 1973a: 376.
21   Kahn (1973a: 9) alludes to what he calls the 'ontological predispositions' of the Greek language.
22   See, for example, Kahn 1969, Kahn 1976 and Kahn 1981.
23   See also von Fritz 1966: 10 and Tugendhat 1977.
24   Kahn 1973a: 372.

language.[25] The theories that eventually came out of these approaches have one thing in common: none of them accepts willingly the basic linguistic facts of the Greek language.

In the *Eudemian Ethics*, Aristotle expresses serious doubts at the very possibility of constructing a science of ontology, because 'to be' can be said in so many ways.

> For the good is <so> called in many ways, indeed in as many ways as being. 'Being', as has been set out elsewhere, signifies what-is, quality, quantity, when, and in addition that <being which is found> in being changed and in changing; and the good occurs in each one of these categories – in substance, intelligence and God; in quality, the just; in quantity, the moderate; in the when, the right occasion; and teaching and learning in the sphere of change. So, just as being is not a single thing embracing the things mentioned, the good is not either; nor is there a single science of being or the good.
>
> (*Eudemian Ethics* 1217b26–36;
> translation M. Woods, Clarendon Aristotle Series, pp. 9–10)

Although Aristotle mostly argues in favour of the unity of a science of being in other texts,[26] the basic linguistic datum is nevertheless that of an embarrassing multiplicity of senses, not a ready-made science of being. Even in the book where Aristotle introduces 'ontology', the science of being *qua* being, his reflections start from the fact that 'being is said in many ways'. In the second chapter of book Γ of the *Metaphysics*, Aristotle postulates that there is something in common to all the various senses of being he has enumerated.[27] To say this, however, it is necessary to go far beyond what language teaches us, even in Kahn's rather subliminal sense.

It would not be a happy idea, I believe, to say that Aristotle and other Greek philosophers had grasped the deep semantic unity of the verb 'to be' in Greek. The truth is, rather, that this verb has been felt as a 'philosophical' problem right from the beginning.[28] The Greek verb 'to be' embodies the most formidable contradiction of all, because language obliges us to use the verb 'to be' even to assert the non-existence of something. Aristotle plainly acknowledges this fact, because he says, after having enumerated all the different ways in which being 'is called':

> '[...] that is why we assert that even what is not *is* a thing that is not' (*dio kai to mê on einai mê on phamen*).
>
> (*Metaphysics* Γ 1003b10)

The same problem appears also in the *Sophistical Refutations*.

---

25   See von Fritz 1966.
26   The text just quoted from the *Eudemian Ethics* is indeed one of the most difficult to interpret in the whole Aristotelian corpus; see Woods 1982: 70–75.
27   This doctrine probably corresponds to a later stage in Aristotle's thought.
28   On this problem, see also Tugendhat 1977: 175–76.

For example, 'if that which is not is an object of opinion, then that which is not *is*'; for it is not the same thing 'to be something' and 'to be' absolutely. Or again 'that which is not, if it is not one of the things which are, e.g. if it is not a man.' For it is not the same thing 'not to be something' and 'not to be' absolutely; but, owing to the similarity of the language, 'to be something' appears to differ only a little from 'to be', and 'not to be something' from 'not to be'.

(Aristotle, *Sophistical Refutations* 167a1–8; translation E. S. Forster,
Loeb edn; cf. *ibid.* 180a33–34; *Rhetoric* 1402a3–6)

Aristotle here directly accuses the Greek language, which obscures the difference between 'not being something' and 'not to be absolutely'. Plato likewise does not refrain from saying that non-being somehow *is*.[29] But for him, this statement is less troublesome, for he has already given a new sense to the notion of being: there is a kind of being that truly and completely is, and other forms of being, that are more or less.[30]

The philosophically really embarrassing fact is that the Greek language itself tolerates that being is ascribed to non-being, because that which is said not to exist is said to *be* something that does not exist. 'Being', in other words, is used as wrongly by the Greeks as 'becoming' and 'perishing'.

The philosopher feels a contradiction between the demands of philosophy and the Greek ways of speaking.[31] Some thinkers even proposed radically to amend the Greek language and stop using the verb 'to be' altogether:

Thinkers of the more recent past also were much agitated lest things might turn out to be both one and many at the time. Therefore some, like Lycophron, did away with the word 'is' (*dio hoi men to estin apheilon*); others sought to remodel the language, and say, not that the man is pale, but that he pales (*hoti ho anthrôpos ou leukos estin alla leleukôtai*), not that the man is walking (*badizôn estin*), but that he walks (*badizei*), for fear that by inserting 'is' they would render the one many […].

(Aristotle, *Physics* 185b25–31; translation W. Charlton,
Clarendon Aristotle Series, 1984, p. 4, slightly changed)

This is, in my eyes, a quite extraordinary testimony pertaining to the Greek philosophers' attitude to language. The semantic and intellectual connotations they attribute to the verb 'to be' make it clear that they see a contradiction in the very use of it.

Parmenides, the first Greek philosopher of being, had been scandalized by such an 'illogical assertion'. This, however, did not prevent him from *speaking* about non-being. The really difficult part in Parmenides' poem is not to understand that what is *is*, but, rather, how it is possible to say that what is not *is* not.[32] When he says that we cannot point to or say something about things that do not exist, he cannot avoid speaking about those things that do not exist.

---

29   *Sophist* 258C–E.
30   Bröcker 1959; Vlastos 1979.
31   Aristotle, in particular; see Wardy 2000: 72.
32   Brown 1994: 218.

Come now, and I will tell you (and you must carry my account away with you
when you have heard it) the only ways of enquiry that are to be thought of. The one
that [it] is and that it is impossible for [it] not to be (*hê men hopôs estin te kai hôs
ouk esti mê einai*), is the path of Persuasion (for she attends upon Truth); the other
that [it] is not and that it is needful that [it] not be (*hê d' hôs ouk estin te kai hôs
khreôn esti mê einai*), that I declare to you is an altogether indiscernible track: for
you could not know what is not – that cannot be done – nor indicate it.

(Parmenides 28 B 2 DK = 291 KRS; p. 245 for the translation)

There is a paradox in Parmenides' formulation: while saying *ouk esti mê einai*
'non-being is not' one is somehow obliged to refer to what does not exist.[33]
Gorgias, the sophist, and author of a famous treatise, *On Non-Being*, playfully
echoes this formulation when he declares flatly that:

> 'non-being *is* non-being' (*to mê einai esti mê einai*).
> (*De Melisso Xenophane Gorgia* 979a25; ed. B. Cassin 1980: 445)

The most impressive testimony, however, is certainly Plato's *Sophist*. The
programme, as he declares himself, is to arrive at a correct way (*orthologia*) of
speaking about what is not,[34] implying thereby, of course, that normal Greek ways
of speaking are utterly incorrect. Plato finds himself confronted by the standard
Greek usage of the verb 'to be' which does not normally allow for a clear distinction between existent, real and true. The whole argumentation developed in the
Sophist, however, aims at a clear distinction between what is real and what is true.[35]

Greek ontology, in the face of these testimonies, owes its birth rather to the
problems encountered – and partially solved – by the first philosophers than to
a supposed favourable influence of the Greek language. Parmenides, in his
poem, offers a complete reconstruction and redefinition of the concept of
being, stating how it should be understood, as opposed to the inconsistent
notion that resides in normal ways of speaking.

Plato goes even further and creates totally new senses for the expression 'to
be' in Greek. He establishes, for the first time, a difference between the being
that really is[36] and the other kinds of being that are and are not. Knowledge
must have as its object something that really and truly is (*pantelôs on*),
whereas opinion has as its objects things that are and are not.

> [Socrates] 'Tell me this: does one who knows know something, or nothing? You
> answer me on this behalf.'
>   [Glaucon] 'I answer that one who knows knows something.'
>   'Does he know what is, or what is not?'

---

33   Brown 1994: 217–20. See also Plato, *Sophist* 238E–239A.
34   *Sophist* 239B4.
35   'It seems, however, that in the passage we are here considering [*Sophist* 240A–C] the
      symbiosis between truth and being is beginning to break up, which in itself is a significant
      step towards conceptual differentiation.' (Seligman 1974: 18)
36   *Phaedrus* 247C.

'What is. For how could something that is not be known?'

'Then we are sure of the following, however we may look at it, that what fully is is fully knowable (*to men pantelôs on pantelôs gnôston*) and what is not in any way is totally unknowable.'

'Absolutely.'

'Fine. Now if there is something such that it both is and is not, would it not lie between that which purely is and that which in no way is?'

'Yes.'

'Then knowledge is matched with what is, ignorance necessarily with what is not, and we need to search for something between knowledge and ignorance to be matched with this thing which is between <what is and what is not>, if indeed there is such a thing.'

(Plato, *Republic* 476E6–477B1; translation Brown 1994: 221)

If there are degrees of knowledge, there must also be degrees of reality, that is, some things *are* more than other things. What can it mean for a thing *to be* less than another thing, or *to be* more than another thing? Plato here interprets the notion of being as *being real*, not as being in the sense of existing. He thereby also fundamentally reinterprets the ordinary meaning of these terms. Plato's attitude is continuous with that of the Presocratics.

The basic impression one is left with is that none of the first Greek philosophers was satisfied with the linguistic raw material he had at his disposal. Every philosopher has criticized language, has proposed to add or to remove expressions, has introduced new words or proposed to change the sense of existing ones. If the Greek language has had an influence upon the ways in which Greek philosophy has evolved, this influence was necessarily indirect and oblique. The first Greek philosophers have always reacted *against* language.

I shall leave here the Greek ontologists and turn to the Chinese aspect of the problem. Kahn's theory implies, as he has said himself, that the discovery of ontology within a linguistic substratum different from ancient Greek is, if not impossible, then at least much more difficult. This raises the question whether the Chinese language is at all able to develop a science of ontology and express its basic tenets. We are at a loss to answer this question, because there is no Chinese ontology. It would be rash, however, to try to explain this absence by linguistic factors alone. Chinese philosophy, as I have already argued, did not have the same starting-point as Greek philosophy. We cannot rule out, on linguistic grounds alone, the very possibility of ontological speculations in China. These speculations perhaps did not arise simply because they were not needed in the context of early Chinese philosophy. Nothing forces us to admit that there *should* have been ontology in China, unless we would want to affirm that Western ontology is the only possible and the only sensible form philosophy could take.

On precisely this point, Kahn is not at all clear. He seems to admit that the principles of ontology are latent in the Greek language and that there is continuity between language and philosophy only in the Greek domain.[37] The

---

37   Kahn 1979: 32.

philosophies of other cultures, having failed to develop ontologies, thereby resemble seeds that have not developed. But we have to free ourselves from the obsession that ontology should have grown everywhere.

Graham's approach implies that ontology, in the Western sense of the term, could not develop in China because the arguments based on the Western notion of being were simply not translatable into Chinese: 'Nevertheless, Western philosophers do tend to confuse functions of "to be" which, in addition to being separated in Chinese, have different logical implications in their own languages. In such cases, the failure of the Chinese translation shows up the flaw in the argument, in the same way that the difficulties of English translators sometimes expose confusion in the thought of the Chinese.'[38] Graham starts, as I have already indicated, from the conviction that many arguments of Western ontology are simply logical errors. If these are not translatable, the Chinese language, be it logical or not, cannot be held responsible for this situation.[39]

Graham shows, however, in another part of his work, that the expressions *you*[l] 'there is' and *wu*[m] 'there is not' as well as *shi*[n] 'consider as true' and *fei*[o] 'consider as false' give rise, in ancient China, to a set of problems that can be considered as 'analogous' to those of Western ontology.[40] But there is no possibility of directly comparing with each other these two forms of 'ontology' and there is not even any justification for giving the name 'ontology' to both. Are we then to conclude that China had a different, a *Chinese* ontology?

In my opinion, it is not fair to say that the Chinese had developed 'a different ontology'.[41] The discipline of ontology corresponds to a specific stage in the development of Western philosophy. We cannot present this discipline as a universally valid standard by which to judge other cultures. We should not, therefore, take the discipline as a whole, but isolate within it specific philosophical problems, like the one of negative existentials, for example, and then look for counterparts of it in China. If we can show that problems of this type had been raised in ancient China – not necessarily within the framework of an 'ontology' – we can at least conclude that there were no epistemological obstacles that could have prevented the rise of ontology. If we can show that there *could* have been ontology in ancient China, the hypothesis of linguistic relativism loses much of its credit and, above all, finally leaves the ground open for new, and potentially much more complicated ways of explaining the differences.

On the Chinese side, my argument will be twofold. On the one hand, I would like to show that the Chinese language, contrary to what Kahn and others might believe, does not lack the conceptual potentialities of constructing arguments where the notion of 'being' is involved and that

---

38   Graham 1986d: 351.
39   Graham (1986d: 256) writes: 'It is curious to watch Chinese translators struggling to reproduce Western fallacies in a language which, whatever its defects, does not permit them to make these particular mistakes.'
40   Graham 1986d: 331–51.
41   On this problem, see also Mazaheri 1992: 423–25.

resemble those of the Greek philosophers, the Eleatics in particular. These arguments, as we shall see, often do not even rely on linguistic expressions that could be considered as Chinese equivalents of the Greek verb 'to be'.

On the other hand, the so-called Chinese equivalents of the Greek verb 'to be', *you*[p] and *wu*,[q] or *shi*[r] and *fei*,[s] have also a different part to play, because they are fundamental concepts of Daoism. Although these problems have to do with the conceptual analysis of the notion of 'what is', it would be highly misleading to range these doctrines under a discipline called 'ontology'. There is also considerable disagreement among the Chinese philosophers about the conceptual implications that can or cannot be derived from the notions *you* 'there is' and *wu* 'there is not'.

Let us first look at a few examples of Chinese texts where problems that may be considered as cognate to those of Western ontology are treated. I shall be particularly interested in the problem of the reference to things that do not exist. Let me recall, as a start, Parmenides' principle.

> For thou couldst not know that which is not – that is impossible – nor point it out.[42]
>
> (Parmenides DK B2; KRS 344)

It is important, from a comparative point of view, not to read straightforwardly an ontology into this passage. It expresses a kind of elementary logical principle that says, simply, that it is impossible to apprehend something that is not there. The problem is, that this is counterintuitive, because we do speak of things that do not exist and refer to them. We are faced with a conceptual dilemma. It is not necessary, however, to have a discipline called 'ontology' to deal with that, as the following texts from the book *Zhuangzi* will teach us. There is, first, a curious story about a person whose name is 'Nothing's-there' (*wuyou*[t]).

> Lightflash put a question to Nothing's-there: 'Are you existing, sir? Or not?'
>
> Getting no answer, Lightflash looked thoroughly at the form and the appearance. Mysteriously empty! Looking at it unceasingly, he did not see it; listening to it, he did not hear it; grasping at it, he did not seize it.
>
> 'The utmost!' said Lightflash, 'which of us can attain to this? I can consider nothing as something, I cannot yet conceive nothing as nothing. But to reach the point where what is there becomes nothing, who can follow this path?'
>
> (*Zhuangzi*, ch. 22, p. 143, *Zhuzi jicheng* edition; translation Graham 1981: 163–64, slightly changed)

Here we have a kind of conceptual experiment. Through the technique of personification of abstract notions (like 'knowledge' and 'beginning') which he applies consistently throughout the whole chapter, the unknown author of these lines invites these notions to disclose their definitions and give explanations by forcing them to speak about themselves. With the person named 'Nothing's-there', this proves to be difficult but he is finally

---

42   The Greek *phrasais* means 'point' rather than 'speak' or 'utter' (Klowski 1967: 226).

up to his task and acts coherently with his status as a non-existent by doing strictly nothing.

Although this text looks playful, like so much in the *Zhuangzi*, its theme is serious. The human mind cannot conceive the nothing as nothing. Whatever his problem with the nothing, he has to consider it as something, to be able to think and speak of it and refer to it. There must, therefore, be a basic flaw in discursive knowledge, because it is not capable of adequately knowing the nothing as nothing. It cannot, as the last sentence says, consider this last bit of something also as nothing, as it should have done. This conclusion perfectly squares with the general drift of the passage whose goal it is to show the radical inadequacy of any form of discursive knowledge.

The same goal is also pursued in another text from the second chapter of the book *Zhuangzi*.

> If there was a beginning, then there was a time before the beginning. <If there was a time before the beginning, then> there was a time before the time of the beginning. If there is something, then there <has been a time when there> has been nothing, <and if there is a time when there has been nothing, then> there has been a time before there has been nothing, <and if there has been a time before there has been nothing, then> there has been a time before there has been a time when there has been nothing.
>
> <Let us suppose that> suddenly the something is the nothing, then I do not know anymore which of both, the something and the nothing, is which. Currently, I have already given the name 'something' to the something, but I do not know if what I call the something really is called the something, or rather is called the nothing.
>
> (*Zhuangzi*, ch. 2, p. 12, *Zhuzi jicheng* edition)

There is one important element for our present investigation that emerges clearly out of this difficult[43] text: the concept of 'nothing' (*wu*) introduced here is not an absolute nothing, at least not a nothing like the one imagined in Western philosophy, because the hypothesis of 'something' that is prior in time to this 'nothing' is evoked. The problem, here, is a problem of naming: what I call *something* might be a *nothing* for somebody else, and vice-versa: the empty space left in the vessel gives it its usefulness.[44] It depends upon the point of view. Names, as the second chapter of the *Zhuangzi* argues, function like demonstratives.[45] 'Something' and 'nothing' are the same kind of words as 'left' and 'right'. What is 'something' for me, might be 'nothing' for somebody else. The debate, here, has primarily to do with the functioning of names and our ways of knowing the meaning of these names. We use the terms *you* 'there is' or 'something' and *wu* 'there is not' or 'nothing' in a correlative way: *you* cancels a prior *wu* and vice-versa. If we follow this path of

---

43   See the commentaries on this passage drawn together by Le Blanc (1987). In the *Huainanzi* this same text is completely reinterpreted in terms of stages of development of the universe.

44   *Daodejing*, ch. 11.

45   Graham 1969–1970: 142.

reasoning, our intellect runs into trouble, because we would also have to get to a state prior to what is not. But it would be absurd to suppose that this state would then be even less than nothing to permit the nothing to come out of it. Still more absurd would be the hypothesis that there is an alternation of 'something' and 'nothing', one producing the other in turn. If something and nothing are viewed from a cosmological point of view and if it is asked which one is prior during the process of cosmic transformations, the problem is even more difficult. In the two texts from the *Zhuangzi* quoted so far, we are, however, still in the domain of conceptual analysis, because the subject under discussion is the one of the mutual dependence of *you* and *wu*. This aspect is also confirmed by a text from the *Mohist Canon*.

> *Canon*: Being lacked does not necessarily require being had. Explained by: what it is said of.
> *Explanation*: In the case of lacking some of something, it is lacked only if it is had. As for the lack of cases of the sky falling down, they are lacking altogether.
> *(Mohist Canon*, B 49; Graham 1978: 418)

The goal of this text seems to be to refute a sophism: namely that we can only say of things that once have existed that they do not now exist anymore. We also touch here on the problem of negative existentials: the thing that is said not to exist anymore, necessarily once has existed, otherwise we could not even talk about it. But there is, then, the counter-example of the collapsing of the sky. This is something that has never existed, and yet we can refer to it. It is wrong, therefore, to say that something must have been there before we can say that it does not exist anymore.

This is much more evident in the case of events that have never happened. It is easy to think and speak about events that might happen or that might have happened. If we refer to these events, we necessarily also refer to something that does not exist.[46]

> Something might not have happened, but when it has occurred it cannot be got rid of. Explained by: having been so.
> *(Mohist Canon*, B 61; Graham 1978: 433; translation slightly changed)

There is another interesting passage on being and non-being in the second chapter of the book *Zhuangzi*.

> To try to fix true and false before they have grown in the mind,[47] is like going to Yue today and arriving there yesterday. *This would be to consider what is not as*

---

46   It is worth noting that the Later Mohists associate here and in the next example the idea of events or processes with the terms *you* and *wu*, and not primarily things. The Chinese *you* means 'there is' as well as 'it happens'. I am indebted to Bobby Gassmann for this remark.

47   In this second chapter, Zhuangzi always argues that there are no absolute judgements. I have already discussed this passage in the essay 'The Origin of Logic in China'.

what is. To consider what is not as what is, even the daemonic Yu could not be made to understand this.

(Zhuangzi, ch. 2, p. 9, *Zhuzi jicheng* edition)

This is a somewhat astonishing passage, because the notions of *you* and *wu* are considered here in an absolute sense. One could be tempted to observe that being and non-being are expressed, in Chinese, by two completely different words, which could obscure the fact that there is a deep link between them. But this is certainly not true in the present case, because both are associated. The phrase *wu you*ᵘ 'what does not exist' here indicates clearly something that does not exist *at all*. What does not exist at all is unknowable, for Parmenides as well as for Zhuangzi. This principle, however, is not quoted here with a specifically metaphysical or 'ontological' intention.[48]

To know something, or to point at it, requires the existence of this object. The problem of pointing at things that do not exist seems also to be at the heart of a treatise of the sophist Gongsun Long, the famous *Zhiwulun*ᵛ 'Treatise on Pointing Things Out'.[49] What happens, Gongsun Long asks, if we say of something that it does not exist? Do we still point at the thing? But how could we point at something that does not exist? If we do not point at it, how can one then say that there was a pointing at this object?

Let us suppose that there is a pointing at something that does not exist in the world. Who would rashly affirm that it fails to point?[50]

But something not existing in the world, who would rashly affirm that it is pointed out?

If there is a pointing that points at something that does not exist in the world, who would rashly affirm that it is a pointing that fails? Who would rashly affirm that it fails to point out something that is not there?

Moreover, if a pointing functions inherently and by itself as a pointing that points at nothing, why should it further depend upon a thing to link to to become a pointing that points?

(Zhiwulun, end; *Daozang* edition)

Gongsun Long here seems to go through all the alternatives to the problem. One cannot deny that the pointing that points at something that does not exist is a pointing that truly points. But how can such a pointing point since if it points truly there is nothing there to point at. The conclusion, then, is that there exists a kind of pointing that is a true and successful pointing but that does not point at some *thing*. It is indeed perfectly logical to assume that if the pointing at something that does not exist succeeds, there is no thing at the other end.

Gongsun Long had also seen the logic that is behind the Eleatic discourse on change. There is, indeed, also in the book *Gongsunlongzi,* a chapter,

---

48   We shall see below, however, that the expression *wu you* must be translated quite differently in other portions of the *Zhuangzi,* namely as 'that which is without anything'.
49   See my new interpretation of this chapter (Reding 2002).
50   Or: 'that it points at nothing'.

*Tongbianlun*ʷ 'Thinking Through Change', that has at its beginning a short treatise on change. This text tries to establish that it is impossible to designate a changing object without contradicting oneself.

> Is there I (one) in II (two)?
> There is no I in II.
> Is the I over on the right in II?
> No.
> Is the I over on the left in II?
> No.
> If neither the I over on the left nor the I over on the right is in II, how is it that II is the I over on the left combined with the I over on the right?
>
> Is it admissible that the I over on the right be called II?
> Inadmissible.
> Is it admissible that the I over on the left be called II?
> Inadmissible.
> Is it admissible that the I over on the right combined with the I over on the left be called II?
> Admissible.
> Is it admissible to affirm that what has changed has not changed?
> It is not.
> When the I over on the right enters into a combination, may it be called changed?
> Admissible.
> Which one changes?
> The right.
> If it has changed from being the I over on the right, how can it [still] be called the I over on the right? If it has not changed, how can it [then] be called changed?
>
> > (*Tongbianlun*, beginning; *Daozang* edition;
> > text partially transposed according to Graham 1986b; Chinese textˣ)

This short dialogue on change may be divided into two parts. In the first part, the exchange is conducted in terms of *you* and *wu*ʸ (there is – there is not); in the second part, it is conducted in terms of *ke wei* and *bu ke wei*ᶻ (can be called – cannot be called).

If two units (I + I) are associated to form a new total (II), they disappear in it, for otherwise we could not say that the two units form a new combination. The new total, therefore, does not have I + I anymore, for it would then not be II. The same reasoning applies to the left and the right. If the left and the right vanish into the whole that both contribute to form, there is no sense in saying that left and right still are in this whole, for otherwise it would not form a new encompassing total. We would still be with left and right, and not with a new compound. If we assume this reasoning, we hit upon a paradox: how can we assure the 'ontological continuity' between the units and the total? When should we cease to call the left and the right 'left' and 'right' and call them II? But there is also the other aspect: the unit has been formed by I + I, or by left and right, and these two elements must somehow be preserved in the total, because what distinguishes the new total is that it is formed precisely by the two units I + I, or by left and right. The total therefore is and is not left and right, I and I.

In the second part, the paradox is much more visible, because it is expressed on the level of naming. The total (II) cannot anymore be called 'left' or 'right', for it is something different from both. It is the union of both that can be called II. In this treatise, we also see once again one of these 'logical clauses' ('Is it admissible to affirm that what has changed has not changed?') that are frequent in the *White Horse Treatise* and in *Thinking Through Change*. This is to underline the stringency of the argument.

The reasoning that generates the paradox can be reconstructed as follows: if the right (*you*) enters into a combination, it undergoes some change (*bian*), because it loses its identity in the new total. If the right side changes, it becomes something different from what it used to be before, and if it is something different, it is not the right that we had started with. And there is the dilemma: either the right has not altered – but then it has not entered into the combination II either – or it has altered – but then it is not the right side anymore.

This argument has affinities with the Eleatic arguments against the possibility of change and becoming, for the proof tries to establish that the concept of an object that changes is contradictory in itself, because it becomes what is not it. In the *Euthydemus*, an early Platonic dialogue that can at the same time be considered as an anthology of sophistic paradoxes, we find a chain of reasoning that comes astonishingly close to the short dialogue on change of the *Thinking Through Change*.

> 'Well now,' he proceeded, 'you wish him to become wise, as you say?'
> 'Certainly.'
> 'At present,' he asked, 'is Cleinias wise or not?'
> 'Not yet so, as he says; but he is no vain pretender.'
> 'But you,' he went on, 'do you wish him to become wise, and not to be ignorant?'
> We agreed.
> 'In this way, you wish him then to become what he is not, and to be no longer what he is now.'
> When I heard this I was confused; and I was even more confused when we went on.
> 'Of course then, since you wish him to be no longer what he now is, you wish him, apparently, to be dead.'
>
> (Plato, *Euthydemus* 283C–D)

If Cleinias changes from an uneducated man to a wise man, he will cease to be what he is now. He will cease to exist as he is now, which could mean that the uneducated Cleinias 'dies' whereas the educated Cleinias will be a totally different man. This paradox from the *Euthydemus* hinges on exactly the same mechanism as the paradox on the assembled 'ones' in *Thinking Through Change*. The formulation, however, is different: whereas the Greek paradox is built upon the opposition between being and becoming, the Chinese paradox is entirely conducted in terms of 'can be called' or 'cannot be called'. It seems evident, therefore, that the paradox in itself is not dependent upon any linguistic peculiarities of either Greek or Chinese.

Another instance of it can be found in the second list of paradoxes in chapter 33 of the *Zhuangzi*.

> An orphan colt never has had a mother.
>
> (*Zhuangzi*, ch. 33, p. 224, *Zhuzi jicheng* edition)

If the colt loses its mother, it undergoes some change. It changes from a colt with a mother to a motherless colt. Can we say, then, that it is the orphan colt that has lost its mother? This is not possible, since an orphan is, by definition, already motherless. If it is the colt that loses its mother, it is not a colt anymore, but already an orphan colt. We arrive at the conclusion that it is impossible to describe correctly a changing object. If we use two different names – the colt with mother and the orphan colt – we cannot say that one of them has changed, since we talk of two different objects. If we keep the same name, we cannot affirm that something has changed, since there was no change in the name.[51] The paradox could also have been formulated the other way round: a colt never can lose its mother. If it does, it is not a colt anymore, but an orphan colt.

The beginning of *Thinking Through Change* follows the dilemmatic model of the *Treatise on Pointing Things Out*, except that, this time, the fundamental aporia is generated with the concept of change as its target. Here again, no metaphysical conclusion is drawn. Gongsun Long had no philosophical intentions whatsoever. Nevertheless, his paradoxes are extremely interesting for us, because they show all the philosophical and logical potentialities of the Chinese language, even without the support of the magical expression 'to be'. The Chinese language then cannot have been an obstacle to the discovery of ontology or metaphysics in the Greek sense, as is generally affirmed.[52] With Gongsun Long's paradoxes, we have the proof that there could have been ontology and metaphysics in the Greek sense in ancient China. Had Gongsun Long applied his arguments in the same way as Parmenides, Zeno and Plato, no doubt we would have had a Chinese ontology. The absence of ontology in ancient China cannot, then, be attributed to the structure of the Chinese language alone.[53]

From this point of view, Gongsun Long's example shows even more, because it also sheds light, though in rather an oblique way, on Greek philosophy. Parmenides has often been accused of confusing the existential and the predicative sense of 'being' (*einai*). The whole argument collapses, it is said, if this distinction is respected. As the present investigation shows, Parmenides' 'error' cannot solely be due to some intrinsic feature of the Greek language, since the same argument is possible also in classical Chinese,

---

51   The argument is reminiscent of *Phaedo* 96E–97B.

52   See, for example, Gernet 1991: 323.

53   Mazaheri (1992: 425) has arrived at the same conclusion.

a language that possesses an entirely different conceptualization of the verb 'to be' from ancient Greek.

That the doctrines of Gongsun Long and Parmenides are embedded in totally different philosophical contexts cannot subtract anything from their comparative value. As a matter of fact, Gongsun Long is, intellectually speaking, much closer to the sophist Gorgias than to Parmenides. Gongsun Long's book must be considered as a collection of rhetorical exercises that shows – much in the style of the sophists in ancient Greece – that on any matter, even the most difficult ones, two opposite arguments can be defended.[54] Gongsun Long's goal was only to produce paradoxical statements to demonstrate the precedence of rhetoric over philosophy. He uses, also in the *White Horse Treatise*, the dialectical method of the Later Mohists in a self-destructing manner, just as Gorgias had tried to ruin the arguments of Parmenides and Melissus in his famous treatise *On Non-Being or On Nature*.

A question, however, arises here. If the Chinese language is not in itself an obstacle to the discovery of ontology or metaphysics in the Greek sense, how can we explain then the fact that it is impossible to render correctly Greek ontological arguments into Chinese? If we look at a Chinese translation of Parmenides' fragments, we cannot but agree with Graham.[55]

> Come now, and I will tell you (and you must carry my account away with you when you have heard it) the only ways of enquiry that are to be thought of. The one that [it] is and that it is impossible for [it] not to be, is the path of Persuasion (for she attends upon Truth); the other that [it] is not and that it is needful that [it] not be, that I declare to you is an altogether indiscernible track: for you could not know what is not – that cannot be done – nor indicate it.
>
> (Parmenides 28 B 2, B 3 DK = 291 KRS;
> p. 245 for the translation; Chinese text[aa])

The expression *estin* 'is' in the Greek text is translated invariably by the Chinese *cunzai*.[ab] This ruins, as is to be expected, the philosophical acumen of the whole passage.[56] *Cun* means something like 'to resist change', whereas *zai* means 'to stay in a place'. The Greek text does not say by itself that being is; it only says, impersonally, or with an understood subject, 'that [it] is' (*estin*). The 'it' has to be supplied in the translation. To translate Parmenides in a

---

54   The sophistic movement that can be detected in both cultures is characterized only by rhetorical and philosophical themes that happen to be common to both traditions (Reding 1985). The sophistic movement does not obey any phylogenetic law, as Graham seems to admit: 'In both traditions we meet thinkers who delight in propositions which defy common sense, and consequently are derided as frivolous and irresponsible. In both, these thinkers belong to the early period when reason is a newly discovered tool not yet under control, seeming to give one the power to prove or disprove anything.' (Graham 1989: 75)

55   Graham 1986d.

56   The radical insufficiency of some of the modern Chinese translations of Western philosophical texts is also recognized by Trauzettel 1970.

more faithful way, we should only say *you*[ac] '[it] is there' and then coin the unhappy expression [*you zhe*] *wu wu you*[ad] 'there is no not-being [for it]'. Even if it is impossible for us to check the grammatical correctness of this retrospective translation, we can be sure that it is in no way standard classical Chinese.[57] It has, though, one thing in common with Parmenides' text: it is just as hard to understand, because it corresponds to a totally new way of using language. It is nearly as paradoxical as Parmenides' original text itself – and for the very same reason. The special problems of translation generated by Western philosophical texts – above all those from the ancient Greek tradition – are mostly due to the semantic innovations introduced by the philosophers. This is the reason why these texts then become almost as difficult to translate into modern languages like German, French or English as into Chinese. Of Parmenides' poem, there are more rival translations than of any other Greek philosophical text. To translate this text faithfully into Chinese, we would then also be forced to change the Chinese language in the same way as the first Greek philosophers had changed the Greek language.[58] This is, indeed, what the Greek philosophers had achieved, because we still use their philosophical 'innovations': terms like 'existence', 'essence', 'substance', 'category', 'actual', 'potential' and so on have become part of our everyday vocabulary.

The lesson that is to be learnt from this is that Graham's method of checking Chinese translations against their Western originals is inconclusive. We cannot arrive, from the impossibility of translating such texts, at the conclusion that the Chinese language is incapable of holding within itself the fundamental notions of ontology. The truth is, precisely, that the Greek language – as a natural, non-philosophical language – could not express these new concepts either, but had first to be changed by the philosophers. Translation, in such cases, is not possible without interpretation. A native Chinese speaker has thus to know many things about Greek philosophy before he will be able to understand these Greek texts – even in translation. Without a certain degree of interpenetration of cultures, translations of such texts must remain meaningless.[59] But once this groundwork is achieved, there should be no obstacle to percipient translations of Western philosophical texts into Chinese.[60]

Moreover, arguments invoking an incapacity of translation can also be made to work in the opposite direction. We could equally well observe that the arguments of the Daoists are not translatable into Western languages,[61] proving thereby that Western languages are as ill suited for Daoism as

---

57   According to Graham, these attempts lead inevitably to a 'deterioration of syntax' (Graham 1989: 13–14).

58   This is also proposed by Yu Jiyuan 1999: 448–54.

59   On this problem, see also Wardy 1992 and Wardy 2000.

60   After having examined modern Chinese translations of Plato, Harbsmeier is much less pessimistic on this issue than Graham; see Harbsmeier 1998: 164–70. See also Wardy 2000: 87, who shows that there would have been room enough, also in classical Chinese, to accommodate already existing structures to the linguistic needs of ontological theories.

61   This is denied by Graham (1976).

Chinese is for ontology. Now we begin to see where the real outcome lies, for we have to give an answer to this crucial question: is it more important for a language to be able to translate Daoist texts or to be able to render the fine nuances of ontology? Or, to put it in a cruder and more absurd way: which of the two philosophies is the more *valuable*? The reason why Kahn's and Graham's approaches proved perplexing in the end was that each gave a different answer to this question, since each of them only valued his own discipline.

In the present context, however, the value of ontology is not at issue. All we need to show is that there *could* have been ontology in ancient China. We have already seen that Gongsun Long had developed a set of arguments that we can qualify without hesitating as ontological, because they are in tune with those of Parmenides. There are, in addition, also arguments resting upon the notion of being and that are more typically Chinese, because embedded in contexts for which there are no Western counterparts. This observation applies more specifically to the notions of *you*[ae] 'there is' and *wu*[af] 'there is not' that had a crucial role to play in the philosophy of Daoism. Most problems arise in conjunction with the exegesis of a famous text in the *Daodejing*:

Tianxia zhi wu sheng yu you. You sheng yu wu.[ag]
The creatures in the world are born from something, and something from nothing.
(*Daodejing*, ch. 40, p. 25, *Zhuzi jicheng* edition, Wang Bi text)

The notions of *you* 'there is' and *wu* 'there is not' are here integrated into a philosophical framework that is completely different from Western concerns. Nevertheless, there is no trace of a violation of the principle *ex nihilo nihil* in this text. The notion of 'nothing' still refers to some kind of being, but to a being that is completely undetermined, without anything and without a name, as the next text says.

At the extreme beginning, there was nothing. Without anything, without a name. The One has grown out of it.
(*Zhuangzi*, ch. 12, p. 73, *Zhuzi jicheng* edition)

In later strata of the book *Zhuangzi*, the notions of being and non-being seem to be located already in an *onto-cosmological* framework.

The Gate of Heaven is that which is without anything (*wu you*[ah]); the myriad things go on coming forth from that which is without anything. Something cannot become something by means of something, it necessarily goes on coming forth from that which is without anything; but that which is without anything is forever without anything.
(*Zhuangzi*, ch. 23, p. 151, *Zhuzi jicheng* edition;
translation Graham 1981: 103)

Here it seems as if we have definitely left Parmenides' Eleatic logic behind us. The text contradicts Parmenides on two very essential points: that being originates from nothing, and that being cannot come from being. The notion of *wu you*, translated as 'that which is without anything' by Graham cannot designate non-being in Parmenides' sense. *Wu you* rather means the absence of any shaped things.[62] Becoming then also means taking shape rather than originating from nothing. Hence the Chinese concept of 'nothing' is still a being, but a being that is completely without shape or determination.

Views that could be considered as cognate to those of the Eleatics are to be found only much later in Chinese intellectual history. When the Neo-Confucians criticize the Daoist doctrine that the Dao comes out of the Nothing, they invoke arguments that are not unlike those formulated by the Greek philosopher Parmenides.

The Neo-Confucian philosopher Cheng Hao, who attacks the Daoist thesis that the Dao comes out of Non-Being (*wu*[ai]), writes:

> If you say there is Nothing (*you wu*[aj]), the *you* (there is) is a word too many; if you say there is no Nothing (*wu wu*[ak]) the *wu* (there is not) is a word too many.
> (*Henan chengshi yishu*, p. 134, *Basic Sinological Series*;
> quoted in Graham 1986d: 344)

Cheng Hao's target is chapter 40 of the *Daodejing*: 'The creatures in the world are born from something, and something from nothing.' If this 'Nothing' really is nothing, Cheng Hao argues, we cannot say anything about it at all, neither that it is nor that it is not. If we say 'there *is* (*you*) nothing', we seem to confer existence on something that by definition does not exist. In this case, we should refrain from using the expression 'there is' altogether, as Cheng Hao reminds us.

On the other hand, to say of the 'Nothing' that it is not there (*wu*) is either a tautology or another contradiction, if our saying implies that the 'Nothing' nevertheless has some kind of existence. If we concede that the 'Nothing' has existence after all, then there is no sense in saying that it does not exist! This, it seems to me, is not far from what Parmenides had declared.

The paradoxes that surround the Chinese notions of *you* and *wu* have also been felt very clearly by Wang Fuzhi.

> What is there in the world really which can be called Nothing? If you say there is no hair on a tortoise, you are talking about (something on) a dog, not (nothing on) a tortoise. If you say there are no horns on a hare, you are talking about (something on) a deer, not (nothing on) a hare. A speaker must set something up before he can argue successfully. Now if he is to set a Nothing in front of us, he can search everywhere above and below, North, South, East and West, in the past and the present, the surviving and the lost, without ever finding it.
> (*Siwenlu*, ed. Wang Boxiang, Beijing, 1956, p. 11;
> quoted in Graham 1986d: 349–50)

---

62   On this point, see also the essay 'Words for Atoms – Atoms for Words' in this collection.

The solution to the problem of negative existentials proposed here comes close to the one devised by Plato in the *Sophist*: if it is impossible to refer to things that do not exist, references to such things always are references to something 'other'.[63] Not to be a horse, or not to be Socrates does not mean to be a 'non-horse' or a 'non-Socrates', but only something different from Socrates or from a horse. There is a formal resemblance between the Greek and the Chinese approaches to the notion of being, in the sense that both cultures had hit upon the same paradoxes. These ontological paradoxes, however, had little importance in China, because they had not been discovered in the same context.

One final example from the book *Mozi*, one of the earliest philosophical texts from ancient China, is worth quoting. Mozi argues against those who hold that ghosts and spirits do not exist.

> Since we must understand whether ghosts and spirits exist or not (*ji yi guishen youwu zhi bie*[al]), how can we find out? Mozi said: 'The way to find out whether anything exists or not is to depend on the testimony of the ears and eyes of the multitude. If some have heard it or some have seen it then we have to say it exists. If no one has heard it and no one has seen it then we have to say it does not exist. So, then, why not go to some village or some district and inquire? If from antiquity to the present, and since the beginning of man, there are men who have seen the bodies of ghosts and spirits and heard their voice, how can we say they do not exist? If none have heard them and none have seen them, then how can we say they do?'
>
> (*Mozi*, ch. 31, p. 139, *Zhuzi jicheng* edition; translation Mei Yi-Pao 1929: 161)

Mozi's problem is not an ontological problem in the Western sense. The issue at stake is whether ghosts and spirits do have an influence on human life and society. In this context, the criteria invoked by Mozi, namely what people have seen and heard, clearly establishes the existence of ghosts and spirits. Mozi nevertheless arrives here at an abstract concept of 'existence' and coins, for the first time in ancient China, the notion of existence. Note that abstract notions like 'size' or 'quantity' are generally expressed in Chinese by the juxtaposition of the two relevant antonyms: *daxiao*[am] ('size', literally 'large-small'), *duoshao*[an] ('quantity', literally 'many-few'). Mozi coins *youwu* 'existence'.

Let us go back, now, to Kahn's original tenet: the Greek language, he said, had exerted a decisively favourable influence upon the first Greek philosophers, because it offered them, 'ready-made', the groundwork of ontology by using one and the same word ('to be', *einai*) for expressing the notions of predication, existence and truth. The internal unity of this system appears all the more clearly if we look at the way other languages, especially those lying outside the Indo-European influence, have handled these same features. All these languages use a great variety of different notions for the unique Greek expression 'to be'. It was thus, for the native speakers of these 'exotic' languages, much more difficult, if not impossible, to have the same insight

---

63   *Sophist*, 257B9–257C3.

into the unity of predication, truth and reality that eventually led to the foundations of Greek ontology. Chinese, as we have seen, uses at least six different expressions to render the unique Greek *einai* 'to be'.[64]

1　*Existence*

Sentences asserting that X exists or does not exist are mainly rendered by the Chinese expressions *you*[ao] 'there is' and *wu*[ap] 'there is not'.

> Even if there were no men in the world, master Mozi's words would still stand.
> (*Mozi*, EC 2; Graham 1978: 247)

2　*Expressions with a copula*

It is somewhat improper to speak of a Chinese copula.[65] We have already stated the reason why the term 'copula' had been introduced by grammarians of the Greek language: in Greek, the juxtaposition of two nominal elements to form a sentence leaves the impression that this sentence is somehow incomplete and is in need of a verb. In Greek, as in most Indo-European languages, this role had been delegated to the verb 'to be'. In Chinese, however, there are two basic types of sentences: the verbal sentence, negated by *bu*[aq] and the nominal sentence negated by *fei*.[ar] Nominal sentences, however, are not felt as incomplete sentences in Chinese. Although classical Chinese does not have a 'positive' copula, nominal sentences are nonetheless generally marked by the final particle *ye*.[as] This constellation, it has to be noted, did not prevent the Later Mohists from discovering the concept of a sentence.[66]

> *Bai ma ma ye.*[at]
> A white horse is a horse.
>
> *Yuan, yi zhong tong chang ye.*[au]
> *Circular* is having the same lengths from a single centre.
> (*Mohist Canon*, A 58; Graham 1978: 307–309)

In negative sentences, we have *fei*[av] 'is not', which can be, improperly though, as I have already indicated, considered as a negative copula. In preclassical Chinese, there was perhaps once a 'positive' copula, namely *wei*.[aw] The negative copula *fei*[ax] could well have arisen out of a contraction[67] of *bu* + *wei*.[ay]

64　Graham 1986d. See above.
65　I am indebted to Bobby Gassmann for these remarks.
66　On this problem, see Graham 1978: 480–83; Bosley 1997.
67　See Pulleyblank 1959.

Mao fei ji ye. Ji fei mao ye.[az]
A lance is not a halberd; a halberd is not a lance.

(*Lüshichunqiu*, ch. 19.1)

3 *Roles and functions*

For roles and functions, mainly expressed by the copula in Greek, classical Chinese often uses the term *wei*.[ba]

Ren jie keyi wei Yao Shun.[bb]
Everyone can be a Yao or a Shun.

(*Mencius*, VI,B,2)

4 *'Copula' with adjectives*

Adjectives function in Chinese mainly like verbs. Simple sentences like:

Ma bai.[bc]
The horse is white.

Ren xing shan.[bd]
Human nature is good.

are, from the Chinese point of view, verbal sentences. There is no need to mark them separately by devices that would resemble the Greek copula.

5 *Locative constructions*

In these cases, classical Chinese uses the word *zai*,[be] but also, and perhaps even more frequently, the expressions *you*[bf] 'there is' and *wu*[bg] 'there is not'.

Suo wei dao, wu hu zai? Zhuangzi yue: Wu suo bu zai.[bh]
What we call the Way, where is it? Zhuangzi said: 'There is no place where it is not.'
(*Zhuangzi*, ch. 22, p. 141, *Zhuzi jicheng* edition)

6 *Identity*

Identity statements are sometimes expressed in classical Chinese by the particle *ji*.[bi]

Er zi zhe yan ze xiang fei, xing ji xiang fan.[bj]
The words of these two are directly opposed, as are also their actions.
(*Mozi*, ch. 25, p. 105, *Zhuzi jicheng* edition)

There can be no doubt about the conclusion intended by Graham when he lists all these different senses: there is no Chinese notion of 'being'. But Graham, like Kahn, starts from the otherwise unsupported conviction that the linguistic uniformity of the verb 'to be' must also guarantee its conceptual unity and, conversely, that there can be no conceptual unity without linguistic uniformity. The conceptual unity, however, if it has ever been achieved, has mainly been the work of the philosophers in ancient Greece. This task, as we have seen, had been accomplished rather by fighting against language than by following its lessons. The importance of ontology in ancient Greece can only be measured against the formidable obstacle that the Greek language represented to the first philosophers.

There is, then, an interesting experiment to be conducted. I shall try to bring together the findings of Kahn and Graham and see how far one can be used to enlighten the other. If we start, not from the Greek verb 'to be', but rather from Kahn's notions of predication, truth and existence, and if we try to see how these notions are rendered in Chinese, we begin to notice that there is a considerable overlap in the Chinese terminology as well, sufficient, even, to draw also the attention of the philosophers to a possible underlying unity of these three concepts. It will appear, indeed, that the notions of *you* and *wu*, *shi* and *fei*, and *ran* are not only cognate in that they translate the Greek 'to be', but also in that they render Western notions of truth, predication and existence.

There is, in particular, a strong association between existence and truth in Chinese. To say 'it is true' or 'you are right', we can have simply the answer *you*[bk] 'there is such a thing' in Chinese.[68] Mencius, for example, after having told a story to King Xuan of Qi asks at the end of it:

Bu shi you zhu? Yue: you zhi.[bl]
[Mencius asked:] I wonder if this is true?
The King said: It is [there has been such a thing].

(*Mencius*, I,A,7)

Existence and truth are asserted at the same time. On another occasion, the King answers in a slightly different way.

Cao Jiao wen yue: ren jie keyi wei Yao Shun you zhu? Mengzi yue: ran.[bm]
Cao Jiao asked, 'Is it true that all men are capable of becoming a Yao or a Shun?'
'Yes', said Mencius.

(*Mencius*, VI,B,2; translation Lau 1983: 172)

To confirm the truth of the statement, Mencius here uses the term *ran*,[bn] also one of the equivalents of the Greek 'to be' in Graham's list. Its meaning is: 'it is as you say', as an answer to the question 'is there such a thing?'

The notion of predication is harder to analyse. It seems obvious, though, that predication is not necessarily attached to the verb 'to be' in Greek, nor to the nominal sentence in Chinese. That predication is implicit in nearly every sentence with a verb had been noticed by Aristotle.[69] The connection between

---

68   For examples, see Harbsmeier 1989: 130–37.
69   See Aristotle, *Metaphysics* Δ 7; 1017a27–30.

truth and predication in any language is too obvious to need special consideration.

Another term used to translate the Greek 'to be', namely *shi*[bo] can also mean 'to consider something as true'.

Yi shi qi suo fei er fei qi suo shi;
yu shi qi suo fei er fei qi suo shi.[bp]
To want to consider as true what they consider as false and consider as false what they consider as true by considering as true what they consider as false and by considering as false what they consider as true.

(*Zhuangzi*, ch. 2, p. 9, *Zhuzi jicheng* edition)

Here is another text, from the book *Xunzi*, illustrating the same concern.

Shi shi fei fei wei zhi zhi. Fei shi shi fei wei zhi yu.[bq]
To consider what is true as true and what is false as false, this is what is called 'knowledge'. To consider as false what is true and as true what is false, this is what is called 'ignorance'.

(*Xunzi*, ch. 2, p. 14, *Zhuzi jicheng* edition)

There has been a sharp debate between Harbsmeier and Hansen on the problem of whether the Chinese had a notion of truth or not. Hansen has maintained that the Chinese philosophers seldom employ semantic concepts of truth but prefer, on the whole, pragmatic concepts like appropriateness, assent, assertibility.[70] As a result, no theory of truth in the Western sense of this term could develop in ancient China. Hansen's thesis has been sharply criticized by Harbsmeier, who answers with a huge list of counter-examples of Chinese sentences where the notion of semantic truth is to be found.[71]

The Chinese *fei*[br] 'is not' is also of some philosophical interest, for it can be used as a verb signifying 'to consider something as false'. The antonym of *fei*, namely *shi*,[bs] is a demonstrative in classical Chinese that means 'this', but also means 'to consider something as true', as we have seen. It is precisely this *shi*[bt] that has developed into the copula of modern Chinese. There is, in this case, at least an indirect connection between the notions of predication and truth, on the one hand, and 'being' on the other.

In another text, we can see the relation between truth and cause.

Every thing's being so must necessarily have a reason. And when one does not know the reason, then even though what one says fits-the-facts (*dang*[bu]), this is the same as ignorance. [...] That the water comes from the mountains and flows towards the sea is not because the water hates the mountains and loves the sea, it is the declivity that causes it to be so (*dang*[bv]).

(*Lüshichunqiu*, ch. 9.4)

---

70   Hansen 1985.
71   Harbsmeier 1989. See also Harbsmeier 1998: 193–209.

In this case, the term *dang* 'fit (the fact)' can also mean 'true'.

All these examples show that the Chinese language offers many linguistic 'bridges' between the notions of truth, predication and existence, even if there is no single term encompassing all of them. The conceptual framework that was needed to construct an ontology in the Western sense of the term was then also to be found – though not quite 'ready-made' – in classical Chinese. The fact that the notions of predication, truth and reality are distributed over different terms and not expressed, as in Greek, by one and the same expression[72] is counterbalanced by the functional diversity of the key terms *shi/fei*, *you/wu*, *ran* and *dang*. Each of these terms, as we have seen, can be made to express in turn predication, truth or existence.

My conclusion then is that there were no epistemological barriers that could have prevented the rise of ontology in ancient China. In ancient China, philosophical thinking simply focused on economical, political and anthropological theories, and in this context ontology in the Western sense of the term was not needed. I disagree, therefore, with Graham who implicitly argued that the Chinese language was not adapted to ontology.

But I also disagree with Kahn whose views imply that the birth of Greek ontology had been favoured by the structures of the Greek language. We have seen that the unity of the Greek verb 'to be' proved, in the end, to be illusory. The philosophers had viewed this expression mostly as paradoxical and even as illogical. As a consequence, some philosophers wanted to prohibit its use. Greek ontology could only develop at the expense of language. The Greek philosophers have thus coined many new philosophical expressions and have eventually completely reorganized the senses of 'to be' and replaced the old, pre-philosophical uses, by the new technical language of ontology.[73] It should also be said that our present investigation has reached a conclusion that is just the opposite of what Kahn had maintained. He wrote: 'I would suggest that ancient Greek is one of the most adequate of all languages, and that the possession of such a language was in fact a necessary condition for the success of the Greeks in creating Western logic and philosophy [...]'[74] Only the last part of this sentence is true, but not for the reason Kahn advocates. The Greek language is, on the contrary, an extremely *un-metaphysical* language, full of logical and conceptual pitfalls. It should be obvious, though, that it is precisely because of all these misleading linguistic habits that the Greek culture has produced such a rich philosophical tradition. The more 'illogical' the language, the more philosophy is needed to put it back on the right track.

---

72   We should not forget, however, that there are many other expressions in Greek that can render the notions of truth and existence.

73   That the language of the philosophers is essentially based on neologisms had already been noticed by Cicero. See *De finibus* III, 1.

74   Kahn 1995: 157.

Chinese Characters and Texts

Introduction
a   欲
b   德
c   法
d   禮

Chapter 1   'Contradiction is Impossible'
a   墨子
b   墨經
c   名
d   口
e   夕
f   公
g   八
h   背
i   厶
j   正名
k   假
l   非牛
m   辯
n   狗
o   犬
p   非牛
q   非馬
r   非
s   矛盾
t   悖
u   偃兵
v   兼愛
w   假

Chapter 2   The Origin of Logic in China

a   恩
b   白馬非馬
c   類
d   恩
e   明
f   力
g   類
h   權
i   類
j   辯
k   異類
l   不知類
m   遺類
n   鄰類
o   別類
p   白馬
q   秦馬
r   兼愛
s   愛
t   問
u   同類
v   非我也，歲也。
w   非我也，兵也。
x   俱鬭，不俱二。白馬多白，眇馬不多眇。
y   多盜人非多人也。
z   無盜人非無人也。
aa   惡多盜人非惡多人也。
ab   欲無盜人非欲無人也。
ac   愛盜人非愛人也。
ad   不愛盜人非不愛人也。
ae   殺盜人非殺人也。
af   非
ag   盜人人也。

Chapter 3   Philosophy and Geometry in Early China

a   墨經
b   經
c   說
d   性
e   欲
f   惡

g　利
h　害
i　仁
j　義
k　孝
l　愛
m　愛，體利也。
n　志
o　愛，志利也。
p　仁
q　體
r　兼
s　先知
t　說
u　圜
v　中
w　同長
x　端
y　有厚
z　正
aa　盡
ab　直
ac　參
ad　曑
ae　三
af　參
ag　月令
ah　非P則Q
ai　性
aj　欲
ak　大小
al　多少
am　有無
an　仁
ao　義
ap　道
aq　性

Chapter 4   Greek and Chinese Categories

a	也	
b	非	
c	馬	白
d	孰	
e	誰	
f	何	若
g	何	爲
h	何	時
i	幾	何
j	何	
k	惡	乎
l	何	以
m	何	爲
n	有	
o	性	
p	辯	
q	先	知
r	說	
s	利	
t	害	
u	欲	
v	惡	
w	性	
x	愛	
y	義	
z	仁	
aa	孝	
ab	類	
ac	長	
ad	多	
ae	貴	
af	高	
ag	白	
ah	大	
ai	何	謂 X

Chapter 5   Words for Atoms – Atoms for Words

a   通變論

b   積

c   至大無外，謂之大一。

       至小無內，謂之小一。

d   無厚不可積也其大千里。

e   氣

f   積

g   無厚

h   辯者

i   厚

j   端

k   無久

l   微

m   塊

n   幾

o   人之目以照見之也。以瞑則與不見同。

       其所以爲照所以爲瞑 [同。其所能接所不能接] 異。

       瞑士未嘗照。故未嘗見。

       瞑者目無由接也。無由接而言見謊。

       智亦然。其所以接智所以接不智同。

       其所能接所不能接異。

       智者其所能接遠也。愚者其所能接近也。

Notes to the text

1. For ming 瞑 'close the eyes' read ming 瞑 'darkness' throughout this text.

2. The proposed emendation rests upon considerations of parallelism in the second part of the text.

p   虛名

q   其實

r   虛

s   虛

t   氣

u   無

v   天下萬物生於有，有生於無。

w   有

x   無

y   空

z   空中之無澤陂也。井中之無大魚也。

aa   室無空虛

ab	虛空
ac	化
ad	爲
ae	生
af	死
ag	存
ah	亡
ai	損
aj	益
ak	變
al	易
am	改
an	移
ao	動
ap	革
aq	更
ar	徙
as	變化
at	死生
au	存亡
av	存
aw	變
ax	變乎色
ay	利害之變
az	天不變其常
ba	變言
bb	又吞炭以變其音
bc	變服
bd	易衣
be	今水已變而益多矣。
bf	譬若鍾山之玉。炊以鑪炭三日三夜而色澤不變。
bg	譬之若良醫生。病萬變藥亦萬變。
bh	夫子見禾之三變也。
bi	粟
bj	苗
bk	穗
bl	子夏曰:「君子有三變: 望之儼然,即之也溫,聽其言也厲。」
bm	損益

bn	如水益深，如火益熱，亦運而已矣。
bo	易
bp	古之爲市也，以其所有易其所無者。
bq	以小易大。
br	惠子易衣變冠。
bs	買鬻，易也。
bt	宋人易子而食之。
bu	古者易子而教之。
bv	夷子思以易天下。
bw	化
bx	變
by	易
bz	易
ca	生
cb	萬物有乎生而莫見其根，有乎出而莫見其門。
cc	少知曰：四方之內，六合之里萬物之所生惡起。
cd	生於
ce	亡
cf	化
cg	且比化者無使土親膚於人心獨無忮乎。
ch	其形化其心與之然。
ci	汝
cj	變
ck	爲
cl	化 **爲**
cm	化而爲
cn	身因化爲空桑。
co	魚化而爲鳥。
cp	夫水嚮冬則凝而爲冰。
cq	莊周夢爲胡蝶。
cr	卵之化爲雛。
cs	使木匠化而爲木，不能治木。 使聖人化而爲農夫，不能治農夫。
ct	七日化爲虎。
cu	故李子曰：非狗不得兔。狗化而爲兔則不得兔。
cv	長遷而不反其初則化矣。
cw	化
cx	損
cy	益

cz   易
da   儇 (= 還)
db   運
dc   動
dd   爲
de   變
df   止
dg   必
dh   損
di   損，偏去也。
         偏也者: 兼之(禮)* 體也 。
         其 體 或 去 <或> 存 ， 謂 其 存 者 損 。
dj   益
dk   運易也。
dl   化，徵易也。
         若 黽 爲 鶉。
dm   徵
dn   凡 國 之 存 亡 有 六 徵 。
do   兵 未 戰 而 先 見 敗 徵 ， 此 可 謂 知 兵 矣 。
dp   故 聖 人 見 化 以 觀 其 徵 。
dq   聖 人 之 所 以 過 人 以 先 知 。先 知 必 審 徵 表 。
dr   徵
ds   無 久
dt   徵
du   勢
dv   勢
dw   勢
dx   雖 有 國 士 之 力 不 能 自 舉 其 身 非 無 力 也 ， 勢 不 可 也 。
dy   勢

Chapter 6   Light and the Mirror in Greece and China
a   服
b   勝
c   竊 鈇 也
d   辯
e   夫 水 之 性 清 。 土 者 抇 之 。 故 不 得 清 。
         人 之 性 壽 。 物 者 抇 之 。 故 不 得 壽 。
         (Read 汩 gu for 抇 bo)
f   自 然
g   戕 賊
h   義
i   比 興

j　　辭
k　　言
l　　意
m　　意
n　　直言
o　　彈
p　　說
q　　明
r　　暗
s　　昏
t　　光
u　　知
v　　文候不說。知於顏色。
w　　接
x　　知材也。
　　　知也者，所以知也而必知。「若明」。
y　　慮求也。
　　　慮也者，以其知有求也而不必得之。「若睨」。
z　　智接也。
　　　智也者，以其知過物而能貌之。「若見」。
aa　恕明也。
　　　恕也者，以其知論物而其知之也著。「若明」。
ab　知
ac　智
ad　恕
ae　慮
af　恕
ag　智
ah　明
ai　久
aj　五路
ak　先知
al　辯
am　彰
an　虧
ao　昧
ap　以明
aq　明是非
ar　隱
as　辯
at　照
au　是以聖人...光而不燿。

av   和其光
aw   葆光
ax   明君治國而晦。
ay   隱
az   明
ba   見
bb   照
bc   彰
bd   昧
be   智
bf   照
bg   瞑
bh   人
bi   仁
bj   子曰：人而不仁，如禮何？人而不仁，如樂何？
bk   人
bl   二
bm   仁
bn   人
bo   田
bp   佃
bq   畋
br   艮
bs   根
bt   很
bu   治
bv   治國
bw   治病

Chapter 7   'To Be' in Greece and China
a   有
b   有無
c   ＡＢ也。
d   Ａ非Ｂ也。
e   然
f   當
g   是非
h   在
i   有無
j   Ａ即Ｂ
k   爲
l   有

m	無
n	是
o	非
p	有
q	無
r	是
s	非
t	无有
u	無有
v	指物論
w	通變論
x	曰：二有一乎？曰：二無一。 曰：二有右乎？曰：二無右。 曰：二有左乎？曰：二無左。 曰：二苟無左又無右，二者左與右奈何？ 曰：右可謂二乎？曰：不可。 曰：左可謂二乎？曰：不可。 曰：左與右可謂二乎？曰：可。 曰：謂變非不變可乎？曰：可。 曰：右有與可謂變乎？曰：可。 曰：變隻？(read: 奚變) 曰：右。 曰：右苟變安可謂右。苟不變安可謂變。
y	有無
z	可謂不可謂
aa	來吧,我告訴你我的話你要諦聽只有哪些 研究途徑是可以設想的。 第一條是：存在者存在，它不可能不存在。 這是確信的途徑，因爲它導循真理。 另一條是：存在者不存在，這個不存在必然存在。 走這條路，我告訴你，是什麼都學不到的。 因爲不存在者你是既不能認識（這當然辦不到）， 也不能說出的。 因爲能被思維者和能存在者是同一的。

(From Xifang zhe xue yuanzhu xuandu, Beijing: Shangwu yinshuguan, Vol. 1, p. 31, D4 and D5.)

ab	存在
ac	有
ad	有者無無有
ae	有
af	無
ag	天下萬物生於有，有生於無。
ah	无有

ai	無
aj	有無
ak	無無
al	既以鬼神有無之別。
am	大小
an	多少
ao	有
ap	無
aq	不
ar	非
as	也
at	白馬馬也。
au	圜，一中同長也。
av	非
aw	唯
ax	非
ay	不 + 唯
az	矛非戟也。戟非矛也。
ba	爲
bb	人皆可以爲堯舜。
bc	馬白。
bd	人性善。
be	在
bf	有
bg	無
bh	所謂道惡乎在？莊子曰：无所不在。
bi	即
bj	二子者言則相非，行即相反。
bk	有
bl	不識有諸？曰：有之。
bm	曹交問曰：人皆可以爲堯舜有諸？ 孟子曰：然。
bn	然
bo	是
bp	以是其所非而非其所是，欲是其所非而非其所是。
bq	是是非非謂之知。非是是非謂之愚。
br	非
bs	是
bt	是
bu	當
bv	當

Bibliography

Ackrill, J. L. (1979), *Aristotle's Categories and De Interpretatione*, Oxford: Clarendon Press (Clarendon Aristotle Series).

Allan, S. (1997), *The Way of Water and Sprouts of Virtue*, Albany: State University of New York Press.

Allinson, Robert E. (2001), 'The Myth of Comparative Philosophy or the Comparative Philosophy *Malgré Lui*', in Bo Mou (ed.), *Two Roads to Wisdom*, La Salle, Illinois: Open Court, pp. 269–91.

Ames, R. T. (1983), *The Art of Rulership: a Study in Ancient Chinese Political Thought*, Honolulu: University of Hawaii Press.

—— (1988), 'Confucius and the Ontology of Knowing', in Deutsch, E. (ed.), *Interpreting Across Boundaries: New Essays in Comparative Philosophy*, Princeton: Princeton University Press, pp. 265–79.

Ames, R. T. and Hall, D. L. (1987), *Thinking Through Confucius*, Albany: State University of New York Press.

Ames, R. T. and Rosemont, H. Jr. (eds) (1998), *The Analects of Confucius: a Philosophical Translation*, New York: Ballantine Books.

Aubrey, J. (1962), *Aubrey's Brief Lives*, ed. O. L. Dick, London: Secker and Warburg.

Austin, J. L. (1964), *Sense and Sensibilia*, Oxford: Oxford University Press.

Bachelard, G. (1933), *Les intuitions atomistiques: essai de classification*, Paris: Boivin.

Bao Zhiming (1987), 'Abstraction, *ming-shi* and problems of translation', *Journal of Chinese Philosophy*, **14**, 419–44.

Balme, D. M. (1975), 'Aristotle's Use of Differentiae in Zoology', in Barnes, J., Schofield, M. and Sorabji, R. R. K. (eds), *Articles on Aristotle. Vol. 1: Science*, London: Duckworth, pp. 183–93.

Barnes, J. (1982), *The Presocratic Philosophers*, London: Routledge & Kegan.

Bayley, C. (1928), *The Greek Atomists and Epicurus*, Oxford: Clarendon Press.

Beijing daxue zhexuexi (1981–1982), *Xifang zhexue yuanzhu xuandu* [= A selection of original writings of Western philosophers], Beijing: Shangwu yinshuguan, 2 vols.

Benesch, W. (1997), *An Introduction to Comparative Philosophy: a Travel Guide to Philosophical Space*, New York: St. Martin's Press.

Benveniste, E. (1966), *Problèmes de linguistique générale. Vol. 1*, Paris: Gallimard. (Translated as *Problems in General Linguistics*, Coral Gables, FL.: University of Miami Press, 1971.)

—— (1966a), 'La phrase nominale', in *Problèmes de linguistique générale. Vol. 1*, Paris: Gallimard, pp. 151–67.

—— (1966b), 'Tendances récentes en linguistique générale', in *Problèmes de linguistique générale. Vol. 1*, Paris: Gallimard, pp. 3–17.

—— (1966c), 'Catégories de pensée et catégories de langue', in *Problèmes de linguistique générale. Vol. 1*, Paris: Gallimard, pp. 63–74.

—— (1966d), 'Etre et avoir dans leurs fonctions linguistiques', in *Problèmes de linguistique générale. Vol. 1*, Paris: Gallimard, pp. 187–207.

—— (1966e), 'Coup d'oeil sur le développement de la linguistique', in *Problèmes de linguistique générale. Vol. 1*, Paris: Gallimard, pp. 18–31.

—— (1974), 'Les transformations des catégories linguistiques', in *Problèmes de linguistique générale. Vol. 2*, Paris: Gallimard, pp. 126–36.

Bernal, M. (1987), *Black Athena: the Afroasiatic Roots of Classical Civilization. Vol. 1: The Fabrication of Ancient Greece 1785–1985*, London: Free Association Books.

—— (1991), *Black Athena: the Afroasiatic Roots of Classical Civilization. Vol. 2: The Archaeological and Documentary Evidence*, London: Free Association Books.

Biderman, Sh. and Scharfstein, B. A. (eds) (1989), *Rationality in Question: on Eastern and Western Views of Rationality*, Leiden; New York: Brill.

Binder, G. and Liesenborghs, L. (1966), 'Eine Zuweisung der Sentenz οὐκ ἔστιν ἀντιλέγειν an Prodikos von Keos', *Museum Helveticum*, **23**, 27–43.

Black, M. (1981), 'Metaphor', in Johnson, M. (ed.), *Philosophical Perspectives on Metaphor*, Minneapolis: University of Minnesota Press, pp. 63–82.

—— (1986), 'More About Metaphor', in Ortony, A. (ed.), *Metaphor and Thought*, Cambridge: Cambridge University Press, pp. 19–43.

Bloom, A. H. (1981), *The Linguistic Shaping of Thought: a Study in the Impact of Language on Thinking in China and the West*, Hillsdale: Lawrence Erlbaum.

—— (1989), 'The Privileging of Experience in Chinese Practical Reasoning', *Journal of Chinese Philosophy*, **16**, 297–307.

Blumenberg, H. (1957), 'Licht als Metapher der Wahrheit: im Vorfeld der philosophischen Begriffsbildung', *Studium generale*, **10**, 432–47.

Boas, F. (1911), *Handbook of American Indian Languages*, Washington: Government Printing Office.

Bodde, D. (1967), *China's First Unifier*, Hong Kong: Hong Kong University Press.

Bosley, Richard (1997), 'The Emergence of Concepts of a Sentence in Ancient Greek and in Ancient Chinese Philosophy', *Journal of Chinese Philosophy*, **24**, 209–29.

Brancacci, A. (1990), *Oikeios logos: la filosofia del linguaggio di Antistene*, Naples: Bibliopolis.

Bremer, D. (1973), 'Hinweise zum griechischen Ursprung und zur europäischen Geschichte der Lichtmetaphysik', *Archiv für Begriffsgeschichte*, **17**, 7–35.

—— (1974), 'Licht als universales Darstellungsmedium: Materialien und Bibliographie', *Archiv für Begriffsgeschichte*, **18**, 185–206.

—— (1976), 'Licht und Dunkel in der frühgriechischen Dichtung: Interpretationen zur Vorgeschichte der Lichtmetaphysik', *Archiv für Begriffsgeschichte*, Suppl. 1, 1–446.

—— (1980), 'Aristoteles, Empedokles und die Erkenntnisleistung der Metapher', in *Poetica*, **12**, 350–76.

Bröcker, W. (1959), 'Platons ontologischer Komparativ', *Hermes*, **87**, 415–25.

Bronkhorst, J. (ed.) (2001), *La rationalité en Asie = Rationality in Asia: Actes du colloque de l'Institut International pour les Etudes Asiatiques (IAAS), tenu à Leiden*, Lausanne: Université de Lausanne, Faculté des lettres (Etudes de Lettres; 2001:3).

—— (2001), 'Pourquoi la philosophie existe-t-elle en Inde?', in Bronkhorst, J. (ed.), *La rationalité en Asie = Rationality in Asia: Actes du colloque de l'Institut International pour les Etudes Asiatiques (IAAS), tenu à Leiden*, Lausanne: Université de Lausanne, Faculté des lettres, pp. 7–48.

Brown, L. (1994), 'The Verb "To Be" in Greek Philosophy: Some Remarks', in Everson, S. (ed.), *Language*, Cambridge: Cambridge University Press, pp. 212–36.

Brunner, F. (1975), 'Une théorie de la perception dans l'Advaita Vedanta et quelques comparaisons avec la philosophie occidentale', *Revue de théologie et de philosophie*, **4**, 252–74.

Brunot, F. ([1905] 1966), *Histoire de la langue française des origines à nos jours. Vol. 1: De l'époque latine à la Renaissance*, Paris: A. Colin.

Brunschwig, J. (1991), 'Quelques malentendus concernant la logique d'Aristote', in Sinaceur, M. A. (ed.), *Penser avec Aristote*, Toulouse: Erès, pp. 423–29.

Burkert, W. (1970), 'La genèse des choses et des mots. Le papyrus de Derveni entre Anaxagore et Cratyle', *Les Etudes Philosophiques*, **25**, 443–55.

Canto-Sperber, M. and Barnes, J. (eds) (1997), *Philosophie grecque*, Paris: Presses Universitaires de France.

Cassin, B. (1980), *Si Parménide: le traité anonyme De Melisso Xenophane Gorgia. Edition critique et commentaire*, Lille: Presses Universitaires de Lille.

Cassin, B. and Narcy, M. (1989), *La décision du sens: le livre "Gamma" de la "Métaphysique" d'Aristote*, Paris: Vrin.

Caveing, M. (1993), 'Rationalité et réévaluation des mathématiques anciennes en Europe', in R. Klibanski, R. and Pears, D. (eds), *La philosophie en Europe*, Paris: Gallimard: Unesco, pp. 541–85.

Chan Wing-Tsit (1973), *A Source Book in Chinese Philosophy*, Princeton: Princeton University Press.

Chang, Leo S. and Feng Yu (1998), *The Four Political Treatises of the Yellow Emperor*, Honolulu: University of Hawaii Press, 1998.

Chao Yuanren (1959), 'How Chinese Logic Operates', in *Anthropological Linguistics*, **1**, 1–8.

Charlton, W. (1984), *Aristotle's Physics, Books I and II*, Oxford: Clarendon Press. (Clarendon Aristotle Series).

Cheng Chung-Ying (1965), 'Inquiries into Classical Chinese Logic', *Philosophy East and West*, **15**, 195–216.

Chmielewski, J. (1962–1969), 'Notes on Early Chinese Logic I–VIII', *Rocznik Orientalistyczny*, **26–32**.

—— (1962), 'Notes on Early Chinese Logic (I)', *Rocznik Orientalistyczny*, **26**, 7–21.

—— (1963), 'Notes on Early Chinese Logic (II)', *Rocznik Orientalistyczny*, **26**, 91–105.

—— (1966), 'Notes on Early Chinese Logic (VI)', *Rocznik Orientalistyczny*, **30**, 31–52.

—— (1979), 'Concerning the Problem of Analogic Reasoning in Ancient China', *Rocznik Orientalistyczny*, **40**, 64–78.

Cikoski, J. S. (1975), 'On Standards of Analogical Reasoning in the Late Chou', *Journal of Chinese Philosophy*, **2**, 325–57.

Cordero, N. – L. (1984), *Les deux chemins de Parménide*, Paris: Vrin.

Creel, H. G. (1970), *The Origins of Statecraft in China. Vol. 1: the Western Chou Empire*, London; Chicago: Chicago University Press.

—— (1974), *Shen Pu-Hai: a Chinese Political Philosopher of the Fourth Century* BC, Chicago: Chicago University Press.

Cullen, Chr. (1976), 'A Chinese Eratosthenes of the Flat Earth: a Study of a Fragment of Cosmology in *Huai Nan Tzu*', *Bulletin of the School of Oriental and African Studies*, **39**, 106–27.

—— (1995), *Astronomy and Mathematics in Ancient China: the Zhou bi suan jing*, Cambridge: Cambridge University Press.

Curd, P. (1998), 'Eleatic Arguments', in Gentzler, J. (ed.), *Method in Ancient Philosophy*, Oxford: Clarendon Press, pp. 1–28.

Dancy, R. M. (1975), *Sense and Contradiction: a Study in Aristotle*, Dordrecht: Reidel.

Davidson, D. (1978), 'What Metaphors Mean', *Critical Inquiry*, **5**, 31–47.

Demiéville, P. (1947), 'Le miroir spirituel', *Sinologica*, **1**, 112–37.

Defoort, C. (1997), *The Pheasant Cap Master* (He guan zi)*: a Rhetorical Reading*, Albany: State University of New York Press.

—— (1998), 'The Rhetorical Power of Naming: The Case of Regicide', *Asian Philosophy*, **8**/2, 111–18.

Denyer, N. (1991), *Language, Thought and Falsehood in Ancient Greek Philosophy*, London: Routledge.

Derrida, J. (1971), 'La mythologie blanche (la métaphore dans le texte philosophique)', *Poétique*, **5**, 1–52. (Translated in *Margins of Philosophy*, by A. Bass, Chicago: University of Chicago Press, 1982.)

—— (1976), *Of Grammatology*, trans. G. C. Spivak, London; Baltimore: John Hopkins University Press.

—— (1981), 'The Supplement of Copula: Philosophy Before Linguistics', in Harari, J. V. (ed.), *Textual Strategies: Perspectives in Post-structuralist Criticism*, Ithaca New York: Cornell University Press, pp. 82–120. (Originally published in *Marges de la philosophie*, Paris: Editions de Minuit, 1972.)

Destrée, P. (1998), 'L'être et la figure du soleil. Note sur Parménide, D.K. B 8, v. 43', *Revue des études grecques*, **111**, 304–307.

Deutsch, E. (1970), 'Commentary on J. L. Mehta's "Heidegger and the comparison of Indian and Western philosophy"', *Philosophy East and West*, **20**, 318–21.

Diels, H. (1951–1952), *Die Fragmente der Vorsokratiker*, ed. W. Kranz, 3 vols, sixth edn, Berlin: Weidmann (= DK).

Dumarsais-Fontanier ([1730] and [1818] 1984), *Les tropes*, introd. G. Genette, Geneva: Slatkine.

Dupréel, E. (1980), *Les Sophistes: Protagoras, Gorgias, Prodicus, Hippias*, Neuchâtel: Editions du Griffon.

Feng Jingyuan (1985), 'Qi and the Atom: a Comparison of the Concept of Matter in Chinese and Western Philosophy', *Chinese Studies in Philosophy*, **17**, 22–44.

Feng Youlan (1952), *A History of Chinese Philosophy. Vol. 1*, Princeton: Princeton University Press.

Flew, A. G. N. (1979), 'The Cultural Roots of Analytic Philosophy', *Journal of Chinese Philosophy*, **6**, 1–14.

Fontanier, P. ([1821–1830] 1977), *Les figures du discours*, Paris: Flammarion.

Forke, A. (1901–1902), 'The Chinese Sophists', *Journal of the China Branch of the Royal Asiatic Society*, **34**, 1–100.

Forster, E. S. (1978), *Aristotle, On Sophistical Refutations*, Cambridge, MA: Harvard University Press (The Loeb Classical Library).

Foucher, A. (1949), *Le compendium des Topiques (tarka samgraha) d'Annambhatta avec des extraits de trois commentaires indiens*, Paris: Adrien-Maisonneuve.

Frede, M. (1981), 'Categories in Aristotle', in *Studies in Aristotle*, ed, D. J. O'Meara, Washington: Catholic University of America Press, pp. 1–24. (Studies in Philosophy and the History of Philosophy, vol. 9.)

Fritz, K. von (1955), 'Die ἀρχαί in der griechischen Mathematik', *Archiv für Begriffsgeschichte*, **1**, 13–103.

—— (1966), *Philosophie und sprachlicher Ausdruck bei Demokrit, Plato und Aristoteles*, Darmstadt: Wissenschaftliche Buchgesellschaft.

Fu, Ch. (1973), 'Lao Tzu's Concept of Tao', *Inquiry*, **16**, 376–78.

Furley, D. J. (1967), *Two Studies in the Greek Atomists*, Princeton: Princeton University Press.

—— (1987), *The Greek Cosmologists. Vol. 1: The Formation of the Atomic Theory and its Earliest Critics*, Cambridge: Cambridge University Press.

Gadamer, H.-G. (1972), *Wahrheit und Methode: Grundzüge einer philosophischen Hermeneutik*, Tübingen: J. C. B. Mohr. (Translated as: *Truth and Method*, New York: Crossroad, 1985.)

—— (1999), 'Wieweit schreibt Sprache das Denken vor?', in *Gesammelte Werke. Bd. 2: Hermeneutik II: Wahrheit und Methode. 2. Ergänzungen*, Tübingen: J. C. B. Mohr, pp. 199–206.

Galton, A. (1984), *The Logic of Aspects: an Axiomatic Approach*, Oxford: Clarendon Press.

Gassmann, R. H. (1988), *Cheng ming: Richtigstellung der Bezeichnungen: Zu den Quellen eines Philosophems im antiken China: ein Beitrag zur Konfuzius-Forschung*, Berne: P. Lang.

Genette, G. (1972), 'La rhétorique restreinte', in *Figures*, Paris: Seuil, vol. 3, pp. 21–40.

Gernet, J. (1982), *Chine et christianisme: action et réaction*, Paris: Gallimard. (Translated as: *China and the Christian Impact: a Conflict of Cultures*, Cambridge; New York: Cambridge University Press; Paris: Editions de la Maison des sciences de l'homme, 1985,)

—— (1991), *Chine et christianisme: la première confrontation*, édition revue et corrigée, Paris: Gallimard.

—— (1994), 'Sur la notion de changement', in *L'intelligence de la Chine: le social et le mental*, Paris: Gallimard, pp. 323–34.

Gernet, J. and Vernant, J.-P. (1964), 'L'évolution des idées en Chine et en Grèce du VIe au IIe siècle avant notre ère', *Bulletin de l'Association Guillaume Budé*, **4/3**, pp. 308–325.

Ghiglione, A. (1999), *La pensée chinoise ancienne et l'abstraction*, Paris: Editions You-Feng.

Gloy, K. (ed.) (1999), *Rationalitätstypen*, Freiburg i.Br. [etc.] : K. Alber.

Gourinat, J.-B. (2001), 'Principe de contradiction, principe du tiers-exclu et principe de bivalence: philosophie première ou organon?', in Bastit, M. and Follon, J. (eds), *Logique et métaphysique dans l'Organon d'Aristote: actes du colloque de Dijon*, Leuven: Peeters, pp. 63–91.

Graham, A. C. (1955), 'Kung-sun Lung's Essay on Meaning and Things', *Journal of Oriental Studies*, **2**, 282–301.

—— (1957), 'The Composition of the Gongsuen Longtzyy', *Asia Maior*, **11**, 128–52 (reprinted in Graham 1986b, pp. 126–66).

—— (1964), 'The Logic of the Mohist Hsiao-ch'ü', *T'oung Pao*, **51**, 1–54.

—— (1965), '"Being" in Linguistics and Philosophy: a Preliminary Inquiry', *Foundations of Language*, **1**, 223–31.

—— (1965b), 'Two Dialogues in Kung-Sun Lung Tzu, "White Horse" and "Left and Right"', *Asia Maior*, **11**, 128–52 (reprinted in Graham 1986b, pp. 167–92).

—— (1969–1970), 'Chuang-tzu's Essay on Seeing Things as Equal', *History of Religions*, **9**, 137–59.

—— (1975), 'The Concepts of Necessity and the "a priori" in Later Mohist Disputation', *Asia Maior*, **19**, 163–90.

—— (1976), 'Chuang-Tzu and the Rambling Mode', in Lai, T. C. (ed.), *The Art and Profession of Translation: Proceedings of the Asia Foundation Conference on Chinese–English Translation*, Hong Kong: The Hong Kong Translation Society, pp. 61–77.

—— (1978), *Later Mohist Logic, Ethics and Science*, London: School of Oriental and African Studies; Hong Kong: Chinese University Press.

—— (1981), *Chuang-tzu: the Seven Inner Chapters and Other Writings from the Book Chuang-tzu*, London: Allen and Unwin.

—— (1985), *Reason and Spontaneity*, London: Curzon Press.

—— (1986a), *Yin-Yang and the Nature of Correlative Thinking*, Singapore: Institute of East Asian Philosophies.

—— (1986b), 'Three Studies of Kung-Sun Lung', in *Studies in Chinese Philosophy and Philosophical Literature*, Singapore: The Institute of East Asian Philosophies, pp. 125–215.

—— (1986c), 'The Date and Composition of Liehtzyy' (1965), in *Studies in Chinese Philosophy and Philosophical Literature*, Singapore: The Institute of East Asian Philosophies, pp. 216–82.

—— (1986d), '"Being" in Western Philosophy Compared With *shi/fei* and *you/wu* in Chinese Philosophy' (1960), in *Studies in Chinese Philosophy and Philosophical Literature*, Singapore: The Institute of East Asian Philosophies, pp. 322–59.

—— (1986e), 'Relating Categories to Question Forms in Pre-Han Chinese Thought', in, *Studies in Chinese Philosophy and Philosophical Literature*, Singapore: The Institute of East Asian Philosophies, pp. 360–411.

—— (1989), *Disputers of the Tao: Philosophical Argument in Ancient China*, La Salle: Open Court.

Granet, M. (1934), *La pensée chinoise*, Paris: La Renaissance du Livre.

Guthrie, W. K. C. (1978), *A History of Greek Philosophy. Vol. 5*, Cambridge: Cambridge University Press.

Hale, K. (1986), 'Notes on World View and Semantic Categories: Some Warlpiri Examples', in Muysken, P. and Van Riemsdijk, H. (eds), *Features and Projections*, Dordrecht: Foris Publications, pp. 233–54.

Hall, D. L. and Ames, R. T. (1995), *Anticipating China: Thinking Through the Narratives of Chinese and Western Culture*, Albany: State University of New York Press.

Hansen, Ch. D. (1983), *Language and Logic in Ancient China*, Ann Arbor: University of Michigan Press.

—— (1985), 'Chinese Language, Chinese Philosophy, and "Truth"', *Journal of Asian Studies*, **44**, 491–519.

—— (1987), 'Classical Chinese Philosophy as Linguistic Analysis', *Journal of Chinese Philosophy*, **14**, 309–30.

Harbsmeier, Chr. (1979), *Wilhelm von Humboldts Brief an Abel-Rémusat und die philosophische Grammatik des Altchinesischen*, Stuttgart: Frommann Holzboog.

—— (1981), *Aspects of Classical Chinese Syntax*, London; Malmö: Curzon Press.

—— (1989), 'Marginalia sino-logica', in Allinson, R. E. (ed.), *Understanding the Chinese Mind: the Philosophical Roots*, Oxford: Oxford University Press, pp. 125–66.

—— (1995), 'Some Notions of Time and of History in China and in the West with a Digression on the Anthropology of Writing', in Chun-Chieh Huang and Zürcher, E. (eds), *Time and Space in Chinese Culture*, Leiden; New York: Brill, pp. 49–71.

—— (1998), *Science and Civilisation in China. Vol. 7.1: Language and Logic*, Cambridge: Cambridge University Press.

—— (2001), 'La rationalité dans l'histoire intellectuelle de la Chine', in Bronkhorst, J. (ed.), *La rationalité en Asie = Rationality in Asia: Actes du colloque de l'Institut International pour les Etudes Asiatiques (IAAS), tenu à Leiden*, Lausanne: Université de Lausanne, Faculté des lettres, pp. 127–51.

Hatton, R. (1982), 'A Comparison of Ch'i and Prime Matter', *Philosophy East and West*, **32**, 159–75.

—— (1988), 'Is Ch'i Recycled? The Debate Within the Neo-Confucian Tradition and its Implications with Respect to the Principle of Personal Identity', *Journal of Chinese Philosophy*, **15**, 289–318.

Heidbüchel, U. (1993), *Rhetorik im Antiken China. Eine Untersuchung der Ausdrucksformen höfischer Rede im Zuo Zhuan, Herzog Zhao*, Münster: Eigenverlag.

Heidel, W. A. (1911), 'Antecedents of Greek Corpuscular Theories', *Harvard Studies in Classical Philology*, **22**, 111–72.

Heidegger, M. ([1943] 1987), *Heraklit: der Anfang des abendländischen Denkens, Freiburger Vorlesung, Sommersemester 1943*, ed. M. Frings, Frankfurt a.M.: V. Klostermann.

Helman, D. H. (ed.) (1988), *Analogical Reasoning: Perspectives of Artificial Intelligence, Cognitive Science, and Philosophy*, Dordrecht; Boston: Kluwer Academic Publishers.

Henricks, R. G. (2000), *Lao Tzu's Tao Te Ching: a Translation of the Startling New Documents Found at Guodian*, New York: Columbia University Press.

Henry, E. (1987), 'The Motif of Recognition in Early China', *Harvard Journal of Asiatic Studies*, **47**/1, 5–30.

Hintikka, J. (1983), *The Game of Language: Studies in Game-Theoretical Semantics and its Applications*, Dordrecht: Reidel, pp. 201–31 (= chapter 8: 'Semantical Games and Aristotelian Categories').

Ho Peng Yoke (1985), *Li, Qi and Shu: an Introduction to Science and Civilisation in China*, Hong Kong: University Press.

Holenstein, E. (1994), 'L'herméneutique interculturelle', *Revue de théologie et de philosophie*, **126**, 19–37.

Hountondji, P. J. (1982), 'Langues africaines et philosophie: l'hypothèse relativiste', *Les Etudes philosophiques*, **37**/4, 393–406.

Hu Shi (1922), *The Development of the Logical Method in Ancient China*, Shanghai: Commercial Press.

Hughes, E. R. (1942), *Chinese Philosophy in Classical Times*, London: Dent.

Husserl, E. ([1938] 1977), *La crise de l'humanité européenne et la philosophie = Die Krisis des europäischen Menschentums und die Philosophie*, bilingual edn, trans. P. Ricoeur, Paris: Aubier Montaigne.

Jacquinod, B. (1988), 'Etude de vocabulaire grec: *auxô* et *aôtos*', *Revue des études anciennes*, **90**, 315–23.

Johnson, M. (1981), 'Introduction: Metaphor in the Philosophical Tradition', in Johnson, M. (ed.), *Philosophical Perspectives on Metaphor*, Minneapolis: University of Minnesota Press, pp. 3–47.

Joseph, G. G. (1991), *The Crest of the Peacock: non European Roots of Mathematics*, Harmondsworth: Penguin Books.

Jullien, F. (1992), *La propension des choses: pour une histoire de l'efficacité en Chine*, Paris: Seuil. (Translated as *The Propensity of Things: Toward a History of Efficacy in China*, New York: Zone Books, 1995.)

—— (1995), *Le détour et l'accès: stratégies du sens en Chine, en Grèce*, Paris: Grasset. (Translated as *Detour and Access: Strategies of Meanings in China and Greece*, New York: Zone Books, 2000.)

—— (1998), *Un sage est sans idée ou L'autre de la philosophie*, Paris: Seuil.

—— (2001), *Du "temps": éléments d'une philosophie du vivre*, Paris: Grasset.

Kagame, A. (1956), *La philosophie bantu-rwandaise de l'être*, Gembloux: Duculot.

Kahn, Ch. H. (1969), 'The Thesis of Parmenides', *Review of Metaphysics*, **22**, 700–734.

—— (1973a), *The Verb Be in Ancient Greek*, Dordrecht: Reidel.

—— (1973b), 'On the Theory of the Verb "To Be"', in Munitz, M. K. (ed.), *Logic and Ontology*, New York: New York University Press, pp. 1–20.

—— (1973c), 'Language and Ontology in the *Cratylus*', in Lee, E. N., Mourelatos, A. P. D. and Rorty, R. M. (eds), *Exegesis and Argument: Studies in Greek Philosophy Presented to Gregory Vlastos, Phronesis. Supplementary Vol. 1*, pp. 152–76.

—— (1976), 'Why Existence does not Emerge as a Distinct Concept in Greek Philosophy', *Archiv für Geschichte der Philosophie*, **58**, 323–34.

—— (1978), 'Questions and Categories: Aristotle's Doctrine of Categories in the Light of Modern Research', in Hiz, H. (ed.), *Questions*, Dordrecht: Reidel, pp. 227–78.

—— (1979), 'Linguistic Relativism and the Greek Project of Ontology', *Neue Hefte für Philosophie*, **13**, 20–33.

—— (1981), 'Some Philosophical Uses of "To Be" in Plato', *Phronesis*, **26**, 105–34.

—— (1991), 'Some Remarks on the Origins of Greek Science and Philosophy', in Bowen, A. C. (ed.), *Science and Philosophy in Classical Greece*, New York; London: Garland, pp. 1–10.

—— (1995), 'The Greek Verb "To Be" and the Concept of Being', in Irwin, T. (ed.), *Philosophy before Socrates. Vol. 1*, New York; London: Garland Publishing, pp. 157–77.

Kamenarovic, I. P. (2001), *Le conflit: perceptions chinoise et occidentale*, Paris: Cerf.

Karlgren, B. (1957), 'Grammata serica recensa', *Bulletin of the Museum of Far Eastern Antiquities*, **29**, 1–331.

Katz, J. J. (1986), *Cogitations: a Study of the Cogito in Relation to the Philosophy of Language and a Study of them in Relation to the Cogito*, New York; Oxford: Oxford University Press.

Keightley, D. (1989), 'Craft and Culture: Metaphors of Governance in Early China', in *Proceedings of the 2nd International Conference on Sinology. Section on History and Archaeology*, Taipei: Academia Sinica, pp. 31–70.

—— (1990), 'Early Civilization in China: Reflections on How It Became Chinese', in Ropp, P. S. (ed.), *Heritage of China: Contemporary Perspectives on Chinese Civilization*, Berkeley: University of California Press, pp. 15–54.

Kirby, J. T. (1997), 'Aristotle on Metaphor', *American Journal of Philology*, **118**, 517–54.

Kirwan, C. (1980), *Aristotle's* Metaphysics. *Books Γ, Δ, and E, translation with notes*, Oxford: Clarendon Press (Clarendon Aristotle Series).

Kirk, G. S., Raven, J. E. and Schofield, M. (1983), *The Presocratic Philosophers: a Critical History with a Selection of Texts*, second edn, Cambridge: Cambridge University Press (= KRS).

Kittay, E. F. (1987), *Metaphor: its Cognitive Force and Linguistic Structure*, Oxford: Clarendon Press.

Klowski, J. (1967), 'Zum Entstehen der Begriffe Sein und Nichts und der Weltentstehungs- und Weltschöpfungstheorien im strengen Sinne (I. u. II. Teil)', *Archiv für Geschichte der Philosophie*, **49**, 121–48 (Teil I) and 225–54 (Teil II).

Knorr, W. R. (1981), 'On the Early History of Axiomatics: the Interaction of Mathematics and Philosophy in Greek Antiquity', in *Theory Change, Ancient Axiomatics, and Galileo's Methodology, Proceedings of the 1978 Pisa Conference on the History and Philosophy of Science*, Dordrecht; Boston: Reidel, vol. I, pp. 145–86.

—— (1982), 'Infinity and Continuity: the Interaction of Mathematics and Philosophy in Antiquity', in Kretzmann, N. (ed.), *Infinity and Continuity in Ancient and Medieval Thought*, Ithaca; London: Cornell University Press, pp. 112–45.

Konersmann, R. (1991), *Lebendige Spiegel: die Metapher des Subjektes*, Frankfurt a.M.: Fischer.

Kou Pao-Koh (1953), *Deux sophistes chinois: Houei Che et Kong-Souen Long*, Paris: Imprimerie Nationale: Presses Universitaires de France.

Kwee Swan Liat (1953), *Methods of Comparative Philosophy*, Leiden: Universitaire Pers.

Lackner, M. (1993), 'Les avatars de quelques termes philosophiques occidentaux dans la langue chinoise', *Etudes chinoises*, **12**, 136–60.

Lakoff, G. and Johnson, M. (1980), *Metaphors We Live By*, Chicago; London: University of Chicago Press.

Laks, A. and Most, G. W. (eds) (1997), *Studies on the Derveni Papyrus*, Oxford: Clarendon Press.

Lanérès, N. (1994), 'La phrase nominale en grec: nouvelle approche', *Bulletin de la Société de Linguistique de Paris*, **LXXXIX**, 229–54.

Lasserre, F. (1964), *The Birth of Mathematics in the Age of Plato*, London: Hutchinson.

Lau, D. C. (1952–1953), 'Some Logical Problems in Ancient China', *Proceedings of the Aristotelian Society*, **53**, 189–204.

—— (1963), 'On Mencius' Use of the Method of Analogy in Argument', *Asia Maior*, **10**, 173–94.

—— (1979), *Confucius, The Analects (Lun yü)*, Harmondsworth: Penguin Books.

—— (1983), *Mencius*, Harmondsworth: Penguin Books.

Le Blanc, Ch. (1987), 'From Ontology to Cosmogony: Notes on Chuang Tzu and Huai-nan Tzu', in Le Blank, Ch. and Blader, S. (eds), *Chinese Ideas about Nature and Society: Studies in Honour of Derk Bodde*, Hong Kong: Hong Kong University Press, pp. 117–29.

Leslie, D. (1964), *Argument by Contradiction in Pre-Buddhist Chinese Reasoning*, Canberra: Australian National University, Center of Oriental Studies.

Levet, J.-P. (1976), *Le vrai et le faux dans la pensée grecque archaïque: étude de vocabulaire. Tome I: Présentation générale. Le vrai et le faux dans les épopées homériques*, Paris: Les Belles Lettres.

Lévi-Strauss, C. (1990), *Le cru et le cuit*, Paris: Plon.

Liou Kia-Hway (1965), 'The Configuration of Chinese Reasoning', *Diogène*, **49**, 66–96.

Lloyd, G. E. R. (1962), 'The Development of Aristotle's Theory of Classification of Animals', *Phronesis*, **7**, 91–104.

—— (1966), *Polarity and Analogy: Two Types of Argumentation in Early Greek Thought*, Cambridge: Cambridge University Press.

—— (1979), *Magic, Reason and Experience: Studies in the Origin and Development of Greek Science*, Cambridge: Cambridge University Press.

—— (1990), *Demystifying Mentalities*, Cambridge: Cambridge University Press.

—— (1996), *Adversaries and Authorities: Investigations Into Ancient Greek and Chinese Science*, Cambridge: Cambridge University Press.

Lohmann, J. (1948), 'M. Heideggers "ontologische Differenz" und die Sprache', *Lexis*, **1**, 49–106. (Translated in *On Heidegger and Language*, ed. J. Kockelmans, Evanston: Northwestern University Press, 1972, pp. 303–63.)

Lorentz, K. and Mittelstrass, J. (1967), 'On Rational Philosophy of Language: the Program in Plato's *Cratylus* Reconsidered', *Mind*, **76**, 1–20.

Lu Xing (1998), *Rhetoric in Ancient China, Fifth to Third Century B.C.E.: a Comparison with Classical Greek Rhetoric*, Columbia: University of South Carolina.

Luther, W. (1965), 'Wahrheit, Licht, Sehen und Erkennen im Sonnengleichnis von Platons *Politeia*: ein Ausschnitt aus der Lichtmetaphysik der Griechen', *Studium generale*, **18**, 479–96.

—— (1966), 'Wahrheit, Licht und Erkenntnis in der griechischen Philosophie bis Demokrit', *Archiv für Begriffsgeschichte*, **10**, 1–240.

Lyons, J. (1977), *Semantics. Vol. 2*, Cambridge: Cambridge University Press.

MacCormac, E. A. (1985), *A Cognitive Theory of Metaphor*, Cambridge, MA: MIT Press.

Makeham, J. (1991), 'Names, Actualities and the Emergence of Essential Theories of Naming in Classical Chinese Thought', *Philosophy East and West*, **41**, 341–63.

Mall, R. A. (1995), *Philosophie im Vergleich der Kulturen: interkulturelle Philosophie – eine neue Orientierung*, Darmstadt: Wissenschaftliche Buchgesellschaft.

Martzloff, J.-Cl. (1988), *Histoire des mathématiques chinoises*, Paris: Masson. (Translated as: *A History of Chinese Mathematics*, Berlin; New York: Springer, 1997.)

Masson-Oursel, P. (1911), 'Objet et méthode de la philosophie comparée', *Revue de métaphysique et de morale*, **19**, 541–48.

—— (1913), 'La démonstration confucéenne: note sur la logique chinoise pré-bouddhique', *Revue de l'histoire des religions*, **67**, 49–54.

—— (1926), *Comparative Philosophy*, London: Kegan Paul, Trench, Trubner and Company; New York: Harcourt, Brace and Company. (Reprinted: London: Routledge, 2000.)

—— (1941), *Le fait métaphysique*, Paris: Presses Universitaires de France.

Mauthner, F. (1902), *Beiträge zu einer Kritik der Sprache. Vol. 3: Zur Grammatik und Logik*, Berlin; Stuttgart: J. G. Cotta.

Mazaheri, S. (1992), *Anfänge metaphysischer Spekulation im alten China und im alten Griechenland: eine Gegenüberstellung anhand von Originaltexten*, Diss. Frankfurt am Main. (Reprinted under the title: *Anfänge der Metaphysik im alten China und im alten Griechenland: eine Gegenüberstellung*, Aachen: Shaker, 1997.)

Mei Yi-Pao (1929), *The Ethical and Political Works of Motse*, London: Probsthain (Probsthain's Oriental Series; vol. XIX).

Meillet, A. ([1924] 1984), *La méthode comparative en linguistique historique*, Paris; Geneva: Slatkine Reprints.

—— (1926), 'L'évolution des formes grammaticales', in *Linguistique historique et linguistique générale*, Paris: Honoré Champion, pp. 130–48.

Meillet, A. and Vendryès, J. (1963), *Traité de grammaire comparée des langues classiques*, Paris: H. Champion.

Menn, S. (2002), 'Plato and the Method of Analysis', *Phronesis*, **47**/3, 193–222.

Metzger, Th. A. (1985–1987), 'Some Ancient Roots of Ancient Chinese Thought: This-Worldliness, Epistemological Optimism, Doctrinality, and the Emergence of Reflexivity in the Eastern Zhou', *Early China*, **11–12**, 61–117.

Moritz, R. (1973), *Hui Shi und die Entwicklung des philosophischen Denkens im alten China*, Berlin: Akademie-Verlag.

—— (ed.) (1988), *Wie und warum entstand Philosophie in verschiedenen Regionen der Erde?*, Berlin: Dietz Verlag.

Mou, Bo (ed.) (2001), *Two Roads to Wisdom? Chinese and Analytic Philosophical Traditions*, La Salle: Open Court.

Needham, J. (1954), *Science and Civilisation in China. Vol. 1: Introductory Orientations*, Cambridge: Cambridge University Press.

—— (1956), *Science and Civilisation in China. Vol. 2: History of Scientific Thought*, Cambridge: Cambridge University Press.

—— (1959), *Science and Civilisation in China. Vol. 3: Mathematics and the Sciences of the Heavens and the Earth*, Cambridge: Cambridge University Press.

—— (1962), *Science and Civilisation in China. Vol 4.1: Physics and Physical Technology*, Cambridge: Cambridge University Press.

—— (1968), 'Time and Knowledge in China and the West', in Fraser, J. T. (ed.), *The Voices of Time: a Cooperative Survey of Man's Views of Time as Expressed by the Sciences and by the Humanities*, London: Allen Lane The Penguin Press, pp. 92–135.

Nietzsche, F. ([1885] 1930), *Jenseits von Gut und Böse: Vorspiel einer Philosophie der Zukunft*, Leipzig: Kröner.

Nylan, M. and Sivin, N. (1987), 'The First Neo-Confucianism: an Introduction to Yang Hsiung's "Canon of Supreme Mystery" (T'ai hsuan ching, c. 4 BC)', in Le Blanc, Ch. and Blader, S. *Chinese Ideas about Nature and Society: Studies in Honor of Derk Bodde*, Hong Kong: Hong Kong University Press, pp. 41–99.

Ohji, K. and Xifaras, M. (1999), *Eprouver l'universel: essai de géophilosophie*, Paris: Kimé.

Onians, R. B. (1998), *The Origins of European Thought: about the Body, the Mind, the Soul, the World Time, and Fate. New Interpretations of Greek, Roman and Kindred Evidence also of Some Basic Jewish and Christian Beliefs*, Cambridge: Cambridge University Press.

Ortony, A. (ed.) (1994), *Metaphor and Thought*, Cambridge: Cambridge University Press.

Oshima, H. (1983), 'A Metaphorical Analysis of the Concept of Mind in the Chuang-tzu', in Mair, V. (ed.), *Experimental Essays on Chuang-tzu*, Honolulu: University of Hawaii Press, pp. 63–84.

Owen, G. E. L. (1979a), 'Logic and Metaphysics in Some Earlier Works of Aristotle', in Barnes, J., Schofield, M. and Sorabji, R. R. K. (eds), *Articles on Aristotle. Vol. 3: Metaphysics*, London: Duckworth, pp. 13–32.

—— (1979b), 'Aristotle on Time', in Barnes. J., Schofield, M. and Sorabji, R. R. K. (eds), *Articles on Aristotle. Vol 3: Metaphysics*, London: Duckworth, pp. 140–58.

Pellegrin, P. (1991), 'Le *Sophiste* ou de la division', in Aubenque, P. and Narcy, M. (eds), *Etudes sur le* Sophiste *de Platon*, Naples: Bibliopolis, pp. 389–416.

Perelman, Ch. (1977), *L'Empire rhétorique: rhétorique et argumentation*, Paris: Vrin.

Perelman, Ch. and Olbrechts-Tyteca, L. (1970), *Traité de l'argumentation: la nouvelle rhétorique*, Bruxelles: Editions de l'Université de Bruxelles. (Translated as: *The New Rhetoric: A Treatise on Argumentation*, Notre-Dame; London: University of Notre-Dame Press, 1971.)

Piaget, J. and Inhelder, B. (1978), *Le développement des quantités physiques chez l'enfant: conservation et atomisme*, 4th edn, Paris; Neuchâtel: Delachaux et Niestlé.

Pulleyblank, E. G. (1959), '*Fei, Wei* and Certain Related Words', in Egerod, S. and Glahn, E. (eds), *Studia serica Bernhard Karlgren dedicata*, Copenhagen: International Booksellers, pp. 178–89.

Raphals, L. A. (1992), *Knowing Words: Wisdom and Cunning in the Classical Traditions of China and Greece*, Ithaca; London: Cornell University Press.

—— (1994), 'Poetry and Argument in the *Zhuangzi*', *Journal of Chinese Religions*, **22**, 103–16.

Reding, J.-P. (1985), *Les fondements philosophiques de la rhétorique chez les sophistes grecs et chez les sophistes chinois*, Berne: P. Lang.

—— (1998), 'La philosophie comparée', in *Encyclopédie philosophique universelle. Vol. IV: Le discours philosophique*, Paris: Presses Universitaires de France, section 69, pp. 1203–22.

—— (2002), 'Gongsun Long On What Is Not: Steps Toward the Deciphering of the *Zhiwulun*', *Philosophy East and West*, **52**/2, 190–206.

Reed, N. H. (1972), 'Plato on Flux, Perception and Language', *Proceedings of the Cambridge Philological Association*, **18**, 65–77.

Regamey, C. (1968), 'The Individual and Universal in East and West', in Moore, C. A. (ed.), assisted by Morris, A. V., *The Status of the Individual in East and West*, Honolulu: University of Hawaii Press, pp. 503–18.

Richards, I. A. (1932), *Mencius on the Mind: Experiments in Multiple Definition*, London: Kegan Paul.

—— (1936), *The Philosophy of Rhetoric*, Oxford: Oxford University Press.

Ricoeur, P. (1975), *La métaphore vive*, Paris: Seuil.

Rorty, R. (1980), *Philosophy and the Mirror of Nature*, Oxford: Basil Blackwell.

Rosemont, H. Jr., (1974), 'On Representing Abstractions in Archaic Chinese', *Philosophy East and West*, **24**, 71–88.

—— (1998), 'Appendix II: Further Remarks on Language, Translation and Interpretation', in *The Analects of Confucius*, trans. R. T. Ames and H. Rosemont, Jr., New York: Ballantine Books.

Ross, W. D. (1955), *Aristotelis fragmenta selecta*, Oxford: Clarendon Press.

Ryle, G. (1949), *The Concept of Mind*, London: Hutchinson.

—— (1954), *Dilemmas*, Cambridge: Cambridge University Press.

—— (1971), 'Categories', in *Collected Papers. Vol. 2: Collected essays 1929–1968*, London: Hutchinson.

Sacksteder, W. (1974), 'The Logic of Analogy', *Philosophy and Rhetoric*, **7**, 234–52.

Saffrey, H.-D. (1990), 'Origine, usage et signification du mot IΔEA jusqu'à Platon', in *IDEA: VI Colloquio Internationale*, Roma: Edizioni dell'Ateneo, pp. 1–11.

Scharfstein, B.-A. (1998), *A Comparative History of World Philosophy: From the Upanishads to Kant*, Albany: State University of New York Press.

Scharfstein, B.-A. and Daor, D. (1978), *Philosophy East/Philosophy West: a Critical Comparison of Indian, Chinese, Islamic and European Philosophy*, New York: Oxford University Press.

—— (1979), 'In Answer to Anthony Flew: the Whiteness of Feathers and the Whiteness of Snow', *Journal of Chinese Philosophy*, **6**, 37–53.

Schneider, N. (ed.) (1997), *Philosophie aus interkultureller Sicht = Philosophy From an Intercultural Perspective*, Amsterdam; Atlanta, GA: Rodopi (Studien zur interkulturellen Philosophie; 7).

—— (ed.) (1998), *Einheit und Vielfalt: das Verstehen der Kulturen*, Amsterdam; Atlanta, GA: Rodopi (Studien zur interkulturellen Philosophie; 9).

Schwartz, B. I. (1985), *The World of Thought in Ancient China*, Cambridge, MA; London: The Belknap Press of Harvard University Press.

Searle, J. R. (1981), 'Metaphor', in Johnson, M. (ed.), *Philosophical Perspectives on Metaphor*, Minneapolis: University of Minnesota Press, pp. 248–85.

Segal, Robert A. (2001), 'In Defense of the Comparative Method', *Numen: International Review for the History of Religions*, **48**/3, 339–73.

Seligman, P. (1974), *Being and Not-Being: an Introduction to Plato's* Sophist, The Hague: Martinus Nijhoff.

Shankman, S and Durrant S. W. (eds) (2002), *Early China/Ancient Greece: Thinking Through Comparisons*, Albany: State University of New York Press.

Shorey, P. (1980), *Plato in Twelve Volumes. Vol. 6: The Republic, books VI–X*, London: W. Heinemann (The Loeb Classical Library).

Sivin, N. (1969), 'Cosmos and Computation in Early Chinese Mathematical Astronomy', *T'oung Pao*, **55**, 1–73.

—— (1995a), *Medicine, Philosophy and Religion in Ancient China: Researches and Reflections*, Aldershot: Variorum.

—— (1995b), 'State, Cosmos, and Body in the Last Three Centuries B.C.', *Harvard Journal of Asiatic Studies*, **55**, 5–37.

Slobin, D. I. (1996), 'From "Thought and Language" to "Thinking for Speaking"', in Gumperz, J. J. and Levinson, S. C. (eds), *Rethinking Linguistic Relativity*, Cambridge: Cambridge University Press, pp. 70–96.

Smart, J. J. C. (1953), 'A Note on Categories', *British Journal for the Philosophy of Science*, **4**, 227–28.

Smith, H. (1980), 'Western and Comparative Perspectives on Truth', *Philosophy East and West*, **30**/4, 425–37.

Snell, B. (1978), *Der Weg zum Denken und zur Wahrheit: Studien zur frühgriechischen Sprache*, Göttingen: Vandenhoeck und Ruprecht.

Sorabji, R. R. K. (1979), 'Aristotle on the Instant of Change', in Barnes, J., Schofield, M. and Sorabji, R. R. K. (eds), *Articles on Aristotle. Vol. 3: Metaphysics*, London: Duckworth, pp. 159–77.

Suzuki, D. T. (1914), *A Brief History of Early Chinese Philosophy*, London: Rider and Company.

Swanson, G. (1984), 'The Concept of Change in the Great Treatise', in Rosemont Jr, H. (ed.), *Explorations in Early Chinese Cosmology*, Chico, CA: Scholars Press, p. 67–93.

Szabo, A. (1977), *Les débuts des mathématiques grecques*, Paris: Vrin.

—— (2000), *L'aube des mathématiques grecques*, Paris: Vrin.

Tan Jiefu (1964), *Mobian fawei* [= *The Subtle Unfolding of Mohist Dialectic*], Beijing: Zhonghua shuju.

Tarrant, D. (1960), 'Greek Metaphors of Light', *Classical Quarterly*, **10**, 181–87.

Thom, P. (1999), 'The Principle of Non-Contradiction in Early Greek Philosophy', *Apeiron*, **32**/3, 153–70.

Todorov, T. (1982), 'Comprendre une culture: du dehors/du dedans', *Extrême-Orient – Extrême-Occident*, **1**, 9–15.

Thompson, K. O. (1995), 'When a "White Horse" is not a "Horse"', in *Philosophy East and West*, **45**/4, 481–99.

Trauzettel, R. (1970), 'Zum Problem der chinesischen Ontologie unter dem Aspekt der Sprache', *Zeitschrift der deutschen morgenländischen Gesellschaft*, **119**, 270–77.

Trendelenburg, A. (1846), *Geschichte der Kategorienlehre: 2 Abhandlungen*, Berlin: Bethge (Reedition Hildesheim: Olms, 1979).

Tugendhat, E. (1977), 'Die Seinsfrage und ihre sprachliche Grundlage' [= review of Kahn 1973], *Philosophische Rundschau*, **24**/3–4, 161–76.

Turner, M. (1988), 'Categories and Analogies', in Helman, D. H. (ed.), *Analogical Reasoning: Perspectives of Artificial Intelligence, Cognitive Science, and Philosophy*, Dordrecht: Kluwer Academic Publishers, pp. 3–24.

Unger, U. (1994), *Rhetorik des klassischen Chinesisch*, Wiesbaden: Harrassowitz Verlag.

Vandermeersch, L. (1983), 'Ecriture et langue écrite en Chine', in *Ecritures: systèmes idéographiques et pratiques expressives*, Paris: Le Sycomore, pp. 255–67.

Villard, M. (1984), *Les universaux métaphoriques: étude contrastive de la métaphore en japonais et en français*, Berne: P. Lang.

Vlastos, G. (1979), 'Degrees of Reality in Plato', in Bambrough, R. (ed.), *New Essays on Plato and Aristotle*, London: Routledge & Kegan Paul.

Volkov, A. (1992), 'Analogical Reasoning in Ancient China: Some Examples', *Extrême-Orient – Extrême-Occident*, **14**, 15–48.

Vuillemin, J. (1967), *De la logique à la théologie: cinq études sur Aristote*, Paris: Flammarion.

Waley, A. (1934), *The Way and its Power*, London: Allen and Unwin.

—— (1945), *The Analects* (Lun Yü), London: Allen and Unwin.

Wardy, R. (1992), 'Chinese Whispers', *Proceedings of the Cambridge Philological Society*, **38**, 149–70.

—— (2000), *Aristotle in China: Language, Categories and Translation*, Cambridge: Cambridge University Press (Needham Research Institute Studies; 2).

Waterlow, S. (1982), *Nature, Change, and Agency in Aristotle's* Physics: *a Philosophical Study*, Oxford: Clarendon Press.

Watson, B. (1963), *Hsün Tzu: Basic Writings*, New York: Columbia University Press.

—— (1964), *Han Fei Tzu: Basic Writings*, New York: Columbia University Press.

West, M. L. (1983), *The Orphic Poems*, Oxford: Clarendon Press.

Whorf, B. L. (1956), *Language, Thought and Reality: Selected Writings of Benjamin Lee Whorf*, ed. J. B. Carroll, Cambridge, MA: MIT Press.

Wiredu, K. (1996), *Cultural Universals and Particulars: an African Perspective*, Bloomington: Indiana University Press.

Woods, M. (1982), *Aristotle's Eudemian Ethics, Books I, II, and VIII*, Oxford: Clarendon Press (Clarendon Aristotle Series).

Wu Kuang-Ming (1998), *On the 'Logic' of Togetherness: a Cultural Hermeneutic*, Leiden: Brill (Philosophy of History and Culture; 20).

Wu Xiaoming (1998), 'Philosophy, *philosophia* and *zhexue*', *Philosophy East and West*, **48**, 406–52.

Wunenburger, J.-J. (1997), *Philosophie des images*, Paris: Presses Universitaires de France.

Yu, A. C. (2002), '*Cratylus* and *Xunzi* on Names', in Shankman, S. and Durrant, S. (eds), *Early China/Ancient Greece: Thinking Through Comparisons*, Albany: State University of New York Press, pp. 235–50.

Yu Jiyuan (1999), 'The Language of Being: Between Aristotle and Chinese Philosophy', *International Philosophical Quarterly*, **39**/4, 439–54.

—— (2001), 'Saving the Phenomena: An Aristotelian Method in Comparative Philosophy', in Bo Mou (ed.), *Two Roads to Wisdom*, La Salle, Illinois: Open Court, pp. 293–312.

Yu Mingguang (1993), *Huangdi sijing jin zhu jin yi* [= *A Modern Commentary and Translation of the Four Canons of the Yellow Emperor*], Hunan: Yuelu shushe.

Yu, Pauline (1987) *The Reading of Imagery in the Chinese Poetic Tradition*, Princeton: Princeton University Press.

Yu Yue ([1899] 1967), *Du Gongsunlongzi* [= *On Reading the Gongsunlongzi*], in *Zhuzi pingyi bulu*, Taibei: Zhongguo xueshu mingzhu, p. 26.

Zenker, E. von (1926), *Geschichte der chinesischen Philosophie*, Reichenberg: Stiepel.

Zhang Zhenhua (1991), *Chinesische und europäische Rhetorik. Ein Vergleich in Grundzügen*, Frankfurt a.M.: Peter Lang.

Zürcher, E. (1995), 'In the Beginning: 17th-century Chinese Reactions to Christian Creationism', in Chun-Chieh Huang and Zürcher, E. (eds), *Time and Space in Chinese Culture*, Leiden: Brill, pp. 132–66.

Index

Caveing, M., 49 n1, 58 n25, 59 n31, 61 n44
change, 108f.
Chao Yuanren, 31, 60 n39
Cheng Chungying, 76 n33
Cheng Hao, 188
Chmielewski, J., 31 n5, 60, 76 n33
Chunqiufanlu, 123 n79
Chunyu Kun, 34, 40
ci (proposition, phrasing), 141
Cicero, 50 n6, 194 n73
Cikoski, J. S., 31 n5, 32 n9, 76 n33
circle, 53, 54 n14
class logic, 47
cogito ergo sum, 10
commensurability, 3
comparative method, 1–5, 4 n12, 82
comparative philosophy, 1–5, 7, 82
conceptual analysis, 62
conceptual prerequisites, 100
conflicting appearances, 94, 101, 102, 103
Confucius, 127, 159, 160
    see also Lunyu
congruence, 55 n18
contradiction, 17f., 34, 35, 122, 138 n35
copula, 71, 72, 81, 171, 190, 191, 193
Cordero, H., 72 n24
corpuscular model, 95
correction of names, see *zheng ming*
correlative thinking, 42 n36
cosmology, 102, 105, 116, 187
Creel, H. G., 9 n27
crossbow, 124, 142
crossroads, 130 n10
crucial experiment, 9
Cullen, C., 53 n11, 55 n19
Curd, P., 58 n30

Dancy, R. M., 30 n35
dao, 6
Daodejing, 97 n22, 104, 105, 106, 151, 152 n61, 155, 159 n78, 178, 179 n45, 187
Daor, D., 5 n13, 48 n45, 62 n47
Davidson, D., 166 n92
de (virtue), 8
definition, 63, 64, 85, 92
Defoort, K., 23 n18, 104 n48
degrees of reality, 101, 176

Demiéville, P., 156 n67
Democritus, 23, 24, 62, 92, 94, 101, 102, 156, 161
    see also atomism
demonstration, 59, 64
demonstratives, 20, 42
Deng Xi, 134 n25
Denyer, N., 17 n1
Derrida, J., 9, 10, 13 n39, 73 n27, 163 n86, 165 n90
Derveni, 21, 22 n12
Descartes, 7, 10, 49
Destrée, P., 149 n58
Deutsch, E., 1 n1
dichotomies, 64 n53
differentiae, 85, 88
Diogenes (of Apollonia), 61, 97
Dionysodorus, 17
disjunctives, 59, 60, 61
duan (starting point), 54, 55, 98, 99
Dumarsais, 131 n12
Dupréel, E., 135 n26
durationless, *see wujiu*

einai (to be), 167f., 185
Eleaticism, 57, 60, 181, 188
    see also Parmenides
Empedocles, 107, 127, 161
en (compassion), 40
Epicurus, 94, 102
epistemological obstacle, 95, 141, 194
epistemological optimism, 162
etymology, 21, 22
Euclid, 55 n18, 56, 58 n23, 59
Euthydemus, 17
Ewe, 70, 71
ex nihilo nihil, 97 n21, 107, 108, 110, 114, 125
existence, 63

fa (law), 8
fan (converse), 24, 30
fei (not), 177f., 190
Feng Jingyuan, 97 n21
Feng Youlan, 49 n4
Feuerbach, L., 10
figures of speech, 130, 132, 133, 134
Flew, A. G. N., 62 n47
focal meaning, 86, 87, 89, 90

mentality, 5, 95
metaphor, 12, 23 n19, 127f.
 see also root-metaphor
metaphysics, 168, 169, 170, 194
Metzger, T. A., 162 n82
military science, 124
ming (blind), 158
ming (clear-sighted), 40, 144, 147, 148,
 153, 155, 158
ming (name), *see zheng ming*
mirror, 103 n43, 120, 127f., 143f., 155f.
Mittelstrass, J., 19 n7
Mohism, 116
Mohist Canon, 19, 20, 24, 25, 29, 39,
 43, 46, 49, 50, 52, 58, 59, 83, 87, 96,
 111, 115, 119, 120, 122, 134, 138,
 146f., 180, 185, 190
Mojing, see Mohist Canon
more geometrico, 50, 87, 120
Moritz, R., 97 n20
Mou, Bo, 62 n47
Mozi, 19, 87, 189
Munchhausen (Baron), 9

name, 18, 19 n19, 20, 22, 23, 25, 26, 42,
 43, 64, 104 n48, 107
names, correction of names, *see zheng
 ming*
Narcy, M., 30 n35
natural kinds, 42
necessary condition, 36, 37
Needham, Sir J., 5 n14, 59, 93, 97, 98 n27,
 99, 100, 100 n33,
negative existentials, 181, 189
Neo-Confucianism, 188
neologism, 161 n80, 186, 194 n73
 see also hapax legomena
ni (look askance), 146 n49
Nietzsche, F., 9, 10, 11, 68 n14
Nile (river), 53
nominal sentence, 171
nominalism, 22 n15
non-being, 105
Nyaya-Vaisesika school, 67
Nylan, M., 151 n59

Onians, R. B., 145 n43
ontology, 156, 162, 164, 167f., 178,
 185, 192, 194

optics, 53
ordinary language, 9, 14, 125, 161
Orion (constellation), 56
Orphism, 21
Oshima, H., 156 n67
Owen, G. E. L., 9 n25, 87 n58

pacifism, 28
paradox, 60, 89 n67, 99, 119, 120, 181,
 182, 183, 184, 188, 189
Parmenides, 101, 107, 108, 114, 149
 n58, 161, 170 n15, 174, 175, 178,
 184, 185, 186, 187, 188
passion, 159
Pellegrin, P., 64 n53
Perelman, C., 134, 135 n26, 163
phenomenology, 11
Philodemus, 32 n10
Piaget, J., 93
Ping Yuan, 29
Plaks, A., 100 n34
Plato, 10, 17, 22, 25, 26, 26, 29 n33, 54
 n14, 58 n23, 64, 74, 75, 92, 101, 109,
 127, 128, 132, 139, 140, 143, 149,
 150, 156, 161, 163, 170 n15, 175,
 176, 183, 186 n60, 189
Platonic Academy, 109
poetry, 155 n66, 156
potential infinity, 99
Presocratics, 94, 95, 127, 132, 143
prime matter, 97, 105 n49
Prodicos, 17 n1, 18
proof, 59, 63
proposition, 25, 26, 166, 190
Protagoras, 17 n1
Proto-Indo-European, 2, 3, 3n10, 7, 10,
 11, 67, 71, 81, 114, 169, 171
Pulleyblank, E., 190 n67
Pythagoras, 58

qi (cosmic breath), 97, 104, 105
qiuhao (fine autumn hair), 100 n32
quail, 120
quantification, 44
qude (oblique discourse), 143 n40
Quintilian, 130

Raphals, L. A., 148 n54, 155 n66
rationalism, 6, 15 n41